How to Change 5000 Schools

# HOW TO CHANGE

# 5000

# SCHOOLS

A Practical and Positive Approach
for Leading Change at Every Level

**BEN LEVIN**

HARVARD EDUCATION PRESS
CAMBRIDGE, MASSACHUSETTS

Library of Congress Control Number 2008928885

Paperback ISBN 978-1-934742-08-2
Library Edition ISBN 978-1-934742-09-9

Published by Harvard Education Press,
an imprint of the Harvard Education Publishing Group

Harvard Education Press
8 Story Street
Cambridge, MA 02138

Cover Design: Perry Lubin

The typefaces used in this book are Adobe Garamond Pro for body type and Hypatia Sans Pro for display.

*This book is dedicated to the thousands of leaders
in education in Ontario from 2003 to today,
including elected provincial and local politicians,
administrators, teachers, support staff,
parents, students, and community members,
whose collective efforts have made Ontario schools
stronger and the province a better place to live.*

# Contents

# Acknowledgments

I was privileged to be able to work in Ontario with political leaders who believed deeply in education, particularly Premier Dalton McGuinty and Ministers Gerard Kennedy, Sandra Pupatello, and Kathleen Wynne. The same was true earlier in Manitoba, with Premier Gary Doer and Ministers Drew Caldwell and Diane McGifford. Politicians take a lot of abuse, most of it unfair. The leaders I have named here, and many other elected people I have worked with, deserve much more public credit and thanks for taking on the challenges of public service, especially given its mediocre pay and terrible working conditions!

I benefited greatly in Ontario from working with some very talented political staff as well, led by Gerald Butts, Katie Telford, and Mary Ng. And I worked with a wonderful, skillful group of senior managers in the Ministry of Education who so often did the remarkable, if not the impossible. Civil servants like anonymity, so I won't name them, but they know who they are, and I will always admire them as the best team I have ever worked with.

I have had the enormous good fortune over my career to work with a very large number of talented people who have helped me learn. There have been literally hundreds of such people. The list includes many teachers from elementary school to university, many colleagues at all levels in the organizations in which I have worked, and many friends and acquaintances, all of whom have both supported me and challenged me to be better.

I wish to mention particularly three people who were important in my life and thinking and who are no longer with us.

Don Girard, who died a couple of years ago, was the superintendent in my district when I was a high school "radical." He was a wonderful teacher who exemplified respect for young people without ever condescending or accepting anything other than real effort.

Tom Greenfield was my doctoral supervisor at the Ontario Institute for Studies in Education (OISE). Tom was an outstanding thinker who had the terrible experience of having his important work misunderstood and attacked in unfair ways, but he never lost his belief in the power of good thinking, or his willingness to help students develop their ideas.

Ron Duhamel was the deputy minister of education in Ontario who first hired me into a senior managerial position in 1983, when I was 31. Ron was a great person to work for and someone from whom I learned a lot. He was respected and admired by all who knew him and loved by many for his humanity and greatness of spirit.

I thank Bob Schwartz for connecting me with Harvard Education Press, and Caroline Chauncey at HEP for editing that was always positive and helpful.

# Introduction

Early in 2007 I attended a number of major events looking at different aspects of Ontario's education agenda. I spoke with many system leaders, from teachers, principals, superintendents, and board members to parent leaders. Although these people did not agree on everything, they were agreed on one vital point. Education in Ontario, they said, was an exciting, energizing, and satisfying place to be. Many of them said that they felt the current period was the best time of their entire careers, as student achievement rose at the same time that educator engagement and morale were increasing.

This book is about how to create change of that kind and at that level. Communities around the world, from neighborhoods to countries, are looking for ways to strengthen their education systems. The rationales are familiar—the need for a competitive edge in the global economy, the changing skill requirements of a high-technology world, the demand for more informed and committed citizens to cope with the unprecedented problems of environmental degradation, and population diversity. Many towns, states, or countries now aspire, however unreasonably, to have "the best education system in the world." Public expectations for our schools have never been higher.

High public expectations are both necessary and challenging. As educators we cannot rest on our laurels, and we cannot be satisfied with our previous achievements, no matter how good they are. Public schools everywhere have much to be proud of. Public education is an important achievement in human history. It has benefited millions who, in earlier periods, never had a chance to be educated. It has made important contributions to social development. Public education has served us well, in large part because so many educators have worked so hard on behalf of their students. All that is wonderful, and should be celebrated, but it does not earn educators any free pass into the future. Education, like every other public institution, must find new ways to cope with the new challenges and new contexts that are an essential part of the human condition. The world changes, and so must schools.

The central challenge for public education in the coming years, at every level from school to nation, is to maintain and strengthen public confidence and support for public education so that people will want to send their children and provide their tax money. To succeed in this task, we will have to bring more students than ever before to higher levels of achievement and engagement in learning than ever before. We will have to deal with more diverse needs and interests in our schools than ever before. We will have to communicate more effectively with our communities than ever before. These challenges will, in turn, require high-caliber people and effective leadership at all levels of education to support and bring about the required changes.

Lasting and sustainable improvement means improving student outcomes across a broad range of important areas (not just reading and math, and not just as measured by test scores). It means reducing the gaps in outcomes among different population groups. And it means doing so in ways that support positive morale among educators, students, and parents; that do not demand impossible levels of energy on an ongoing basis; that increase the capacity of the school or system to continue to be successful; and that generate increased public confidence.

Improving schools is hard work. We have plenty of experience with efforts that have either failed to create improvement or failed to last, as discussed more fully in chapter 2. The outcomes of education are shaped to a large degree by factors that schools do not control, particularly poverty and its related ills. Schools, like other large institutions, tend toward the status quo. They are also very busy places, where people by and large are feeling fully occupied and not looking for yet more challenges. Creating real, lasting improvement requires a sound theory of education, which research increasingly provides us. It also requires a sound approach to management, including the ability to manage all the pressures and factors likely to get in the way of change and a commitment to communication with internal and external audiences. Vision is important, but so is the much less glorious work of looking after all the details that make things work.

This multifaceted approach is what I try to describe in this book, which is about leading large-scale, positive, sustainable change in education at all levels. It is intended to be a practical view of what can and should be done, informed by research and shaped by the author's personal experience both in leading change and in analyzing the change efforts of others. It is also intended to be optimistic, holding out a way to make progress while acknowledging the very real barriers and constraints. Leaders, I believe, need to be optimistic and realistic at the same time, as illustrated by the story that concludes this introduction.

Still, a reader might wonder why we need another book on educational change. After all, this is a subject that already has a large and rich literature, including extensive case studies of particular changes and more general discussions of change.

My answer to that perfectly reasonable question is that there are important things still to be said about leading and managing change in education. Indeed, as we have had more experience with large-scale change and learned more about it, new and deeper questions have emerged. One reason why there is so much writing on this subject, including now four editions of Michael Fullan's classic *The New Meaning of Educational Change*, is because new learning and changing circumstances pose new challenges and require us to reflect, think, and—most of all—act in new ways.

I have been fortunate to be able to consider educational change from several perspectives—as an academic studying education policy, as a consultant working with school systems in several parts of the world, and especially as a senior official playing an important part in the renewal of public education in two Canadian provinces. I have had the benefit of reading and learning from the work of others and of participating actively in a number of important change efforts. Based on these experiences, I have become aware of a number of gaps or oversights in the literature, and also usually in practice, which are the major themes in this book.

First, although we have learned quite a bit about change in schools, we know much less about how to create real change at a broader level, across many schools or entire systems, and how to do so in a sustainable way, so that today's changes do not become tomorrow's memories. As Hargreaves and Fink put it, "Sustainability does not simply mean whether something can last. It addresses how particular initiatives can be developed without compromising the development of others in the surrounding environment, now and in the future" (Hargreaves & Fink 2000: 32).

We do know that what works in one school or a few schools will not necessarily work across hundreds or thousands of classrooms or across multiple districts, yet it is the many classrooms and schools that we need to affect, not just a few here and there.

Although in some ways improving one school is a very different task from improving an entire system, in other ways the basic ideas of improvement are the same at any scale. The issues and strategies described in this book apply at every level, from a classroom to a country. Creating real improvement is always challenging at any level, but there is an extra challenge in creating improvement that is both widespread and lasting.

The issue of scale also raises the need to organize change in a way that is manageable for ordinary people. So many accounts of change seem to depend on heroic efforts by seemingly superhuman people. Yet entire education systems cannot depend for their success on having large numbers of extraordinary people—who, by definition, are always in short supply. The standards developed for education leaders in various places, discussed further in the chapter on leadership, seem to call for super-people who can do everything at once at a very high level of proficiency. As a change strategy, this is akin to basing one's retirement income on winning the lottery. Best not count on it. We must therefore consider how to create and sustain change in ways that work for reasonably competent and committed people, not just for superheroes.

Making change manageable also means taking account of the real, daily demands on educators and school leaders. In the world of books or standards documents, it's easy to recommend five steps or eight actions. In the real world of schools it all looks different. Education leaders at all levels face multiple demands and pressures. And even when there is agreement on what to do, how to do it may be far from obvious.

Much of the advice given to leaders in books like this one urges them to do something in particular—and sometimes a long list of things. It's all very well to call for principals to spend more time in classrooms, or to become leaders of professional learning communities, or for superintendents to engage much more in building community support. The question those folks rightly pose in response is, What are they supposed to stop doing? After all, they are not currently heading for home at 3:30 with their work all done! School leaders, along with most teachers, work hard for long hours. If we are going to ask them to change what they do, we have a responsibility to help them see how they can actually do that, given what they take to be the realities of their jobs.

In practice, leadership is always a matter of balancing competing demands, interests, ideas, and approaches. Yes, a common vision or sense of direction is important, but must it be pushed to the exclusion of all else? Yes, it's necessary to focus on teaching and learning, but the building still has to run as well. Yes, greater consistency in teaching strategies is desirable across grades and subjects, but should this be mandatory or voluntary? Yes, more parent involvement is a good idea, but what about the small number of parents who can eat up huge amounts of everyone's time and attention?

A considerable amount of writing on change lays out the things people need to do differently. It has less to say about *how* to do those things. One of the challenges in education, as in other policy fields, is that the pizzazz is around having the seemingly new idea, whereas the real work is in making it happen. While innovations tend to get the profile, the slog work of implementation is what makes the difference in the end, and this work gets much less attention in the literature on education change. As many business analysts would agree, having a great new idea is less important to success than getting ordinary things done correctly and efficiently. Moreover, governments, schools, and systems tend to be much bigger on announcing new initiatives then they are on putting in place all the mechanisms necessary for those new announcements to turn into reality and become permanent features of the landscape.

The right answer to these challenges is rarely clear, and may change from time to time and place to place. Leaders, like teachers in classrooms, have to make constant judgments about what to do next, about when to push and when to let go, about how much direction to give against how much autonomy to allow, about diversity versus consistency. Every idea and every proposal in every book about leading change—including this one—has to be interpreted in the light of real situations with real people. My grandmother, when asked about how much flour or baking powder to put in a cake recipe, used to say "just enough." The problem was that she knew from experience when it was "just enough" while I did not. It's finding the "just enough" in each situation that challenges and perplexes all leaders, whether in education or other fields.

Politics are another important theme in this book. The literature on education change tends to ignore politics or treat it as an exogenous force, yet political factors have a huge impact on which changes get considered, adopted, supported, and maintained. Educators are not particularly political people by and large. They want to get on with the work of helping children learn and succeed. They often see politics getting in the way of their work, bringing unreasonable mandates or pressures on them. But the world of any public institution is inevitably political. For better or worse, and usually for some degree of each, politics is the way through which public decisions get made in democracies, and, as Winston Churchill famously said about democracy, "it is the worst system of government ever devised—except for all the others that have been tried from time to time." We don't have to like politics or accept its many weaknesses, but we do have to recognize that public education is part of the political world. Educational leaders have to see dealing with political factors as a main responsibility in their work. In this book I try to explain some of the inevitable features of the political world, and how they can be managed.

Political pressures are one main reason that worthwhile changes in education do not last or, even worse, why wrong changes are made in the first place. There are, though, some positive signs about school improvement. While educators in the United States have been struggling with the requirements of No Child Left Behind, there has been around the world a positive shift in thinking about education policy. In the 1980s and much of the 1990s education reform was driven in many places by the idea that improvement could be created through changes in governance, or through increased testing and accountability, or by threats and punishments for failure. As discussed more fully in the chapter on barriers, over the last twenty years we have learned, often the hard way, that these approaches do not bring the desired results. Increasingly, governments and educational leaders are recognizing that the central element in any real improvement must be, as Michael Fullan puts it (2006), "capacity building with a focus on results [for students]." We are seeing more effort in more places to help the system get better instead of punishing it for its shortcomings.

This change in political thinking provides an enormous opportunity for educators to do the things we care about. The opportunity is particularly critical in the United States, where No Child Left Behind and other similar policies have at best distracted people from the requirements of real improvement, and at worst have done significant damage to public education. These policies and directions are now up for debate and possible change. The 2008 U.S. presidential election will be followed by a debate over where to go with education policy in the next few years. The requirement to reauthorize or change the existing approach marks an opportunity to move in a new and better direction. It should be possible to continue the focus on better outcomes for all children regardless of origin, while jettisoning the elements of fear and punishment that have had such negative effects on teachers and students over the last few years.

I contend in this book that there are ways to push forward system improvement, even in a large and decentralized place like the United States, that do not rely on simplistic ideas about accountability, that do not make everything dependent on a single test score, that help strengthen the skills and motivation of students and educators rather than demotivating them, and in doing those things also build public confidence in public education.

## THEORY OF ACTION FOR SCHOOL IMPROVEMENT

"There is nothing so practical as a good theory" is a quote attributed to the organization theorist Kurt Lewin. Lewin meant that any practical effort to do something necessarily embodied, whether more or less thoughtfully, some theory about how things work and can be changed.

The same is true of school improvement. An effort to improve must rest on some notion, however inchoate, of how schools work and how improvement can be generated. The ideas in this book rest on the following theory of action:

- Although student outcomes are deeply affected by forces beyond the school, such as socioeconomic status, schools also play an important role in shaping what happens to students.
- We do not know the limits of human capacity to improve; all we know is that we have not reached those limits yet and that people continue to surprise us with their abilities to achieve and their resilience, sometimes in the face of enormous obstacles.
- The heart of school improvement rests in improving daily teaching and learning practices in schools, including engaging students and their families.
- Those improvements are a matter of "will"—people's motivation—and of "skill"—their capacity.
- Improvement can therefore only occur and last where school staff are engaged and committed.

* Improvement in teaching and learning requires sustained effort and support, including the development of new skills and attitudes.
* Everything else in the school organization and operations must support these effective methods of teaching and learning.
* Lasting change in schools requires ongoing support from the public.
* Effective leadership at all levels, including political support, is critical to the whole improvement endeavor.
* Distractions are inevitable but have to be managed to minimize their negative impact.

This is the model that is developed in this book, with each of the above points, and many complementary issues, developed in the various chapters. An initial chapter describes my personal journey in relation to school improvement, and chapter 2 describes in some detail the very positive changes that took place in Ontario, Canada, in the last few years. The other chapters then roughly follow the theory of action here, starting with what we might reasonably expect from our schools (chapter 3), discussing the barriers to change (chapter 4), outlining needed changes in teaching and learning practices (chapter 5) and the organizational practices need to support those changes (chapter 6). Later chapters discuss the political challenge of building and sustaining public confidence (chapter 7), the leadership challenges to implementing the entire agenda (chapter 8), and the important task of leading in an environment full of operational and political distractions and pressures (chapter 9). My conclusion (chapter 10) recaps some of the main ideas and implications of the book.

The chapters can also be read separately, however, or in a different order. The reader may also find a certain amount of recycling of key ideas, much as in a spiral curriculum in schools, and for the same reason. Some of the central themes of the book—such as the vital role of positive motivation, the necessity to take political factors into account, or the importance of internal and external communications—recur at various points in the book because they take different forms related to different aspects of the overall task, and because they are too important to mention once and then leave aside.

I know that it is possible to make real and lasting change that benefits students, and to do so on a large scale. In the early chapters I describe some of my own experiences and also efforts I have seen elsewhere, especially in Ontario in the last few years, that have produced significantly improved student outcomes while being well grounded in evidence, respectful of educators, and widely supported by the public. More examples are provided throughout the book. Even under the restrictive and in many ways negative conditions arising from policies such as No Child Left Behind, some schools and districts in the United States have seen not only marked improvement in results but a whole new positive attitude on the part of staff, students, and parents. Teacher morale can be improved at the same time as student results. If improvement can be made on a sustained basis in some places, then the same can be done in other schools, districts, states, and countries. It is not easy. It takes well-founded plans, careful implementation, political support, and most of all unrelenting effort, but it can be done and it is worth doing—indeed, it is our moral obligation to make every effort to help more students be more successful.

I hope this book will be useful and meaningful to education leaders at all levels, from teacher leaders in a school to the managers of state and national education systems. This may seem arrogant, but in fact the central tasks are the same. There is no magic in these pages. I simply try to assemble and describe what talented and dedicated educators and their allies everywhere have been doing.

### COMBINING VISION, OPTIMISM, AND REALISM

A central concept through this book is the need for balance. So much in education requires balancing competing pressures and demands, to which there is no right answer. How much pressure and how much support? How much local option and how much central direction? How much uniformity of approach versus diversity? How to balance the long and short term? How to be impatient for better results yet understanding of why they are so hard to achieve?

The challenge of reconciling these different pressures was brought home to me by one of my nephews years ago. He was five at the time and had just come back from kindergarten. We were talking to my father, his grandfather, and Daniel announced that when the Messiah comes, lions won't eat lambs any more.

"Is that right, Daniel?" my father asked. "What do you think the lions will eat then?"

"Oh," Daniel replied, "deer, rabbits, whatever they can catch."

He understood the issue. The biblical vision was of peace and a world living in harmony. One had to be optimistic that the vision would be achieved. But one also had to be realistic; lions would not instantly turn into vegetarians. Getting lamb off the menu was, then, a good and reasonable first step.

This is exactly the world in which educators find themselves. We have a grand vision that we want to hold onto and work toward. But sometimes the steps toward it seem rather small. We have to be able to hold onto our vision, retain our optimism, and temper both with realism if we are to be able to continue to come to work each day believing in what we do.

I hope this book will help you do that.

# 1

## A Personal Odyssey

This book grows out of my personal experience and perspective on large-scale change in education. In this chapter, I describe briefly my personal journey in the realm of education change, and then discuss in more detail the Ontario experience from 2003 to today that forms the main foundation for the arguments made about change in this book.

I first got interested in education reform as a high school student. My own memories of school are primarily of boredom, though I had some very good teachers in elementary schools. My high school years, in the late 1960s, were a time of enormous political and ideological ferment. "Student rights" became an important rallying cry. I got involved in my student council through trying to change some of the more repressive aspects of high school and then, in my last year of high school, was elected president of the student council after a campaign focused on increasing student influence on school rules and processes. We had some modest success in this area. I also got involved in an effort to organize a city-wide high school students' union in my home town of Winnipeg, Canada (which had about 30 high schools in nine districts at the time).

My experience in trying to organize this union was powerful in many ways. Many educators were supportive and helpful, including the super-intendent of my district, Don Girard, who became a lifelong friend and taught me a great deal about the realities of organizations. On the other hand, I was amazed at how threatened some school administrators were by the very idea of the union; several of them prohibited me and other student leaders from entering their schools to speak with students. I was equally amazed by how uninterested many students were and by how much individual egos got in the way of collective action. In retrospect, none of this is surprising in the least, but at the time I was young, naïve, and quite taken aback at how ideas that seemed obvious to our group were far from obvious to so many others, even those who we thought would be on our side more or less automatically.

The effort to organize the union was entirely unsuccessful. We lacked the capacity to do the organizing, and students and their leaders in many schools were not interested. But my interest in trying to change schools to be more interesting, stimulating, and friendly places for students had only begun.

Two years after my graduation from high school, the government of Manitoba changed the voting age from 21 to 18, and I decided to run for election to the school board of the Seven Oaks School Division, where I lived and had gone to school. By this time I had already been involved in several provincial and national political campaigns, so when the school board elections came around, my friends and I were able to put together a real campaign, which was unheard of in school board elections. We had signs, pamphlets, and did door-to-door canvassing of the entire district. In 1971 many adults were happy to see a young person running for election, though others objected quite strongly. So at age 19 I was elected to the school board for a three-year term, at that time the youngest school trustee in the country.

This experience, too, turned out to be quite frustrating (Levin 1975). I was one person on a nine-member board and, largely because of my age, often not taken all that seriously by the others. I was unable to effect any significant change in the district, not least because I discovered, again to my surprise, that the board, though officially charged with the governance of the district, seemed to make few decisions of any great consequence. We spent far more time on buildings, property, budgets, and collective agreements than we did on educational matters, on which the superintendent's proposals were generally accepted—as, I later realized, they should be, since a CEO who cannot bring acceptable proposals to a duly elected board probably needs to be replaced. The school board did not seem to be, as I had hoped, an avenue for changing students' experience in schools. At the end of my three-year term, I went off to graduate school in the United States, now firmly committed to making schools more interesting, relevant, and supportive places for students. I finished a master's degree in education, worked in a small education research organization for a few years, and then, increasingly interested in research, went back to school again to do a doctorate in education. By now I was firmly convinced that research could play an important role in improving education policy and practice.

As I was finishing my doctorate I was hired as the first "chief research officer" in a large Ontario school district. School district research units were largely, I discovered, about the management of testing programs and the analysis of data. They were not much about bringing emerging knowledge based on research into the mainstream of education practice and policy. As one of the senior managers in my district said to me early on, "We're going to get along well. I'll tell you the findings I need, and you can do the research to produce them." To which I responded that his position was quite common, but I appreciated his honesty in stating it. This district, like every other organization, was mostly taken up with keeping things going, managing operations, and dealing with pressures and crises; research was a minor part of the whole enterprise.

After two years in this role, which, despite its frustrations, I quite enjoyed, I was recruited to be director of research and planning for the Manitoba Department of Education, and we moved back from Ontario to Manitoba. A new government had taken office in Manitoba about a year earlier, with ambitious plans for improvements in education, many of which fit my predispositions. I joined the senior management group of the department, which was led by a wonderful deputy minister named Ron Duhamel, one of the very best managers I have ever encountered.

I spent six years with the MDE in three different jobs: research, line management of the community college sector, and policy management of the university sector. Manitoba is a small place—about a million people—so any relatively senior civil servant has quite a bit to do with ministers, senior political staff, public and stakeholder groups, and the attendant politics. During these years I came to appreciate much more fully the incredible demands and constraints on politicians, and the difficulties in creating and pursuing a political agenda. I also realized that most stakeholders really had no idea of how the political process worked. Even university presidents, whom I thought would be a well-informed group, turned out to be quite ignorant about political forces and realities, convinced as they seemed to be that if they only stated their needs loudly enough, often enough, and with enough numbers, governments would fork over the requested money. Years of failure did not seem to lead to any change in this strategy.

In 1988 Manitoba elected a Conservative government. About a year later a tenure-track position in my field came up at the University of Manitoba, so I moved from government, where the new regime's agenda was not very consistent with my beliefs, to academia, to work on education policy, politics, and economics. I spent the next ten years at the university, including a few years as dean of continuing education, a position that gave me a wonderful opportunity to learn about the exciting world of adult education.

In 1999, after 11 years of the Conservatives, Manitoba changed governments again, reelecting the mildly left-of-center New Democratic Party. The premier-elect, Gary Doer (still premier today, after winning two further elections), asked me to take on the role of deputy minister for the Department of Education, where I had worked in the 1980s as a senior manager. The new government had a significant education agenda, though primarily in postsecondary and adult education. I was once again ready to shape education policy and practice in the real world, not just teach and write about them as an academic.

I have described my experiences as deputy minister in Manitoba elsewhere (Levin 2005). My original commitment was to stay two years, but in the end I stayed nearly three years, years that were exciting, rewarding, frustrating, challenging, and draining all at once, as government so often is. The Manitoba government's agenda gave higher priority to postsecondary and adult education (which were also my department's responsibility) than to schools. Still, we were able to make some important and worthwhile changes and, perhaps more importantly, to undo some mistakes and avoid making other mistakes that seemed common elsewhere (Levin and Wiens 2003). Many of the approaches in Ontario after 2003 were either shaped by or highly consistent with the things done in Manitoba a few years earlier, albeit at a much smaller scale, including a respectful approach to stakeholders, a strategy focused on teaching and learning changes, and a consistent, public plan over several years. Ironically, while deputy minister in Manitoba, I watched education developments in Ontario with dismay and remember remarking that it could take Ontario 20 years to recover

---

### A Note on Canadian Government Roles and Titles

Education is the responsibility of each of Canada's ten provinces and three territories; there is no national or federal department or ministry of education in Canada, although the federal government is involved in education in a variety of indirect ways.

Each Canadian provincial government is headed by an elected premier (rather like a governor in the United States), who appoints the cabinet, made up of ministers. Unlike cabinet officers in the U.S. and some other countries, Canadian provincial ministers are drawn from elected members of the provincial legislature.

Each province also has a ministry or department of education that funds schools, makes policies, sets curriculum, and so on—somewhat like state governing boards in the United States. These departments are headed by deputy ministers, who are civil servants appointed by the government. Typically, deputy ministers are career civil servants, though sometimes they are appointed because of their connections to a particular party or government.

Canadian provinces also have local school districts with elected boards, much as in the United States, but in Canada most funding for schools comes from provincial governments, not local sources.

from the policies being put in place by their Conservative government in the mid- to late 1990s. It never occurred to me that I would have any role in this recovery.

In 2002 I left the Manitoba government and returned to my academic position at the University of Manitoba, and two years later was recruited into the Canada Research Chair at the Ontario Institute for Studies in Education at the University of Toronto, Canada's largest and most research-intensive education faculty. However, in June 2004, before I could begin my duties at OISE, I was approached by a search firm seeking a new deputy minister of education for the recently elected new government of Ontario. Ontario had been going through a difficult time in education.

### THE CHALLENGE OF EDUCATION IN ONTARIO

From the early 1990s on, education in Ontario went through a very troubled decade. Two successive governments introduced measures that put pressure on the system and deeply offended teachers. Over a few years almost every aspect of the system was changed quite dramatically. The entire governance system was changed in 1996 and 1997, including reducing the number of local school districts from about 140 to 70, removing taxation powers from local districts coupled with a move to 100 percent provincial financing, and removing school principals from the teacher unions. Funding to schools was cut significantly for several years, leading to the reduction or elimination of many programs and services, often with the worst consequences for the most vulnerable students, such as recent immigrants. These cuts were made worse by other changes in social policy, such as sharp reductions in many social support programs like housing and youth services. Schools were less able to support students at the same time that students needed more support.

At the same time, many program changes were introduced, including the provincial testing of all students just mentioned, but also new and supposedly more rigorous curricula in every grade and subject. The high school program was compressed from five years to four.

Perhaps most importantly, the government was vigorously critical of schools and teachers in public, including broadcasting television ads that portrayed teachers as overpaid and underworked. This view was carried over into policy. Budget cuts led to reductions in staffing levels. Increased workloads for teachers were mandated by legislation. Compulsory pencil-and-paper qualifying tests were put in place for all new teachers, compulsory professional development was required for all teachers, the number of professional development days was cut in half, and a more intensive program of teacher evaluation was legislated, including compulsory input from students and parents. These steps angered teachers greatly and led to substantial labor disruption, including many strikes and sustained "work to rule" campaigns as well as lower morale and higher teacher turnover. In 1997 teachers across the province stopped work for two weeks in response to government legislation bringing in more changes. Many students in the late 1990s went through four years of high school without ever being in a climate of normal labor relations and extracurricular activities.

As another aspect of the government's education program, private schools were encouraged through having minimal regulations, and in 2002 the government passed legislation giving tax credits for tuition at private schools. Years of this environment led to significant public dissatisfaction, increasing private school enrollment, and poor morale among teachers. Parents were divided, often disliking the government's policy measures but equally unhappy with continued disruption in their children's school lives. In short, nobody was happy with the state of public education, as illustrated in public polling undertaken by the Ontario Institute for Studies in Education. For example, a 1998 poll showed a significant proportion of the Ontario population feeling that the quality of education had declined in the previous five years (Livingstone, Hart, and Davie 1998).

These problems showed up in student achievement. Only about 55 percent of Ontario elementary school students met the relatively demanding provincial standard in grades 3 and 6 literacy and mathematics. High school graduation rates actually fell in the late 1990s when a new high school program was introduced; by 2003 only about 60 percent of students were graduating in the "normal" four years.

It was no surprise, then, that education was a main issue in the 2003 provincial election. The Liberal opposition won the election, with the renewal of public education one of its highest priorities and an ambitious set of policy commitments around improving education. The party had spent significant time while in opposition thinking through its education program. Michael Fullan, a University of Toronto expert on education change, played an important role in working with the Liberals. The party's leader, Dalton McGuinty, and the education critic Gerard Kennedy, as well as some of their political staff, were deeply involved in planning the education platform. They came into office in October 2003 with high expectations from the education sector, but also after having been out of government for 13 years.

This was the situation in the first half of 2004, when I was approached about taking on the Ontario deputy minister (chief civil servant) of education position. The job seemed to me to be extraordinarily difficult. Moreover, working in government was, for me, less personally satisfying than academic life, which offers more autonomy and much less stress. So I told the search firm that I was not interested in the job. Nonetheless, after quite a bit of back and forth, in early September 2004 the search firm asked me to come to Toronto to meet the premier, Dalton McGuinty, and the minister of education, Gerard Kennedy.

Although I still did not think I would take on the job, I did think it would be a great opportunity to meet the premier and education minister in my new province of residence. It turned out to be an extraordinary day. These two men, so different in their personal styles, shared a deep commitment to improving public education in Ontario. They had put together a strategy for doing so that seemed to me to be sensible, well grounded, and feasible yet at the same time also very ambitious. They were entirely clear about the priority they gave to education, with the premier saying to me what I heard him say many times later (and act on consistently): that improving public education was the most important single thing his government was trying to do. Gerard Kennedy had an astounding grasp of education policy and politics. It was clear that he understood deeply what needed to be done, both educationally and politically, and that he also had a keen understanding of the strategy necessary to achieve the desired results. Although I thought I had quite a bit of knowledge about education, talking to Gerard that day was something like attending a seminar with a brilliant thinker. It was impossible to refuse the invitation to be part of such a worthwhile endeavor, so I agreed that if the University of Toronto would give me a leave of absence—before I even started working there!—I would return to government for a fourth time, as deputy minister of education for Ontario, a job I started in the late fall of 2004.

# 2

# The Ontario Education Strategy

## THE ONTARIO CONTEXT

Ontario is Canada's largest province, with an area of 400,000 square miles, or 1 million square kilometers, and a population of nearly 13 million, or nearly 40 percent of the Canadian total. Its area is about the size of the combined states of North and South Carolina, Tennessee, Mississippi, Alabama, Florida, Georgia, and Louisiana, while its population is about the same as that of Illinois or Pennsylvania. The population is highly urbanized, with 80 percent of the people living in or near metropolitan areas.

Ontario has about 2 million children in its publicly funded education system. That system is organized into four sets of locally elected school boards with overlapping boundaries, reflecting Canada's constitutional requirement for public support of minority language (in Ontario, this means French) and religious minority (in Ontario, this means Catholic) schools. On the other hand, unlike most Canadian provinces, Ontario provides no public financial support to private schools. The complexities of school governance, language, and religion in Ontario and Canada are beyond the scope of this book, but anyone interested can find a fuller description and discussion in Young, Levin, and Wallin 2007.

All four school systems are publicly governed by elected boards and 100 percent publicly financed. Thirty-one English public school boards serve about 1.3 million students; 29 English Catholic boards serve about 560,000 students; 8 French Catholic boards have some 60,000 students; and 4 French public boards have 13,000 students. This means that any given area of the province will be served by four boards, one from each sector, automatically introducing a degree of choice into the system.

Ontario school districts range in size from a few hundred students to about 250,000 students in the Toronto District School Board, one of the largest in North America. The six largest urban districts in Ontario combined have about a third of all the students in the province. However, many districts cover large territories with very small populations, particularly in the north of the province. In total across the systems there are nearly 5000 schools, many of which are small—the average elementary school has about 350 students and the average secondary school fewer than 1000, and many schools are much smaller than that.

Because the province is home to about half of Canada's immigrants, Ontario's school enrolment is very diverse, with 27 percent of the population born outside of Canada (a third of whom have arrived in the last ten years), and 20 percent visible minorities. The Toronto area, which has nearly 40 percent of the province's population, is one of the most diverse urban areas in the world and receives more than 125,000 new immigrants each year from dozens of different countries. Many urban schools across Ontario have students from 30 or more ethnic groups who speak dozens of different languages.

Ontario's 120,000 teachers are organized in four unions that roughly correspond to the four school systems. Teacher unions are large organizations that have significant political influence. Most of the 70,000 support staff—caretakers, secretaries, maintenance staff, education assistants, and professional support workers such as social workers—are also unionized. Collective agreements are made at the district level, though in the last round of bargaining in 2005 the province played a critical role (as will be described later).

Canadian education systems are more centralized than those in the United States, but less centralized than in many other countries. The

Ontario government through the Ministry of Education sets curriculum, determines many major policies for schools, and provides 100 percent of the funding to school boards in an effort to ensure equity in the allocation of resources across the province. Local school boards do play an important role, however. They are the employers of all staff. They appoint principals and senior administrators such as superintendents. They set annual budgets and make priority decisions on programs. They manage their capital assets. They are the first line for parent involvement and for resolution of local issues. The importance of local boards is clear from the substantial differences in culture across Ontario's 72 districts.

Two other independent agencies should be mentioned. An independent and self-financing College of Teachers, created in the 1990s, controls certification and qualifications for teachers and educational administrators. The province also created the Educational Quality and Accountability Office (EQAO) in the 1990s as an independent agency responsible for the substantially increased testing program that was put in place in those years, although in the end provincial testing was limited to language and mathematics in grades 3 and 6, mathematics in grade 9, and a literacy test in grade 10.

One of the main influences on the Ontario strategy was the experience of the new Labour government in England, which gained power in 1997. Both Michael Fullan and I had been involved in evaluating the British government's Literacy and Numeracy Strategy from 1998 to 2002, and our exposure to that large-scale change effort shaped much of Michael's thinking and advice to the Liberals prior to the election. As opposition leader, Dalton McGuinty also visited England to look at their education strategy. So before describing the Ontario strategy in more depth, let us consider the English experience.

## ENGLAND, 1997–2003

The education system in England has more than 20,000 secondary schools, with more than 8 million students and nearly 400,000 teachers. Schools in England are part of local education authorities, similar to school districts, but since the 1980s have had a high degree of autonomy, including having their own governing bodies, hiring their own principals and staff, and looking after their own physical facilities. Unlike in Canada or the United States, districts in England have little or no influence over schools' staffing or budgets.

Students in England may apply to go to any elementary or secondary school, although they will not necessarily be accepted by a school of their choice. Most if not all teachers are members of one of the several teacher unions in the country, but collective bargaining for teachers was eliminated in the 1980s, and teacher pay is still set by a government advisory committee.

In 1997 a New Labour government was elected under Tony Blair, who had declared his top three priorities to be "education, education, and education." The English education system had been through a decade or more of rapid and large-scale change under the previous Conservative government, which, like the Ontario Conservatives, had been very critical of the schools. The Conservatives had introduced major changes in education, including much greater autonomy for individual schools, choice for parents and competition among schools, a national curriculum, national testing with public reporting of results, and regular external inspections of all schools with publication of the results. Collective bargaining for teachers had been abolished. Many educators felt battered by all the change. (These changes are described much more fully in Levin 2001 and Lawton 1994.)

The new Labour government elected in 1997 also had ambitious goals for education. In particular, it was determined to improve student outcomes in literacy and numeracy and to increase the proportion of students getting good high school qualifications and going on to postsecondary education.

In its first term in office (1997–2001), to the disappointment of many of its supporters in the education sector, the new government kept most of the main Conservative changes but also introduced a large number of its own changes and initiatives. The most important initiative was a Literacy and Numeracy strategy intended to improve students' results in the early years. (Stannard and Huxford 2007 provide a detailed account of the National Literacy Strategy from its inception through 2005.) The minister of the day, David Blunkett, promised that the proportion of children reaching the national standard for literacy at age 12, as measured by annual national tests, would rise from about 55 percent to 80 percent within four years. A target of 75 percent was set for numeracy.

The government, through the Department for Education and Skills (as it was then; it has been renamed several times since 1998 and is now the Department for Children, Families and Schools) launched a serious effort to bring this change about. The Literacy and Numeracy strategy was intended to affect daily teaching and learning practices—hence student results—in all 20,000 elementary schools in England. The government brought in a trusted advisor, Michael (now Sir Michael) Barber, to head a new Standards and Effectiveness Unit in the department, which would lead the government's key education reforms. In 2001, when Barber moved to the prime minister's office, a highly respected academic and expert on school change, David Hopkins, was brought in to lead the SEU.

The Literacy and Numeracy strategies were an unprecedented effort to change school practices as well as policy. Some elements of the strategies were quite prescriptive. For example, every classroom was required to have a literacy hour every day, divided into three parts as outlined in department documents. Schools were given detailed guides to literacy and numeracy content that should be taught each year and term. These provisions were enforced through the school inspection system, in which inspectors made particular note of schools' and teachers' adherence to the guidelines. Districts and schools were also given targets for achievement improvements by the department, and were under considerable pressure to achieve those targets.

However, unlike most previous change efforts in most countries, Labour understood that improved teaching and learning could not be brought about just by fiat, testing, or blaming but required investing in the capacity of the system to do better. So in addition to clear guidelines, prescription, and inspection, schools were also given quite substantial resources and supports. Every school and teacher was provided with new materials and curriculum resources, including print and video examples of good teaching practice as well as materials and ideas for use by teachers. Several days of professional development were provided each year to each school, and a cascade model was used to provide support to all schools and teachers. Three hundred literacy consultant teachers and 300 numeracy consultant teachers were hired to work more intensively, especially with schools with lower levels of achievement. The country was organized into ten regions, each of which had a regional infrastructure to provide this support. The department provided a whole variety of grants to support these and a range of other programs and initiatives for which schools could apply. So in addition to pressure, there was substantial support for change.

In addition to these strategies, the government launched a wide range of other initiatives to improve schooling. Some of these were complementary to the strategies, such as the creation of the National College for School Leadership to work on strengthening leadership across the sector, or efforts to improve early childhood education, or a family literacy initiative, or a number of initiatives to improve the situation in Britain's most depressed urban areas. The government had related strategies to improve early childhood development and reduce child poverty. Other education priorities dealt with such important areas as special education and repairing school buildings. Still, as in Ontario, the overall result was that schools felt subject to a large number of initiatives, some of which seemed to them to be competing for their energy and attention.

In 1998 the Department for Education and Skills commissioned an external assessment of the implementation of these strategies to give them an independent view on how the strategies were developing and how they could be made more successful. This was a brave move, in that a public, independent evaluation carries high political risks for any government. After all, such a review, no matter how positive its overall results, will almost always have some suggestions for improvement (if not, why bother having the review?), yet any suggestions for improvement are likely to be seized on by the media and the political opposition as evidence of the initiative's failure, or at least serious shortcomings. The political attention to negative results of any study is a main reason that more governments do not emulate the British effort. In any case, I was part of the team, headed by Michael Fullan, that won this contract and, from 1998 through 2003, had the opportunity to look carefully at how the strategies were developing (see *www. standards.dfes.gov.uk/primary/publications/literacy*).

The early years of the strategies produced impressive gains in achievement and particularly significant increases in many low-performing districts and schools. However, after the first few years, the gains stopped and results were flat for 3 or 4 years. There are varying explanations as to why this happened (Barber 2007), ranging from a reaction to the relatively narrow focus on the strategies to a lack of focus amid many distracting issues. It is certainly the case, as noted by our evaluation, that schools were being asked to attend to many other issues beyond literacy and numeracy. However, in 2003 the government refocused its efforts, and since then results have again begun to improve. Charts of achievement in England show that in 1998 only a handful of districts had 75 percent or more of their students reaching the approved level at age 11, whereas in 2004 the vast majority of districts had reached this point (Hopkins 2007). Overall, 79 percent of students were reaching the standard in English in 2005, compared to 63 percent in 1997. There is controversy in England as in many other jurisdictions about the improvements, with critics arguing that the tests do not assess the right skills or have been made easier for political reasons, an issue discussed further in the chapter on public confidence.

The English reforms had a strong influence on the Ontario strategy in a number of respects. The Ontario strategy borrowed some main elements from England, particularly their strong focus on building capacity in the system through professional development and resources. Ontario also recognized the need to build a provincial system and infrastructure to do this work, and to surround the main strategy with necessary complementary elements such as leadership development. At the same time, the Ontario strategy deliberately did not adopt some other elements of the English approach. Ontario chose to be less directive on the details of the policy and to give schools and boards more flexibility in how they addressed the priorities. Ontario also decided to be less punitive in setting targets, public reporting of results, and to focus on support rather than punishment for schools or districts that were not making enough progress quickly enough.

### THE ONTARIO EDUCATION STRATEGY

The Liberal election platform of 2003 contained more than 20 specific promises around education. These became the foundation for the new government's education strategy. My role, from late 2004 until early 2007, as deputy minister, or chief civil servant for the Ministry of Education, was to advise the government on policy and to oversee and ensure effective implementation of its programs through the Ministry of Education.

The two most important goals in Ontario from a system point of view were the commitment to improve elementary school literacy and numeracy outcomes and the commitment to increase high school graduation rates—the latter called the Student Success Strategy. A third major focus of our attention was to implement the government's promise to reduce real class sizes in the primary years. These core priorities were complemented by a range of other promises. Some of these, such as strengthening school leadership or changing curricula, were necessary to support the key goals. Other initiatives, including provincial support for the negotiation of four-year collective agreements with all Ontario's teachers, were essential so that all parties could focus on improving student outcomes instead of being consumed by labor issues. Still other initiatives, such as attention to safe schools and healthy schools, sustained public support for improved outcomes by letting people know that the basic needs of students were also being attended to.

This comprehensive strategy was also intended to be implemented in a way that would be coherent, provided the necessary supports and resources, was respectful of educators, and engaged the broader public. That is, the education strategy was fully complemented by an equally carefully considered political strategy.

---

## The Ontario Education Strategy in Brief

*Key goals*
- Improve a broad range of student outcomes.
- Reduce the gaps in achievement.
- Increase public confidence in public education.

*Main strategies*
- Improve teaching of literacy and numeracy across 4000 elementary schools; 75 percent of students to reach provincial standard at age 12—up from 55 percent.
- Improve graduation rates across more than 800 high schools; 85 percent of students to graduate within five years of starting ninth grade—up from 68 percent.
- Reduce class size in primary years to maximum of 20 in at least 90 percent of classes.

*Other strategies*
- Safe schools
- Parent involvement
- Aboriginal education
- Leadership development
- Labor peace
- Using data effectively
- Special education
- Community use of school facilities
- School buildings renewal
- Teacher development—induction, more professional development
- Enrichment—arts, music, physical activity

---

## IMPROVING STUDENT OUTCOMES IN ELEMENTARY
## AND SECONDARY SCHOOLS

The two strategies—Literacy/Numeracy in elementary grades and Student Success in high schools—shared many common elements.

The government set public targets for improvement in at least three areas. For Literacy/Numeracy, the goal announced by the government was to have at least 75 percent of grade 6 students able to read, write, and do mathematics at the expected level on the provincial test by the spring of 2008. This level was considerably higher than mere competence; a comparative analysis of the Ontario standards with those in other jurisdictions, done by EQAO in 2005 (EQAO 2005; see also *www.eqao.com*), showed that "Level 4" represents considerable skill and fluency in reading and writing. The target represented a substantial gain from the approximately 55 percent of students who met the standard in 2003 (after several years of static results) and was regarded as quite ambitious by education system leaders. However, the political reality is that the public will not accept, and the education system cannot be satisfied with, a situation in which even one in four students fails to develop key skills that they will need to participate fully in our society. As one minister said to me about this target, "Well Ben, it's not really all that ambitious a goal, is it? It seems like our goal is to get a B." This gap between what educators see as realistic and what the public expects from schools is an important issue that will be discussed later in greater depth.

In secondary schools the province has set a target of having at least 85 percent of entering grade 9 students graduate from high school in a timely way by 2010. As of 2003–4 only about 60 percent of Ontario students were graduating from Ontario's 800 high schools in the normal four years, and only about 70 percent were graduating even after taking an extra or fifth year. These are clearly unacceptable levels in a knowledge society. Achieving the 85 percent target would put Ontario near the top among Canadian provinces but would still leave the province below a number of other Organisation for Economic Co-operation and Development countries (OECD 2007).

In each case, the ministry created a dedicated infrastructure to lead and guide the overall initiative. In the case of Literacy/Numeracy, a new secretariat led by an outstanding educator, Dr. Avis Glaze, was created as a stand-alone unit to lead the reform. The idea was to free the secretariat from the usual bureaucratic routines and constraints so it could focus more on working directly with schools to improve outcomes. The secretariat recruited about forty outstanding educators to work as Student Achievement Officers who work in teams with school districts to design and implement improvement strategies.

In the high school sector the infrastructure was organized differently. Each school district receives funds to hire a "Student Success Leader," usually at a superintendent level, to coordinate work on high school change. Ministry staff, working with some key external resource persons, bring the Student Success Leaders together regularly to share experiences and ideas across districts. Ministry staff are also central to creating the policy and planning framework that guides the overall Student Success initiative.

Both strategies have as a central element engaging school and district leaders to set ambitious but achievable targets for their system and to develop plans for gains in student achievement. The focus has been less on developing planning documents than on building the strategy and culture in districts to set and work toward significant improvement. Although some Ontario districts were already well on this road and needed little beyond a measure of support and encouragement, in other districts the whole idea of a focus on steadily improving performance was a new feature, and considerable work was needed to help districts move in this direction. Student achievement officers in the Literacy and Numeracy Secretariat, and ministry staff in the Secondary Schools Programs Branch worked closely with district staff on a local basis, taking into account the particulars of each district's situation and capacity. The goal was to push each district a little further than it thought it could go, but to do so in a supportive and collegial way, which assisted and motivated districts, rather than in a commanding or punitive way.

A leadership team was put in place for each strategy in every school district and every school. Not only was each district required to have a team working on each strategy, but every school also had to explicitly create a team to lead the initiative. We have found that having several people with a designated responsibility for improvement in every school itself creates a useful change in culture.

The Ontario strategies give a central place to building system capacity for improvement. This meant providing and funding extensive, carefully targeted professional development for tens of thousands of educators to support the strategies through improved instructional practices. Both strategies spent substantial money and effort on creating high-quality, sustained learning opportunities for teachers and principals. A wide variety of capacity-building strategies were used, ranging from standard professional development events, provision of high-quality resource materials to schools and teachers, creation of networks of teachers and principals within and across districts, and province-wide events that build energy and morale to online webcasts that could be used at school or district staff meetings. Professional development was not seen primarily as a matter of professional development events, although the province did restore two professional development days to the school calendar from those cut by the previous government. Instead, the strategies sought to connect professional development with ongoing school practice through support for initiatives such as coaches and teacher leaders, and by working with school principals to ensure that professional development was supported by school practices such as planning time, staff meetings, or walk-throughs.

Beyond these common elements, each of the main strategies had some unique elements appropriate to the particular challenges that are different in elementary and secondary schools.

In the elementary sector, one of the main components was the reduction of primary class sizes as per the government's election pledge. By 2007, 90 percent of Ontario's primary classes (kindergarten to grade 3) had 20 or fewer students, and the other 10 percent had 23 or fewer. This initiative brought some 5000 new teachers into the elementary school system. In addition, as part of the collective agreements signed in 2005, the government supported 200 minutes weekly of preparation time for all elementary teachers. This agreement led to the creation of about 2000 new teaching positions for specialists in areas such as music, art, physical education, and languages, resulting in significant renewal of these program areas and giving tangible evidence of the government's commitment to a rich and broad elementary school curriculum.

Ontario had initiated a "turnaround schools" program before the 2003 election. This program, working with a small number of low-achieving elementary schools that volunteered to participate, provided expertise and resources to help these schools improve their performance. The program had significant success in most schools, such that by 2006 the number of very low-achieving schools had dropped by 75 percent and the "turnaround" program could be merged into the overall Literacy and Numeracy strategy for greater synergy and effectiveness.

The Student Success strategy, like the Literacy/Numeracy strategy, also had a primary focus on setting goals, developing plans, creating leadership teams, and building local capacity. However, it added some unique elements, recognizing that in most places it has been more difficult to create lasting change in high schools than in elementary schools. The ministry put considerable effort into analyzing the research on high school change and designing a change strategy that took account of the realities of high schools, including their larger size, subject specialization, focus on content, weaker relationships between adults and students, lower degree of parent involvement, and so on.

To combat the anonymity that many students experience in high schools, the Student Success Strategy did several things. First, as mentioned, each school put in place a leadership team that was focused on keeping track of students' success. The ministry developed a set of key indicators that schools were expected to use for this purpose. In particular, each school was expected to keep track of how many students were at risk of not earning all their credits in grades 9 and 10, since falling behind even by one or two credits is a very strong predictor of failure to graduate. So for the first time, every school now knows at all times how many students are on track and, more importantly, makes plans to intervene early in support of those students who are struggling.

Another part of this effort was the creation, again as part of collective agreements in 2005 with secondary teacher unions, of new positions in every high school for "Student Success Teachers." Every Ontario high school now has a half- or full-time position for a teacher whose job it is, in the vernacular, to worry about those students who need attention and are not getting it. Student success teachers are used in varying ways, including advocating for students, providing "credit recovery" (discussed more below), collaborating with parents, and helping classroom teachers understand and adapt their teaching to the needs of particular struggling students. They are also usually members of each school's Student Success Leadership Team. They are key elements of the strategy's intent to ensure that every student in high school is well known to and supported by at least one adult on staff.

The ministry made several programmatic changes to the high school program as well in order to support Student Success. Resources, materials, and professional development were provided to support attention to literacy in all areas of the curriculum. Program options for students were increased through adding more cooperative-education opportunities, the ability to earn credits for genuine external learning, and the introduction of dual credit/dual enrollment programs with colleges and universities. Modifications were made to some curricula that had been introduced in the earlier reorganization of high schools and were found to be unreasonable for the majority of students. For example, the number of topics in the grade 9 advanced mathematics curriculum was reduced to allow greater depth in the key areas students need for their future mathematics and related courses.

A major issue in secondary education has been the appropriate place for technical and vocational programs. It has long been recognized that a significant number of students simply do not like or do well in a traditional abstract and academic curriculum. The problem has been to create options that do not result in students being streamed into lower-status programs that do not give them real options either for employment or for postsecondary education, which has unfortunately been the result of many vocational education efforts over the years and around the world (World Bank 2005). The growing importance of and participation in postsecondary education in all countries makes this dilemma even more important.

The Ontario solution to the dilemma is something called the "High Skills Major." Without going into detail, the High Skills Major allows schools and districts to work with employers and community groups to create packages of courses leading to real employment and further learning. High Skills Major programs in areas such as mining, manufacturing, tourism, or agriculture include components such as links with colleges for future postsecondary activity, real credentials required for the workplace such as safety or equipment training, and a package of courses that are recognized by the industry as necessary and sufficient for employment in meaningful jobs. The first High Skills Majors began in the fall of 2006, and demand both from schools and from industry has been far greater than expected. The intent is to have at least one High Skills Major in every secondary school in the province.

To signal the seriousness of its intent to increase high school graduation rates, the government introduced legislation in 2005 to require all students who had not graduated from high school to continue in an appropriate learning program until the age of 18, with learning programs including not only high school enrollment but also college enrolment or participation in a recognized workplace learning program. Some of the challenges around this legislation are discussed more fully in chapter 6.

The ministry made a specific decision early in the planning for the Student Success Strategy to focus on grades 9 to 12 rather than beginning with grades 7 and 8. We wanted high schools to have to take ownership for Student Success rather than pushing the responsibility off to the elementary sector. However, we recognized that we would eventually have to pay attention as well to transition issues, so in 2007 work began to improve transitions from junior high to senior high through a variety of mechanisms.

### Other common elements

When these initiatives began in 2003–4, Ontario as a whole and many schools and districts lacked the data necessary to understand and improve current performance. Indeed, in 2004 Ontario was the only Canadian province that was unable even to report a provincial high school graduation rate. Both strategies worked hard to improve the data available. Schools and districts were expected to gather and analyze data on key achievement indicators. The ministry built a new student information system that is now providing all schools with current data on student performance, including high school graduation. For the elementary system, the ministry created a "Statistical Neighbours" information system that allows districts and schools to compare their performance with other schools in the province with similar demographics. Substantial effort has also gone into training people in school systems to understand and use data more effectively to guide improvement planning.

The strategies recognized that the improvement targets could only be met if we paid careful attention to some of the groups whose achievement was lagging significantly behind. Specific strategies were developed through extensive consultation in areas such as boys' literacy and Aboriginal (Canadian Indian) education. New policies and resources were developed around English as a Second Language in recognition that Ontario's significant immigrant and second-language population needed more support. Even within the ESL approach, some more specific approaches were needed for particular communities where the challenges to better achievement extend beyond language to cultural factors.

Special education was another area of significant concern. Ontario, like most jurisdictions, has seen a steady increase in the proportion of students being referred to special education, especially in the areas of learning disabilities and behavioral issues. Special education was growing steadily as a proportion of total education spending as well, but we had little or no evidence as to whether all this activity was effective; the gap in outcomes between students in special education and the overall population was quite large. So as part of the overall improvement strategy, the minister created a Working Table (discussed a little later in the section on dialogue) to look at ways of improving outcomes for special-education students. Special education is a particularly difficult policy area, for reasons too complex to take up in this book, but through this process we were able to get broad agreement that more focus in special education should be placed on improving student outcomes rather than only on the provision of services, that paperwork requirements needed to be reduced significantly, and that it was necessary to work toward greater integration and alignment between special education and the mainstream system.

These ancillary strategies, as well as the overall orientation to improvement, assumed that schools could not do it alone. We saw the merit in working closely with community groups so that schools could benefit as well from their expertise and experience and vice versa. So districts and schools were encouraged to reach out to youth agencies, ethnic organizations, and faith communities as partners in the work of engaging and supporting students. As one example, Frontier College, an adult literacy organization, was supported to recruit and train community members as tutors to work with struggling students in high-challenge communities.

The strategies also gave attention to ways of increasing the knowledge and engagement of parents in supporting their children. A variety of information materials were produced for parents, in multiple languages. The ministry also launched a parent involvement strategy with a focus not on governance but on helping parents understand the school system better and support their own children's learning.

As yet another element, the government was committed to basing its policies on current evidence and research to the greatest extent possible. The ministry created a series of "expert panels" in important areas such as literacy, mathematics and special education to bring the best available research evidence to the attention of the system. These reports, available online (*www.edu.gov.on.ca/eng/policyfunding/reports. html*), continue to be widely read and used across Ontario and helped build consensus on desirable practices. Both the Literacy/Numeracy and Student Success strategies included significant research components, which were linked to the development of an overall Ontario Education Research Strategy. Each of the strategies also commissioned, borrowing from the English experience, an independent external evaluation of its impact, both in the shorter and longer term (Canadian Language and Literacy Research Network 2007; Ungerleider et al. 2007).

The government recognized that changing practice in thousands of schools, and tens of thousands of classrooms, would require some additional resources. The two main strategies—Literacy/Numeracy and Student Success—were each supported with about $80 million per year. While this may seem like a large amount of money, it amounts to less than 1 percent of total spending. (These amounts do not include the costs of additional teaching positions as determined through the collective bargaining agreements.) As discussed later in this book, small amounts of money, carefully applied, can lever large changes in practice and in effectiveness.

## THE POLITICAL AND ORGANIZATIONAL INFRASTRUCTURE TO SUPPORT IMPROVEMENT

In addition to its comprehensive educational elements, the Ontario approach embodies the key principles mentioned earlier in this chapter. It was intended to be respectful, based on partnership, coherent, and aligned, as elements that would make the changes significant, broadly acceptable, and sustainable.

### Respect for staff and for professional knowledge

The Ontario strategy was intended to contrast sharply with the previous government's antagonistic relationship with teachers and other educators. The government began with the belief that staffs in our schools are committed professionals who have enormous skill and knowledge to contribute to school improvement. Respect for professionals was shown in a variety of ways.

Most important, and as discussed more fully in chapter 6, the government undertook to end the climate of conflict in labor relations by facilitating the signing in 2005 of unprecedented four-year collective agreements with all Ontario's teacher unions. These agreements created the climate of "peace and stability" in labor relations that was essential to achieve the government's goals for students and to sustain public confidence. In addition:

• The public statements of the government and ministry are constantly supportive of public education and the work of educators and support staff.

• Almost immediately on taking office, the government abolished some policy elements, such as paper-and-pencil testing of new teachers and the compulsory professional development requirement, which had been seen by teachers as punitive. These were replaced with policies—such as an induction program for all new teachers and a simpler system of teacher performance appraisal—that are supportive of professionalism.

• Despite significant declining enrollment across the province, staffing—both teachers and support staff—has increased substantially, teacher workload has been reduced, and preparation time has been increased.

• Both strategies build on successful practices in Ontario. Almost everything in the strategies draws on or is based on practices that were already underway in schools somewhere in the province. Schools are seen as allies and partners in change, not obstacles to it.

• The focus on capacity-building means that there are many opportunities for teacher learning at all levels, from schools, families of schools, and districts to provincial activities.

### Coherence and alignment through partnership

An explicit part of the Ontario approach involves building strong relationships and close connections with districts, schools, teachers, and other organizations.

The Ministry of Education has put in place several mechanisms for consultation with partners. A Partnership Table brings the minister of education together with all the major stakeholders on a regular basis in a forum in which all partners—teachers, school boards, superintendents, principals, support staff, parents, and students—can interact with one another and with the minister. Most major policy issues are discussed at the Partnership Table prior to their finalization and announcement. The Partnership Table has also sponsored the creation of several "Working Tables" that have allowed a fuller discussion of some of the more important issues facing the system. Working tables were established for Literacy/Numeracy, for Student Success, for special education, and for teacher development (including changes in teacher performance appraisals, the introduction of an induction program for new teachers, and an examination of professional development needs). Each Working Table includes representatives of main stakeholder groups, and the tables report to the larger Partnership Table.

In addition to this formal mechanism, the minister, political staff, and senior ministry staff also meet regularly with the main provincial organizations, including teachers, principals, and superintendents. Parent and student organizations also play an important role in policy development and implementation. There is constant communication so that the partners feel, rightly, that they have significant input into ministry and government decisions.

Given the problems created in Ontario education over the last decade because of conflict with teachers and support staff, particular steps were taken to involve teachers and their organizations. The ministry works closely with the teacher federations by involving them in policy development and has provided them with funds to recognize their important role in professional development. Efforts are also made to work more closely with support staff groups and to recognize their need for involvement and for professional development.

Principals also play a vital role in the Ontario strategy, since they are widely recognized as playing key roles in school improvement. Ontario principals were forcibly removed from the teacher unions in the late 1990s, creating some difficult relationship issues. Professional development for principals has been expanded, and efforts are being made to improve some of their key working conditions, though the job of principal remains extremely challenging. In late 2005 the minister issued and began to implement a discussion paper on the role of the principal that will improve principals' working conditions as well as strengthening their professional development opportunities.

Changing the negative and combative public discourse around education in order to build public confidence was itself an important policy goal. However, the efforts to build and sustain strong partnerships all take place within the common emphasis on improving student outcomes. They therefore have a common value core and a strong focus on building capacity everywhere in the system to support students' success more effectively.

## Capacity in districts and the ministry

The Ontario strategy required improved capacity not only in schools but also in districts and in the ministry. Over the first two or three years it was clear that districts varied enormously in their capacity to understand and implement improvement. In some districts, management was entirely taken up with administrative matters such that almost no attention went to education programs and practices. In some districts the administrative functions—such as transportation or management of buildings or budgeting—were so weak that they could not support the education program properly. Over the years since 2004, the ministry has steadily provided more support and direction for both education and administrative leadership and operations in boards, including the use of consultants to help boards improve administrative operations, and leadership networks to help directors (chief superintendents) in struggling districts provide better leadership around pedagogical issues.

The ministry, too, faced challenges in its ways of operating if it was to support the improvement agenda appropriately. Under the previous government, the ministry, like most ministries I have encountered, was primarily occupied with issuing policies, distributing money, enforcing rules, and dealing with problems as they arose. While these are all important functions, they cannot provide the impetus for the kind of system change we were pursuing in Ontario. Moreover, like any large organization, the Ministry of Education had the inevitable problems of internal jealousies and rivalries, unwillingness to share information, excessive hierarchy and deference, and inadequate research capacity. A main part of my role as deputy was to try to improve this situation, primarily through measures that are described in later chapters, such as increased team building, more open communication, clear focus on a few key goals, and so on. In the context of government, which is inevitably pulled toward being hierarchical, deferential, risk averse, and weak on evidence, this is a never-ending challenge.

### Impacts of the strategy

The Ontario strategy has had a significant impact in a very short time. Results on Ontario's provincial assessment have improved substantially and broadly over the last three years. Overall about 10 percent more students, or 15,000 per grade, are now achieving the provincial standard at grades 3 and 6. The number of schools with very low performance has fallen by three-quarters, from nearly 20 percent of all schools to less than 5 percent. The system as a whole is halfway toward the target of 75 percent, though that target itself is not an end-point. Nor are these results just a matter of test-taking. Gains on tests only matter if they represent real improvements in students' skills, and teachers across the province confirm that we are seeing real skill improvements for students, not just increases in test results. Ontario has avoided a focus on test preparation and drill. Moreover, the test results are strongest on basic skills but leave most room for improvement in higher-order

---

**Main Outcomes of the Ontario Reforms**

Proportion of students reaching provincial standard increased from 54 percent to 64 percent in four years.

- Number of very low-performing schools dropped by 75 percent.
- High school graduation rate has risen by 7 percent over four years.
- Attrition among young teachers dropped by half.
- Early retirement among teachers declined sharply.
- Public confidence increased notably.

In short, Ontario has significantly improved student outcomes while simultaneously improving teacher morale!

---

skills, so narrow test-preparation approaches will be ineffective in producing further gains.

The indicators for high school improvement are also positive. Graduation rates are rising—from 68 percent in 2003 to 75 percent in 2006–7. Results on the provincial grade 10 literacy test—not a particular focus of the changes—have improved substantially. Credit accumulation in grades 9 and 10, which strongly predicts graduation, is also improving, so there should be further significant improvements in graduation rates in the next few years.

As mentioned earlier, independent external evaluations of both strategies were commissioned to gauge their impact. The first reports of these evaluations (Canadian Language and Literacy Research Network 2007; Ungerleider et al. 2007) were highly positive about the impact of the strategies on school practice and on educator morale.

The Literacy and Numeracy evaluation said:

> Overall, the evidence gathered over the course of Evaluation Phase 1 . . . indicates that those in the LNS [Literacy and Numeracy Secretariat] have worked intensely . . . to build capacity and improve student achievement. These efforts have had positive impacts in school boards and schools. The LNS has created and sustains a "Sense of Urgency" that permeates the educational language being spoken throughout boards. This sense is not diminishing but rather is growing. At the same time, there is a general sense that the Ministry of Education, through the LNS, is providing the much-needed resources and opportunities that boards require to move their schools forward. Overall, the LNS is providing a valuable service, supporting the education of Ontario's children. This model is effective and the service should continue. (Canadian Language and Literacy Research Network 2007: 8)

The Student Success evaluation concluded:

> The evaluation team is of the view that Ontario has created a . . . strategy that integrates a wide range of programs and encourages considerable programmatic innovation and professional autonomy on the part of educators. There appears to be considerable mutuality and complementarity among the elements in the strategy that, although in its

early stages of development, appears to be succeeding in providing a more respectful and responsive school environment for students and increased opportunities for them to remain in and benefit from secondary schooling in ways that provide a foundation for work and study following high school. (Ungerleider et al. 2007: 4)

Just as important, there is a level of energy and enthusiasm in Ontario schools that has not been seen for quite some time. The number of young teachers leaving the profession in their first few years has dropped dramatically. Moreover, the proportion of teachers choosing early retirement at the first opportunity has also dropped substantially. Ontario had a teacher shortage a few years ago but now has an overall surplus. Resources used to train and recruit new teachers can be used to improve those who are staying. Thousands of teachers are participating voluntarily in summer professional development programs offered by the teacher unions and school districts. More teachers are giving positive responses to surveys of their level of satisfaction with their work. These are all important and tangible indicators of improved teacher morale at the same time that student outcomes are improving.

In the fall of 2007 a group of U.S. chief state school officers spent a day in Toronto examining the Ontario strategy. They were able to meet with a wide range of stakeholder organizations including principals, school trustees, parent organizations, and teacher union leaders as well as ministry leaders. What most impressed the visitors was the consistent message they heard from all the groups about the enormous improvement in the climate of Ontario education, the focus on student outcomes and success, the respectful way in which policy was being developed and implemented, and the spirit of optimism that had replaced the conflict and divisiveness of a few years earlier.

### Adjustment over time: Phases

No change of this magnitude occurs without challenges. Leaders of the Ontario strategy assumed that adjustments would be necessary as we proceeded; we were determined not to embark on a path with no room for modification to fit changing circumstances and accommodate feedback from the system. The strategies have been modified continually as they have developed. The various dialogue vehicles mentioned earlier provide many ways for stakeholders to provide feedback on the strengths and limitations of the government's approach.

One important instance is the role of school- or board-based projects. In the first phase of each strategy, we felt it was important to build local commitment by inviting and funding project proposals from across the province. This would allow schools to generate and implement ideas. Significant funds were devoted toward this end in 2005 and 2006.

As the strategies developed, however, it became clearer to all parties that some approaches were more productive and effective than others. So in subsequent years fewer new or local projects were funded, and more emphasis was placed on broader implementation of strategies that were being found to have more impact. The strategies could thus become more prescriptive without alienating teachers or districts, because the latter were very involved in determining which kinds of changes and approaches would be most beneficial to students. This approach stands in marked contrast to many change initiatives that dictate to schools and teachers their use of particular programs or teaching approaches.

In Ontario primary classrooms today, some practices—such as guided reading, shared reading, use of leveled books, shared writing, data walls to track student progress—are pretty well universal. This is not because the Ministry of Education dictated their use, but because teachers have found them to be beneficial to students. This means that the practices would persist even if the support mechanisms for them largely disappeared.

The same would be true of some secondary school practices, such as monitoring of student progress from early in the first term or the use of student success teams. Having changes in practice that are owned and supported by educators is sustainable educational change.

Another adjustment, already mentioned, was the integration of the Turnaround Schools program into the Literacy and Numeracy strategy, in recognition that having two distinct programs was confusing to school districts and an inefficient use of resources. Moreover, as the number of very low-performing schools fell rapidly, the main challenge shifted to supporting schools whose achievement levels, while not terrible, were equally not as high as they could or should be—for example, schools in relatively affluent areas that had 65 percent of students reaching the standard when they should have been at 85 percent.

There is no question that Ontario schools and teachers are being confronted with many initiatives all at the same time. Even though people are positive about the elements of change, putting them all together has brought stress. One might describe the situation as being a bit like eating all the Halloween candies at once; each one tastes good, but too many at one time does not produce a happy result!

This situation is improving as there are fewer new initiatives and more focus on deeper implementation of those already underway. Ongoing capacity-building and support also reduce the stress of the new. Nonetheless, at all levels of the system the need for more alignment and coherence remains and will remain an important consideration.

Changes in approach are not an indication of weakness or failure; they are an indication of learning. Sometimes the original approach was not as well designed as it could have been. Sometimes the situation changes so that new approaches are needed. Most importantly, the willingness to adjust the strategy, even in the face of political criticism for doing so, builds trust with the education sector since it shows the government's genuine desire to work in partnership and to learn from each other.

With the Ontario strategy outlined, the next chapter moves to considering the reasons why large-scale, sustained change is so important yet so difficult to do.

# 3

## How Much Can We Expect from Public Education?

Nobody reading this book needs to be reminded of how important education is. If we did not believe education mattered, we would not be spending our time working in it or thinking about it. For generations, if not centuries, education has been seen as the route to success and a vehicle for upward mobility. In the last ten years or so, however, important new evidence has emerged about the benefits of education and the possibilities for extending those benefits more widely. Positive outcomes related to education go far beyond the usual mantras of being able to compete in a global economy. As Sue Berryman (1992) put it,

> For the first time in our history, the education needed to function effectively in labour markets in both high- and low-skill jobs looks similar to that needed to participate effectively as citizens, to work through moral dilemmas, or to make intelligent purchases of often complex goods and services. . . . The educative challenge common to these disparate activities is to prepare individuals for thoughtful choice and judgment. (345)

### DO WE EXPECT TOO MUCH FROM SCHOOLS?

Educators often feel that schools are either being blamed for all the ills of the world, expected to make up for all the deficiencies of society, or both!

Continued economic prosperity is said to depend on our schools, as are remedies for health afflictions such as obesity or drug abuse, social norms such as civility and citizen engagement, and the task of remedying the corrosive effects of poverty and discrimination. In some ways the description of all the positive outcomes of education listed on pp. 52–54 may exacerbate the pressure on schools. Even more, educators have often justified calls for more support and resources for education by appealing to all the positive outcomes that can arise, so the education system has to some degree created the multiple expectations about which it now complains.

What is it reasonable to expect from our schools? The stance in this book is clear. Schools cannot do everything, but they can do some important things and almost certainly can achieve more than we typically think possible.

Let's start with the limits of education. Most societies have deep inequalities and problems that affect the work of schools. Poverty, poor housing, racial discrimination, too many low-wage jobs, too much food that is not healthy, lack of adequate health care—all these hurt the future of children and families and make it harder for children to benefit from their education. Richard Rothstein's 2004 book, *Class and Schools*, lays out compellingly for the United States the inequalities that show up in schools due to inadequate health care, poor housing, lack of infant nutrition, and so on. The English-speaking countries— the United States, Canada, England, Australia, and New Zealand— have greater inequalities in these areas than do most western European countries, and the inequalities have in some cases been getting bigger in the last twenty years rather than smaller. When UNICEF (2002) rated the well-being of children in twenty rich countries using data on six different outcome areas, the U.S. and UK were at the bottom of the list. Many other countries with less overall wealth are able to have both higher and less unequal outcomes for children at all ages.

Schools did not create these problems, and schools alone will not solve them. The blame sometimes placed on schools for failing to redress all the negative impacts of poverty, for example, is entirely unfair and highly demotivating to good educators. It is unfair to hold schools and educators responsible for social ills such as discrimination or crime, just as it is unfair to expect every individual student to rise above his or her circumstances just by dint of effort. If our basic social institutions are highly unequal, then we must expect that inequality to show up in educational outcomes as well.

A reality of politics and public attitudes is that it's often easier to try to address social problems through schools than it is to deal with the real underlying factors. Adults appear to be unwilling to adopt good eating habits, so we'll make kids in schools eat better by banning junk food or eliminating pop from vending machines. Adults don't exercise enough, so we'll make kids exercise every day in schools. Our streets and families may have too much abuse and violence, so we will teach students not to bully in our schools. There is nothing wrong with any of these educational initiatives except the feeling of hypocrisy that we are imposing on young people things that we as adults are not prepared or able to do ourselves.

Intractable social problems can create pessimism about schooling. Some researchers have argued that schools can only make a small difference, reinforcing the views of educators who feel it's really the kids' or parents' problems. Some take that view because they feel schools are being blamed unfairly for failing to fix the problems of society. For example, Whitty and Mortimore (1997) and Thrupp (1999) have documented the ways in which poverty makes it harder for schools to do their instructional work even as it also brings to them students who have more need for more support. But whatever the reasons, this position can have the effect of decreasing educators' motivation and sense of efficacy.

The limits of school impact are real and have to be acknowledged. Educators should be active in lobbying for improved public policy in areas such as employment, housing, and social benefits. But there is another side as well. For several reasons, educators cannot simply say "it's not our job" or "you are asking too much of us." To say that we cannot do everything does not absolve us from doing as much as we can.

First, improving student outcomes is the very purpose of the education system. If schools are unable to alter the life chances of the students who come to them, why invest in public education at all? We have a great deal of evidence that schooling does affect those life chances. No matter what background people come from, more education and higher levels of literacy are associated with better outcomes.

Although educators know the importance of education in principle, they do not always have at the fingertips the facts supporting their belief. Former Ontario education minister Gerard Kennedy was a firm believer in the importance of data for political communications, looking for pieces of evidence that were powerful in shaping public attitudes, what he called "killer facts." The examples below (and many other similar studies could have been cited) show how powerful the case is for the importance of high-quality education and good outcomes for all students.

### Education and earnings

"A U.S. study (Spasojevic 2003) estimated that a year of schooling is equivalent to an increase in income of nearly USD 1,700 in terms of its health effect." (175)

"Studies from the U.S., the UK, Ireland, and Canada all show that an additional year of education increases annual earnings by about 10 to 14 percent." (Oreopoulos 2006)

### Education and civic engagement

"Education has a causal relationship to multiple forms of engagement, including voter turnout, group memberships, tolerance, and the acquisition of political knowledge. . . . Classroom climate, or the degree to which students are able to discuss political and social issues in class . . . has a positive impact on every dimension of engagement . . . knowledge, skills, intention of being an informed voter, intention of being civically engaged, intention of being politically engaged, institutional trust, and tolerance." (Campbell 2006)

### Education and health

"Education is strongly linked, with much evidence that the link is causal, to health and to determinants of health such as health behaviours, risky contexts and preventative service use. . . . Empirical investigations often find that the effect of education on health is at least as great as the effect of income." (Feinstein et al. 2006: 172)

"For individuals born in the United States between 1914 and 1939, an additional year of schooling reduces the probability of dying in the next 10 years by 3.6 percentage points." (Feinstein et al. 2006: 174)

"More than 80% of the differences in the child mortality between high-income and low-income U.S. families can be accounted for by differences in socioeconomic status, in particular education." (Feinstein et al. 2006: 246)

"One year of college education decreases smoking prevalence by 4.0 percentage points and increases the probability of smoking cessation by 4.1 percentage points." (Feinstein et al. 2006: 252)

"In Sweden, for the cohort of men born between 1945 and 1955, an additional year of schooling improves the likelihood of having BMI in the healthy range (i.e., BMI greater than or equal to 18.5 and lower than 25) by 12 percentage points (from 60% to nearly 72%)." (Feinstein et al. 2006: 257)

"Effective education interventions may produce significantly more health at a lower cost than all but a handful of health interventions." (Meunig 2007)

## Education and positive behavior

"There appear to be large benefits—both for individuals and for society—attached to education. . . . The importance of good education seems to be underestimated. During the past decade in most western countries, public expenditures on health care and law enforcement have increased more than public expenditures on education. Western countries try to remedy the negative effects and social costs of a relatively low educated population by providing unemployment benefits, law enforcement through policing and higher sentencing, and by increasing health care budgets to counter the detrimental effects of unhealthy behaviour. More and better education could yield savings in health care, law enforcement and unemployment benefits." (Groot and Van den Brink 2006, 362)

## Cost-benefits of education

"The value of just the public benefits embodied in additional tax revenues and reductions in the cost of public health and crime amounts to almost $256,700 per new high school graduate among black males, yielding two to four dollars in public benefits for every dollar spent." (Levin et al. 2007)

All of that evidence—and much more could be cited to the same effect—makes a pretty powerful case for the importance of high-quality education and good outcomes for all students.

Schools can make a significant difference. They may, in fact, make the biggest difference for those with the greatest needs; in other words, schools may have an important role to play in reducing social inequities (Levin 2004). David Livingstone (2004) has developed the idea of the "talent gap." If we assume, as the evidence indicates, that students in disadvantaged communities or from lower-achieving ethnic groups have approximately the same talents and abilities as do higher-achieving groups of students, then their lower level of achievement represents an important loss of talent to our society. These students who do not achieve represent potential artists, doctors, engineers, scientists, teachers, tradespersons, and business leaders who are not getting the opportunity to develop their talents and contribute to our society. Insofar as educators, wittingly or not, underestimate what is possible, we may be doing less than we can or, in some cases, actively participating in counterproductive actions.

### AIMING HIGHER FOR STUDENTS

History tells us that we have often been guilty of underestimating what people are capable of doing or learning. In some ways the history of education can be seen as showing how consistently people's potential to learn and develop has been underestimated. There are many examples of how education was denied to various people on grounds that we now consider completely unjustified. High school graduation a few generations ago was the preserve of relatively few, but now around the world it is widely regarded as a goal that virtually every student should reach. At one time postsecondary education was thought to be suitable only for a select few, but now we find that large numbers of people can benefit from it, and since participation rates around the world continue to rise, we do not yet know what that proportion may turn out to be.

At one time, women were considered (by men, of course) to be unable to benefit from formal education. Now women's achievement is outstripping that of men around the world. In their turn, various minorities were also considered to be less than highly educable. Even as recently as a few decades ago, students with disabilities such as deafness or blindness, or children in wheelchairs, were educated, if at all, in separate facilities. Down's Syndrome children were thought to be uneducable. Though believed sincerely in its time by large numbers of people, including many educators, each of these suppositions has turned out to be quite wrong, which had the effect of denying opportunity to large numbers of children. These experiences should make us very cautious about assuming that we know people's limitations or their capacities.

Educators often feel that we can predict who will succeed in schools based on their present performance. It's common to hear teachers say that they can tell in grade 4 or grade 6 which students will drop out of high school. But people vastly overestimate their ability to predict the future, and are generally quite resistant to evidence showing that their predictions are often wrong (Munro 2004). Let's suppose that about 80 percent of students are successful in first grade, 80 percent are also successful in sixth grade, and we have an instrument that allows us to predict which first graders will do well in sixth grade with 75 percent accuracy. Most of us would say that was a pretty good rate of prediction. But as table 3.1 shows, if we made predictions randomly, we would be right 68 percent of the time, so all the work of prediction has only added 7 percent more accuracy, and may well have incorrectly predicted a greater number of students.

In the aggregate, previous performance does predict later performance, but predictions that are accurate for populations are not accurate

**TABLE 3.1**
**Accuracy of Prediction with Random Assignment**

|  |  | Sixth Grade | |
|---|---|---|---|
|  |  | Successful (80%) | Unsuccessful (20%) |
| First Grade | Successful (80%) | 64% | 16% |
|  | Unsuccessful (20%) | 16% | 4% |

for individuals. A correlation of .7 between, say, grade 1 achievement and grade 6 achievement is considered very high, but it still means that the prediction will be wrong almost as much as it is correct for individual students. Munro (2004) shows how even predictive instruments with high reliability can still produce surprisingly large numbers of false predictions for individuals. Gleason and Dynarski (2002) demonstrate that even multiple predictors of dropping out of school fail to discriminate accurately those students who really need assistance.

More importantly from the standpoint of schools, surely one of the goals of education is to render negative predictions less valid. That is, we want to intervene in ways that increase the likelihood of success even for those students who seem to have everything working against them. If grade 4 or 6 achievement always did predict high school graduation, that would be a condemnation of what we achieve in our schools.

Much recent evidence is helping us to see that there is more potential for good educational outcomes than we may have thought. Consider the impact of the Access Programs established in the province of Manitoba, Canada, some thirty years ago to increase the numbers of people from disadvantaged backgrounds, especially Aboriginal people, in key professions (described more fully in Levin and Alcorn 2000; Sloane-Seale, Wallace, and Levin 2004). These programs recruited into university programs—such as education, nursing, social work, law, engineering, and medicine—adults from inner-city and remote northern communities who were motivated but did not meet normal entrance requirements. Students were selected through a process involving not only university staff but also local community people. Once admitted, the students were supported financially (through a living allowance), academically (through tutoring), and personally (through counseling when needed). Some basic courses, such as biochemistry for premedical students, were redesigned and lengthened to accommodate students' lack of background without in any way reducing standards or expectations.

These programs have over the years produced a substantial number of university graduates and professionals in people who were not, at the start, even acceptable for admission let alone for graduation. Over some 35 years, Manitoba has graduated hundreds of Aboriginal teachers and social workers, about half of the Aboriginal engineers, and about one-third of all the Aboriginal physicians in Canada. In total, well over a thousand students who were considered inadmissible were able to succeed, graduate, and become professionals and role models for their communities. These programs, and others like them in other places, show clearly how much potential is underutilized and how much more many people can do than they have had the opportunity to show.

Children's backgrounds and family situations remain powerful influences on their education everywhere. But some places seem to have found better ways of managing those challenges than others. Differences in effectiveness show up in just about every study of school outcomes, whether in countries or districts. A large literature has grown up describing cases of unexpectedly positive outcomes. While on average schools with high poverty levels have worse outcomes, for any given set of socioeconomic circumstances, the range of outcomes among schools is very wide. To put it in statistical terms, the within-group variance (differences among schools with similar poverty levels) is larger than the between-group variance (the average difference between schools with lower or higher poverty levels). To put it another way, even with similar demographics, some schools and districts consistently generate much better outcomes than others.

If some schools are able to do better for kids, even under difficult circumstances, then surely we all have an obligation to learn from those examples. Much of the popular evidence on this point comes from sto-ries of "schools beating the odds." For example, the Education Trust (*www.edtrust.org*) promotes schools that are able to show high success rates despite high poverty. Similarly, Douglas Reeves (*www.middleweb. com/MWLresources/accountaction.html*) often talks about 90/90 schools that have very high poverty and high success rates.

Advocates often cite Ron Edmonds's (1979) famous assertion that the success of a few schools shows that the same could be done in all schools if we had sufficient desire.

That does not seem a reasonable assertion, however. The fact that someone can high-jump 2 meters, or play Chopin on the piano and bring tears to our eyes, or indeed reach any pinnacle of accomplish-ment, does not imply that everyone could do so. Schooling is a mass institution. We must have improvement in thousands of schools, not just a few. So the means of improvement have to be replicable across many schools and settings. They cannot depend on extraordinary tal-ent or effort by a few unusual people, since such qualities cannot easily be replicated on a large scale. Studies of individual schools that have excelled are important because they can show us potential avenues for improvement, but it is a fallacy to assume that what can be done in one school can necessarily be done in all.

Stronger evidence about possible improvement comes from large-scale evidence more than from studies of individual schools. Emerg-ing international evidence from studies such as TIMMS, PIRLS, and PISA show that in some countries students' socioeconomic status has much less impact on their educational outcomes than in others. For example, in PISA 2006, Korea, Finland, and Canada had better over-all results than the United States or New Zealand while at the same time the socioeconomic status of students had a much smaller impact on outcomes in the former countries than in the latter. Some of those differences appear to be due to features of the school systems (dis-cussed more fully in chapter 4). Similarly, the significant improve-ment in student outcomes brought about through thoughtful effort and investment in places such as Ontario or England shows that we can do better.

The reality is that in learning—as in so many other areas of achievement—we do not know what the boundaries of human capability are. What we do know is that barriers that seem impossible are, eventually, broken, and performance gets better. We do know that many people can achieve far more than was anticipated if they have the right opportunities and supports. There are good grounds for thinking that we are likely still underestimating the potential of many students, even of entire groups and communities.

The whole case is put so clearly in the story a colleague told about his daughter partway through first grade. One of the boys was struggling to read, prompting the teacher—rather unprofessionally, one might add—to make the comment: "I see you are not going to be one of my star readers." Whereupon my colleague's daughter piped up from the back of the room: "And whose fault is that?"

An orientation to increased success is important for schools because, as suggested in the introduction, schools, like other public institutions, must be attuned to what citizens want, since it is the citizenry that determines in the end the health and even future of schools. Internationally, successful schools and school systems have created a virtuous circle in which high levels of achievement and low levels of inequality are linked with higher levels of public support and confidence, more respect for teaching as a profession, and more willingness to invest public funds in education. In other cases the circle is downward, with poor outcomes fueling poor morale and fewer resources. The benefits of the former situation are obvious to any educator, but they do not come as a result of talking about how difficult the work is—even though educating children well is remarkably hard work.

## WHAT COUNTS AS SUCCESS?

I advocate in this book for a broad definition of educational success. The outcomes people want from schools go well beyond short-term measures of academic achievement. As every study of educational goals shows, people want much more from our children's schooling than the traditional "three Rs" (two of which, remarkably, do not start with the letter *r*). We want children to have a broad understanding of the world, in such areas as science, history, psychology, government, and economics. We want them to have an appreciation of and experience in the arts as vital and enriching elements of individual and community life. Even more, we want them to have the broader skills and attitudes necessary for a good and useful life—the ability to work with others, problem-solving skills, a positive attitude, the desire and ability to keep on learning, a sense of confidence in their own capacities and future, the understanding of what it means to be a good neighbor and citizen. People do not want to have to choose among these goals, either. We want them all, and we want them for all children. To put it bluntly, we want schools to make every child perfect!

To say that the goals of schooling are multiple, however, is not to say that each goal has the same weight or importance. Reading is not the only important thing children need to learn; still, it is not only important in its own right but fundamental to achieving many other goals, such as problem-solving skills or citizenship. In the 1970s I can remember some people arguing that it didn't matter so much if children learned to read well as long as they had a positive self-image, and that achievement would follow if children felt good about themselves. Of course self-concept does matter. We want our children to see themselves as worthwhile people with a contribution to make, but surely the relationship is largely the reverse, with self-image substantially shaped by skills and performance. It is difficult to see how one could have a positive self-image without the ability to read well, for example.

High levels of achievement across a number of domains are a vital purpose of schools, but the distribution of those skills is also important. It is not enough to have small numbers of students with very high levels of education; the challenge today is to have almost all children reach those high levels of competence. Young people who do not get a good education will have much more difficulty both participating in and contributing to our societies. They will not get the benefits of education described earlier in this chapter. This is not only their misfortune—it is ours as well, since having large numbers of people with lower levels of education creates costs for everyone else, including lost productivity, poorer health, and more costs for social assistance, unemployment, and crime. Moreover, these costs are intergenerational, as the children of those with poorer skills are more likely to repeat the experience. So, in addition to wanting strong levels of achievement in multiple areas, we should also aim for low levels of inequity in achievement so that the gap between the top and bottom of the achievement distribution is as small as we can make it—what is often called "raising the bar and closing the gap."

The expectation of good results for essentially all students is a huge change in historical terms. For almost all of human history, education has been an activity for elites. It was presumed that only a relatively small number of people either required or could benefit from formal education. The shift in the last few decades to thinking that all young people both deserve and need a substantive formal education is an enormous change in perspective, and nobody should be surprised that it is turning out to be difficult to do.

Education is an activity as well where it is not only the goal that matters, but how that goal is achieved. People would not be satisfied with an education system that produced highly skilled people using unethical means. If someone invented a "knowledge drug" that would fill students' heads with facts if they took pills, most citizens would not be happy with such a form of education. We don't want children to learn by cheating their peers or at someone else's cost. We want an education to be something that takes work, that is earned and deserved. The enterprise of schooling itself has to be conducted in ways that fit our ethical sensibilities and standards.

We hear a great deal about the importance of sustainable development, the need to preserve the natural environment while also trying to live well. There is an educational equivalent of sustainability, which is the idea that increasing success for students must be done in a sustainable way; that is, in a way that can continue indefinitely given reasonable levels of skill, energy, and money for public education. Too often in the past, education reform has been proposed or done on the backs of educators, either demanding superhuman effort or involving punishment for failure to achieve imposed goals, no matter how arbitrary or unreasonable the goals were in the first place.

Jurisdictions that have adopted this top-down and punitive approach to "improvement" have discovered that it does not work. States or countries that made teaching a much more difficult job, whether in regard to pay or working conditions or morale, discovered that they could not attract or retain talented people in their schools, dooming any prospect for lasting improvement. As discussed more fully later, fear does not produce superior performance, either for students or for educators, and an institution based on fear will not be sustainable.

However, the alternative to punitive approaches is not the absence of scrutiny or full autonomy for professionals. Successful and sustainable public education requires public support, which itself depends on people's belief that schools are providing the right outcomes in the right ways. Citizens are entitled to want—indeed, it is their duty to want— their public schools to develop the high and equitable skill levels just described. Where that is not the case, citizens have the right and the obligation to demand improvement. After all, the schools are educating their children with their money. The very idea of public schooling requires a public voice as to how the system operates.

To put it succinctly, then, the goal for public schools should be real and meaningful gains, across a wide range of desirable student outcomes, with greater equity in those outcomes, in a way that builds and supports positive morale among all those involved in schools and also supports high levels of public confidence in public education.

That is a worthy and challenging objective. The rest of this book is about how to achieve that goal.

# 4

## Why Improving Schools Is So Hard to Do

One of the biggest challenges in leading school improvement involves realistically assessing the likely barriers and constraints. Reformers tend to be optimists and visionaries who are not hardheaded enough at the outset about all the things that can go wrong or get in the way of their plans. It may seem excessively negative to have a whole chapter on problems, but the balance between vision, optimism, and realism advocated at the end of the introduction makes it vital to be sober-minded about what is required for real and lasting improvement. This chapter is about the obstacles and how to address them.

Schools are often described as being resistant to change. Looking at the historical record, that seems like a wrong description. In reality, there can be few institutions that have been subject to more change initiatives over time than public schools in many parts of the world. Consider the following list:

| | |
|---|---|
| open-area classrooms | ungraded classrooms |
| individualized instruction | direct instruction |
| differentiated staffing | back to basics |
| mainstreaming/inclusion | parent involvement |
| middle schools | semesters and trimesters |

integrated thematic teaching

new math

integrated services/
   school as service hub

language across the curriculum

magnet schools

charter schools

data-based instructional
   planning

character education

whole language

community schools

character education

school improvement planning

school choice

assessment for learning

career academies

small schools

after-school and summer
   enrichment programs

Most schools in North America—and many in other parts of the world—have tried to implement many, if not all, of these ideas over the last thirty years. And that list does not include a whole range of specific teaching practices or models, such as the Madeleine Hunter approach, or Reading First, or Success for All, or Accelerated Schools, or Knowledge Is Power, or Talent Development, any of the New American Schools models. Want more examples? Just read through some issues of top practitioner journals such as *Educational Leadership* or the *Elementary Principal* to get more examples of great practices that their advocates say should be used widely if not universally. The reality is that most schools have been inundated with change.

The problem is that many of the changes have not brought the desired positive effects or have not been sustained. Despite all the interventions just listed, most of the basic features of schooling remain largely unaltered even over a century. The main organizational features of schools as buildings, full of classes of children, organized by age, with a subject-based curriculum are a century old. Even many classroom practices around teaching, student assessment, and organization of the day are remarkably stable.

This is hardly a new observation. However, forty years ago there was considerable optimism about what could be accomplished in and through education. In the 1960s many people believed that schools could solve many of the world's problems, from poverty to racism to conflict and violence. Today that optimism looks very much like naiveté or even ignorance. We have learned, often painfully, that creating lasting and positive change in large public institutions, whether schools, hospitals, or governments, is extraordinarily difficult to do. Joseph Murphy jokes about the two routes to school reform—prayer and magic!

Much of the research on change in schools is pessimistic. Going back to the first studies in the 1960s of the implementation of large-scale education reforms in the United States or England (e.g., Sarason 1971; Gross, Giacquinta ,and Bernstein 1971) and proceeding through much more recent work (Levin 2001; Fullan 2007), we have had a succession of reports around the failure of all sorts of initiatives to change schools. A famous book from the 1970s about the failures of the U.S. "War on Poverty" carried the illuminating title: *Implementation: How Great Expectations in Washington Are Dashed in Oakland; or, Why It's Amazing That Federal Programs Work at All, This Being a Saga of the Economic Development Administration as Told by Two Sympathetic Observers Who Seek to Build Morals on a Foundation of Ruined Hopes.*

Milbrey McLaughlin once wrote that "policy cannot mandate what matters" (McLaughlin 1990). In the 1980s and 1990s David Cohen and colleagues (Cohen and Hill 2001) described the challenges in changing classroom practices in the United States. In 1991, in his classic *The New Meaning of Educational Change* and again in the revisions to that title in 2001 and 2007, Michael Fullan has analyzed the ways in which efforts to improve schooling in districts and countries have failed to have the desired impact. In 1990 Seymour Sarason wrote *The Predictable Failure of Education Reform.* And then we have the many studies of smaller jurisdictions, such as reform programs in many U.S. cities (Cuban and Usdan 2003; Stone et al. 2001; Fullan 2006) or the efforts of the New American Schools to create and implement new models of schooling (Datnow and Stringfield 2000). Over and over again, the results of these studies of change have been pessimistic. Either the changes were never really brought into effect, or they did not last long enough to show results, or they did not bring about the intended improvements for students.

## WHY HAS SO MUCH CHANGE YIELDED
## SO LITTLE IMPROVEMENT?

As outlined in the previous chapter, the goal for public schools should be real and meaningful learning, across a wide range of desirable student outcomes, with greater equity in those outcomes, in a way that builds and supports positive morale among all those involved in schools and also supports high levels of public confidence in public education.

When the challenge is put this way, it's immediately apparent why it is so difficult to achieve. The problem is not one of resistance to change, but of making the right changes in the right ways. Making real gains across a range of outcomes means that daily teaching and learning practices have to change across many, if not most, classrooms and schools. Greater equity in outcomes suggests changes in programs and resource allocation. Positive morale means that people need real involvement in the changes rather than being on the receiving end of orders they don't agree with or don't know how to carry out. High levels of public confidence require lots of two-way communication between schools and communities. Success involves much more than choosing a program model and trying to put it in place in a school or district.

Changing institutions is hard for many reasons, but just to get a sense of the challenge, it is worth rehearsing some of the main ones.

- Institutions have ingrained patterns of belief and behavior that are widely accepted as normal or natural no matter how poorly they work—for example, the continued use of "failure" as a normal or desirable part of schooling.
- Institutions may be embedded in intricate systems of laws and regulations as well as competing values that make change difficult. A desire to move things in one direction—for example, to simplify bureaucracy—may run headlong into the equally important desire to secure fair treatment for diverse students and staff, requiring more elaborate procedures. Collaboration across institutions turns out to be inconsistent with privacy laws. And so on.

- Institutions have established interest groups and powerful individuals who seek to preserve their own situations and benefits even when doing so does not serve the institution's goals. As Pfeffer and Sutton (2006) have shown, this sort of behavior is endemic in the private sector as well as the public sector, as in steadily increasing pay for executives that is unrelated to any measures of organizational performance.
- Parents and students may be particularly reluctant to change some of the long-standing features of schools even when these features do not benefit them. A case in point is Mary Metz's wonderful description (1991) of parents' demands for what they understood as "real school" even when their children did not like it and were not successful at it.
- People may not know how to do the new things that are asked of them. Black and Gregersen (2002) point out that people may prefer to look competent at doing the wrong thing than to look incompetent at doing the right thing—something familiar to many teachers in trying to get students to do different kinds of work.
- Institutional longevity or popularity may not necessarily be related to good outcomes for students. Years ago, Meyer and Zucker (1989) wrote about the idea of the "permanently failing organization," showing that an organization can perform badly for long periods of time without necessarily suffering adverse consequences. If a school or district has capable students, it may add little value but still be seen as quite successful.

Even taking into account these difficult organizational dynamics, most educational changes fail for one or more of three main reasons:

1. They are the wrong changes.
2. They do not give adequate attention to political dynamics.
3. They are not effectively implemented.

The list at the start of this chapter contains examples of all three kinds of failures.

## THE WRONG CHANGES

Let's begin by distinguishing "change" from "improvement" and being clear that not every change is an improvement. In fact, many of the changes proposed for or made in schools are the wrong changes. Schools are facing many demands and pressures, and will never have enough people or money to do everything they are asked or would like. Given inevitably limited resources and multiple demands, changes should be chosen carefully based on two criteria. The first is potential impact—that is, how much difference a given change is likely to make for student outcomes. The second criterion is feasibility—that is, how likely is it that a school or district can implement and sustain this change given the current context? Feasibility includes such considerations as the availability of skills and resources, and the effect of a change on morale and commitment in the system. Both criteria are important, and each modifies the other.

While it seems unnecessary to say that a plan for improving schools should focus on improving student outcomes and be based on evidence of effectiveness, experience—and the list at the start of this chapter—shows that many improvement projects do not have these characteristics, or only partially so. More typically, someone comes across an idea she or he likes and urges its adoption. Sometimes this person is a principal or superintendent, or, at the state level, a governor or a premier. Sometimes it is a staff member or a school board member or an outside consultant. Sometimes it is a small group of people. Often the changes proposed are both single and simple—more testing of students, or loosening certification requirements for teachers, or a particular school improvement model, or penalties for schools where students do not get the desired results.

What schools and systems should do is consider both criteria equally. We should aim to choose those changes that have the most potential to make the biggest difference for the most students with the least effort. A particular change—for example, changing the way student marks are awarded to give more emphasis to revision and improvement—might yield a relatively small effect but could also be fairly easy to do and maintain. Another idea—say to transform the way teachers are evaluated—might in theory yield greater results but is also much more difficult to bring about and sustain. A third idea—say, asking all parents to do 30 minutes of homework each day with students—probably has zero chance of being done. So sometimes it's better to take on something small but feasible rather than trying to do something grand but difficult.

Consider some instances of major reforms in education that lack evidence of impact or feasibility or, even worse, of either. Many reforms at the state or national level have focused on changing governance structures, such as the roles of school boards, more parental choice, charter schools, or changed collective bargaining arrangements. Yet we know that governance changes do not themselves bring about improvements in teaching and learning or in student outcomes. Changes in governance systems may need to be addressed as part of a comprehensive strategy but cannot themselves generate much improvement. Similarly, school choice and charter schools have generated a huge amount of attention, but even their most ardent advocates have to admit that their impact, especially in relation to the time and energy invested, has been modest at best. One can support parents' rights to choose schools as a good idea and still believe that the enormous energy it has taken could have been better used to support other improvements that would have yielded better results with less turmoil.

The same is true of testing and accountability. High-quality evidence on how well students are doing is crucial, as discussed in the chapter on public confidence, but it is misguided to think that more assessment or more punishment for poor results will lead to better outcomes, either for students or for schools and educators. Even if one agrees that incentives do affect behavior—and it would be hard to argue otherwise—the evidence is that negative incentives (penalties) are less effective than positive incentives for success. Yet in education the incentives in accountability systems are typically negative, such as designation as a "failing school." In a world of competition and rankings, a system that produces 50 percent of schools as below average, with negative effects on morale, is not a good strategy. Every school that moves higher in the rankings pushes another one lower. The incentives produced by this system are perverse. Campbell's Law, coined by the great researcher Donald Campbell, says that "The more any quantitative social indicator is used for social decision-making, the more subject it will be to corruption pressures, and the more apt it will be to distort and corrupt the social processes it is intended to monitor" (Campbell 1975; *en.wikipedia.org/wiki/Campbell's_Law*). James March made the same point even more succinctly: "A system of rewards linked to precise measures is not an incentive to perform well; it is an incentive to obtain a good score" (March 1984: 28).

Even some positive incentives, such as monetary bonuses for better student performance, do not accord with the nature or culture of schools, or with teachers' sense of fairness, and so have high non-monetary costs.

Even more significantly, the accountability approach to improvement assumes that educators already know how to improve outcomes but, for whatever reasons, won't do so unless forced. While that might be the case in some schools, it conflicts with expert judgment that for the most part the problem of improvement rests in the lack of skill or knowledge. Most of the top management theorists (such as Deming or Drucker) take the view that system improvement requires system efforts and changes, not just pressure or incentives for individuals to improve. The same is, of course, true for students. Quite a few jurisdictions put lots of energy into failing students who can't meet particular standards, whether in elementary or secondary, despite abundant evidence that failure or retention in grade are entirely unproductive strategies (Field, Kuczera, and Point 2007; Hong and Raudenbush 2005).

Changes focused on structures, then, are not going to produce the desired results. However, even changes focused on teaching and learning practices may not be the right ones if they do not meet the two criteria discussed earlier. Relatively few innovations have convincing evidence of positive impact on student outcomes, especially where one seeks evidence from multiple locations produced by independent third parties rather than by the promoters of the program in question. Education is a field that spends a tiny portion of its total budget on research and evaluation, and does not yet have a strong tradition of basing practice on evidence, although this situation is improving steadily (Levin 2004).

Does this mean that schools should act only where there is strong and independent evidence of effects? The answer to that is no. Where we find problems in achievement, we have a responsibility as educators to act even where we don't have good evidence as to the best thing to do. Most of the time there will not be enough evidence, since the knowledge base in education is simply insufficient. However, under these conditions there are additional requirements to be kept in mind.

First, where there is no reliable evidence, changes should be based on a credible theory of improvement. For example, we may not have convincing evidence that increasing students' choice about the classroom assignments they do will yield better outcomes. There is good evidence, however, that individual choice is related, in many social and work settings, to increased effort, and also good reason to believe that more effort will yield better results. So there are reasonable a priori grounds, including related evidence, for thinking that increasing student choice in their work might yield better outcomes. Indeed, governments and school boards should have a standard practice of requiring a statement of supporting evidence before adopting new policies or initiatives.

Instructional innovations that do not have solid empirical support should be tested or piloted rather than imposed on an entire system. This is both ethical and efficacious. It is generally easier to put a new approach in place in a few classrooms or schools than across a system, which may reduce the problem of internal resistance. Volunteerism among students, parents, and staff can be used to ease the effort.

In this way innovation can be seen as a means of learning. In education, as in every other sector of our society, many changes will fail or will yield less than expected results. The same is true of new products or services in the marketplace, new drugs, or venture capital efforts. Indeed, venture capitalists expect 90 percent of their investments to fail, otherwise they are not taking enough risks. Failure is part of the price of learning, or, to put it another way, we have to try lots of things to learn what works. We are not talking about individual failure, though. After all, we do not fire scientists when their experiments don't work, and we do not fire people whose venture companies go bankrupt. At the same time, failure is only worth the price when there is organized learning. This means that innovations should be evaluated so that we can steadily improve our knowledge about effective policies and practices.

Evaluation of new practices need not involve large formal research projects, although more of these would be welcome, especially for large initiatives, as a way of producing more reliable evidence on change. For many innovations, even a fairly simple pre- and post-test analysis, especially if a comparison or control group can be found, would be helpful even if it falls well short of the standards of a true randomized experiment (which is very difficult to do in education, for many reasons).

Impact is not enough. As discussed earlier, one must consider feasibility as well. A change might lead to better outcomes but be difficult to do or to sustain for reasons of money or skills. For example, changes that demoralize teachers are not sustainable because good people will leave the profession, as has happened in a number of countries. Changes that assume that large numbers of people will quickly alter their behavior in fundamental ways are unlikely to be workable. Similarly, some of the reports of "schools beating the odds" are not feasible on a system-wide basis because they depend on being able to recruit many excellent teachers into a single school, whereas what we need is to improve teacher skills and efficacy across large numbers of schools.

Currently, school systems do not do well on any of these criteria. In adopting new programs, schools and districts often make quick adoption decisions without adequate consideration of whether a particular program is well supported by evidence or is the best way to use scarce time, energy, and other resources. Everyone in education can cite examples, including many of those listed at the start of this chapter. Quite often school systems will spend enormous amounts of time on changes that fail on both criteria—there is no evidence of impact and they are difficult to do. Examples would be revising entire curricula for a school or district, writing performance goals for every topic in every subject, or changing school timetables.

Instead of evidence, decisions about change are often based on testimonials, personal connections, an impressive conference presentation, or outside political pressures. Even more, the economic notions of trade-offs and opportunity costs are virtually unknown in education policymaking. A program is launched because a board member or superintendent likes it, or because the state recommends it, or because some other school somewhere else says it obtained good results with it. All too rarely is an attempt made to assess any given change proposal against the criteria of its demonstrated power to produce lasting results given the resources and effort required. Otherwise, we would not have spent so much time and energy on changes that were so unlikely to deliver the desired results.

An additional problem is that education systems are highly prone to stand-alone projects. The typical pattern is to adopt some innovation, as just described, in one or a few schools, often based on short-term funding or the enthusiasm of a few people. Based on anecdotal evidence, the innovation is called a success but is never implemented widely across the entire system. After a time, it disappears as the funding runs out or the enthusiasts who sustained it move on. While projects can be important as a means of testing ideas and learning about what works, they are only of value if this knowledge is then used across an entire school, district, or system. When it is not, we waste time, effort, and money.

The opposite of the project disease is the whole-school change, or comprehensive school-reform approach. In the United States particularly, a number of models have been developed in the last 10 or 20 years with the idea of having a tested approach adopted across an entire school or district. These models, it should be said, vary enormously in their intentions and approaches. However, whole-school reforms have also run into serious problems (Quint 2008). In some cases the model is only adopted superficially so that it does not produce the desired results. In other cases the model is mandated by school or district leadership but dies when those leaders leave the organization. In general the research on comprehensive school reform has found disappointing results, both in terms of adoption of the models and in their impact on student achievement.

The external and internal pressures around particular changes cannot be entirely avoided, but a school or district with clear criteria rooted in evidence for its program decisions would have a much sounder basis for resisting such pressures, and currently few school systems have such criteria in place.

## Political dynamics

Almost all the literature on education change focuses on dynamics within the school or school system and the steps that should be taken by education leaders and teachers. These are clearly important and also make up a central part of this book. But the direction, success, and sustainability of change in schools really rest as much on political dynamics as on improved teaching and learning practices, leadership, or any of the capacity-building factors just discussed. Because these factors are so important, they are discussed several times in this book, notably in the chapter on public confidence and in the chapter on leading in the face of distractions.

Educators tend to dislike politics, to see it as something that gets in the way of their work. What we need to remember is that politics of various kinds has an enormous amount to do with whether the right changes get adopted, whether they are effectively supported, and whether they last long enough to make a real difference.

Consider the role of large and small "p" politics in any education system. Elected politicians have primary responsibility for shaping large-scale reforms. Since education has assumed high political visibility, governments everywhere have felt compelled to promise improvement and to take action to fulfill such promises. While educators often feel these actions are less than helpful or even downright negative, keep in mind that government directions are not intended to please educators but to appeal to the general public, whose knowledge of and ideas about education are inevitably limited.

No Child Left Behind, which has dominated education policy in the United States since 2001 and has so deeply affected many schools and districts, was clearly the result of the educational views of the Bush administration as tempered by the compromises necessary to get the bill passed by Congress—not all of which were improvements. Many states have also adopted significant education reform programs. Indeed, one of the main obstacles to school improvement is that such plans are often adopted, then poorly supported, and, even worse, abandoned or changed when a new administration comes into office. Many states have seen several different comprehensive reform programs adopted and imposed on schools in a period of only a few years, making it impossible for any system to do well. In Canada, the Ontario government that was in place from 1995 to 2003 had an agenda for education that emphasized higher standards, lower spending, and public attacks on teachers, whereas since 2003 all those have been reversed. Nothing is more destructive of morale in any system than frequent, sudden reversals of strategy or policy, especially when people have worked hard to make the previous policy successful.

Compare those experiences to the comments Ontario premier Dalton McGuinty made to a large gathering of education leaders in the fall of 2005. By this time, halfway into the government's mandate, many important changes had already been made, new resources were flowing to schools, and improved results were already evident. The premier spoke to several hundred superintendents and principals who had gathered to discuss the Literacy and Numeracy strategy. He spoke about the importance of education, about his government's determination to work in partnership with the school system, to recognize the great work done by educators, and to hear and take seriously their views and ideas. But he also challenged them by saying that he was not prepared to accept that any children should or could be "written off" as the inevitable failures of any large system. The room got very quiet when the province's political leader reminded us of our moral obligations as educators, especially because people knew that the government had matched actions to its pronouncements. This speech was an important moment that helped galvanize support and energy for the Ontario strategies.

Politics also matter at the school board level. Who gets elected can make a big difference. A school board that works together well and respects its professionals (which does not mean always doing what the professionals want or recommend) creates a very different atmosphere and sense of direction from a board that is badly split, highly suspicious of its staff, and driven by personal animosities instead of policy concerns.

Consider the case of Philadelphia in the mid-1990s (Christman, Corcoran, and Corcoran 2002). In 1995 Philadelphia hired a new superintendent, David Hornbeck, to improve a school system that had experienced enormous problems. A few months later the system received a $50 million grant from the Annenberg Foundation, matched by $100 million in local contributions, to support large-scale reform. Hornbeck developed a 10-point plan (the points are outlined in chapter 5), called "Children Achieving."

Over the first few years of the plan, results in Philadelphia improved, especially in elementary grades where there was a clear focus on literacy and relatively explicit direction as to instructional practices. As in so many other settings, there was less success in high schools. However, the plan, and Hornbeck's leadership, ran into serious difficulties as bitter public disputes developed between the board and the state government over the funding being provided to Philadelphia schools, debates that "overwhelmed discussions about the progress of instructional reform" (10). It was also difficult to sustain support and interest from the broader community after the first few years, especially when it became evident that improving student results would take years of sustained effort. Business sector support waned as the key people changed roles.

A second political problem was the emphasis on decentralization of authority to schools and clusters of schools. Much time and effort went into figuring out how these new structures would work, and many schools did not have the capacity to take on all the new responsibilities, further distracting school leaders from the instructional role they had also been assigned. As teachers and principals became disillusioned with some elements of the plan, they became less willing participants in the approach as a whole.

In 1999 city voters passed a referendum to have the mayor appoint the school board instead of having it directly elected, diminishing Superintendent Hornbeck's authority. Later that year, the governor of Pennsylvania proposed a school voucher plan that was supported by many business leaders in Philadelphia. In 2000 the state passed legislation to take over failing schools in districts including Philadelphia. By this time the 1995 plan had run out of steam, and Superintendent Hornbeck resigned in the face of budget cuts made by the appointed board.

Many similar stories could be told about other districts or states, along with some contrasting stories. Boston enjoyed ten years of progress in part because of a stable board and strong leadership. Connecticut was able to adopt and implement a strong strategy over a number of years with good results (Wilson, Darling-Hammond, and Berry 2001). Progress is not, as discussed in the chapters on leadership, a matter of having a single person who can turn things around, but a matter of an entire system pointed in the same direction, with all the parts working together reasonably smoothly. The study by Stone et al. (2001) of education reform efforts in ten U.S. cities shows both how difficult and how promising it can be to build political support for meaningful school improvement.

Politics matter not only at the national or state level. Inside a school or district, micropolitics also play a key role. We all know the difference between a school with a cohesive, supportive staff with strong, positive relationships and a school without them. Tensions among people on a staff affect not only working relationships but also the decisions and choices made, and often not for the better. People compete for status or position while student priorities are ignored. Program choices may be made to boost someone's career rather than because of careful thought about students' needs.

Educators may feel that these political processes are beyond their control. It is, certainly, difficult if not impossible for any single organization to change the outcome of a national or state election. As one example, teacher unions in jurisdictions such as California or British Columbia or Australia have been active participants in elections and have spent large amounts of money supporting particular parties or candidates, with uneven success.

At the local district level the picture is rather different. In most places, voter turnout for school trustees is quite low, so a relatively small group of committed volunteers with some modest resources may indeed be able to affect who gets elected. But the central issue here is not so much around electoral politics as it is around all the other political aspects of education that happen outside elections. There is much that educators can do—in fact, that we do whether aware of it or not— that does affect political processes, views, and decisions, in and beyond our own schools and systems.

- *Our communication with internal and external communities.* Is it frequent, open, honest, and focused on our priorities? Or is it infrequent, one-sided, defensive, and focused on everything but what we think is most important?
- *Our approach to stakeholders.* Do we treat all partners, every day, as if we they thought really mattered to us (which does not mean agreeing with them on everything), or are we sometimes dismissive of others' legitimate interests and ideas?
- *Our use of evidence.* Do we pay objective attention to the best available evidence even if it tells us something we don't really like, or are we more motivated by our immediate interests or the pressures on us?
- *Our advice to senior staff and elected officials.* Are we giving the best advice we have, or are we sometimes motivated to avoid tough issues or to soft-peddle what we think in light of what we know about the views of elected leaders?
- *Our commitment to the larger system.* Do we think about our decisions and actions in light of their impact on the education system as a whole, or do we care about our own organization's welfare without much regard to what that might mean for others?

All of us would want to say we do these things well, but experience suggests that few are able to resist the strong pressures and temptations to choose the easy road, at lest some of the time. Yet these and other similar indicators and actions help shape the political climate around education in a school, a district, and even a state or country. They are tangible ways in which educators generate the kinds of education politics we want and need to support real improvement in our schools.

### Poor implementation

While many innovations proposed for schools have not been well considered, and others have failed for lack of political support, neither of these causes is enough to understand the full problem of improvement. In many cases schools and school systems have had good ideas and have had a reasonable degree of support for those ideas, yet the result has still been inadequate. Many of the ideas listed at the start of this chapter fall into the category of "potentially good but never really caught on." A sobering experience is to read through back issues—say, from 20 years ago—of some of the top practitioner journals such as *Educational Leadership* or *Phi Delta Kappan*, and see how many of the great program and policy ideas being proposed then are still being proposed today but have never been broadly or successfully adopted.

Having the right innovations is not enough. There are plenty of good ideas going around as to what schools could do to improve student outcomes. The problem is that even the best ideas can, and do, fail if badly implemented. A few years ago a large consulting company ran television ads in which a couple of hot-shot young consultants were talking with a senior manager, who said that he liked their report and now wanted them to implement it. In the next scene they are leaving the building, laughing to themselves about the bizarre notion that they would be asked to implement the changes they had proposed! It turns out that implementation is much harder than people think but also much more important than most people recognize. Without effective implementation, reforms remain at the level of rhetoric.

But what does "implementation" mean? Forty years ago large-scale reforms were introduced with the idea that if we just gave teachers new curricula or new books, schools would improve. It was soon discovered that these reforms did not result in the changes in practice that their proponents had anticipated. Teachers either did not use the new products, or used them in ways that were different from what had been planned.

Then people came up with "teacher proof" innovations, where teachers would follow prescribed approaches without having to make any judgments of their own. This, too, failed; predictably, since the whole idea fundamentally misjudges the nature of teaching and learning (about which more a little later in this chapter). As the old saw from George Bernard Shaw goes, "Build a system that even a fool can use, and only a fool will want to use it."

As noted earlier in this chapter, when one considers the scale and scope of changing daily practices of thousands of people in hundreds or thousands of schools, the problem of implementation is entirely to be expected. Changing what people do in their daily work clearly involves much more than being told to do something different or being given a demonstration of a new procedure.

In large part, this is because behavior is largely a matter of routines and habits, whether in teaching or any other role. People have procedures or scripts that we fall into automatically, just as there are routine patterns of communication and behavior in our families. These do not change easily, even if we want to change them. Just think about how hard it is to put into practice a new routine in our personal lives, such as regular exercise. We know we should do it, we know how to do it, and yet we still don't.

Change is much harder in a social situation. Schools are busy places with lots of daily pressures, so adding something new, or changing something, requires extra energy and effort. Moreover, we may not be very good at the new practice at first—in fact, if the new practice is challenging, it is likely that we won't be good at it for a while. Any important skill takes lots of practice to learn, and without support people are likely to revert to what they know, even if it does not work as well. Even surgeons have to learn to do surgery, which they do through carefully supervised practice (Gawande 2002). But in schools—whether as a teacher or principal or superintendent—there is no tradition or organization that supports carefully supervised learning of this kind.

Then, too, the challenge of individual change is compounded by pressure from others to remain the same. Other teachers or principals may resist a colleague's change if they think it will make their job harder or put pressure on them to do likewise. Students can also be resistant to new practices for the same reasons. So a teacher's efforts to encourage critical thinking or problem-solving may be met with a signal lack of enthusiasm from students who are used to having clear tasks in order to earn certain grades.

Of course people can and do change their behavior, even habitual or addictive behaviors. Millions of people have stopped smoking, or have taken up regular exercises, or have learned new ways to relate to others. If change in behavior were not possible, there would be no point to having schools. The point is that such change is hard to do, and takes sustained effort and support.

As we have learned more about creating lasting and effective change, it has become clear that "implementation" is the wrong word. Effective change in schools does not come from some kind of blind obedience to a central plan or, as noted earlier, from the beneficent operation of markets, but from thoughtful application of effective practices in particular contexts. It requires the ability to achieve goals in new ways under differing—and changing—circumstances. Although some elements will be common, perhaps even universal, other elements will differ from place to place and time to time.

Schools and school systems provide a particular case of this process. Both teaching and learning require positive energy, and that energy is unleashed when people believe in and care about what they are doing. Gradually and painfully we have come to learn that real change in schools requires will and skill, capacity and understanding and commitment, and that developing these requires considerable and carefully designed effort.

This kind of change is much harder to bring about, but it is the only kind that really works and lasts. The requirements for building engagement and motivation are discussed in later chapters, but it is worth

81

taking some time here to consider what is required in order to build the capacity of a school system to create and sustain real change.

This effort has come to be known as capacity-building. Because capacity-building is so important to the whole line of this book, it's worth being clear about what it means. Among the foremost proponents of capacity-building are Richard Elmore and Michael Fullan. As Elmore (2004) puts it:

> The theory of action . . . might be stated as follows: The development of systematic knowledge about, and related to, large-scale instructional improvement requires a change in the prevailing culture of administration and teaching in schools. Cultures do not change by mandate; they change by the specific displacement of existing norms, structures, and processes by others; the process of cultural change depends fundamentally on modeling the new values and behavior that you expect to displace the existing ones. (11)

And Fullan (2008) has recently written:

> Capacity building concerns competencies, resources and motivation. Individuals and groups are high in capacity if they possess and continue to develop knowledge and skills, if they attract and use resources (time, ideals, expertise, money) wisely, and if they are committed to putting in the energy to get important things done *collectively* and *continuously* (ever learning). This is a tall order in complex systems, but it is exactly the order required. (57)

Capacity-building requires that people have the opportunity to learn new and more effective practices. This is true for classroom teachers but also for principals, support staff, and, indeed, students. Of course, this is why we have professional development in education. But professional development in schools has been roundly criticized for many years, if not decades, by teachers as well as by researchers, because it so often has so little impact on what people actually do. It is abundantly clear that professional development days or sessions do not have significant impact on teaching practice anymore than going to leadership development seminars has much effect on what leaders do in our organizations (Hesketh 1997).

It may seem self-evident that behavior change requires ongoing support, but if so the understanding is rarely put into practice. Many quite complex changes are introduced into schools with the idea that a few days of professional development or a few support documents will be sufficient. Sometimes change is not even supported to that extent; schools or teachers may be sent a memo or a policy document with the expectation that effective implementation will result. Yet we know how hard it is to change practice in large organizations, for reasons already outlined.

Capacity-building requires a thoughtful, sustained approach that will create and support the changes in behavior or practice that we want to see. Because schools are social settings, change is not just a matter of giving people new ideas but of creating the social conditions that foster and support changed practices. This in turn requires what I call infrastructure—the wherewithal to bring about changes in what people do every day. Simply put, there can be no effective or lasting change without careful attention to the infrastructure and supports required for implementation, with "implementation" meaning here both adoption and modification to suit particular contexts.

### What sorts of supports and infrastructure could be considered?

A solid plan for infrastructure would include several components, all of which are necessary to some degree. Many of these elements are discussed further in chapters 5 and 6, but it is worth having some brief mention here as well of four central elements of capacity-building: leadership structures, materials, learning opportunities, and data.

One of the most important aspects of capacity-building is to have structural elements that serve to remind everyone of what the priorities are. For the Ontario Literacy and Numeracy strategy, the Ministry of Education created a special purpose secretariat to lead the initiative, with outstanding educators and leaders seconded to its staff. These "student achievement officers" worked collaboratively with school districts to help the districts define and focus their work on literacy and numeracy so that goals got translated into actions. They were well versed in ideas of capacity-building and spent a great deal of time working with district and school leaders on how greater local capacity could be created and sustained. The student achievement officers had no authority to require districts to do particular things but did have some degree of moral suasion and could apply some pressure. In some cases these relationships were smooth while in others there was considerable tension with districts that did not necessarily share the ministry's focus on literacy and numeracy, but in every case their work strengthened attention to capacity-building in the districts.

Analogously, each district was both pushed and supported in developing its own leadership team for literacy and numeracy, with whom the student achievement officers worked. These teams varied depending on the size, culture and structure of each district, but they typically included at least one very senior person such as a superintendent in addition to consultants (where such positions existed) and often one or more experienced principals. These teams worked in quite different ways in each district in terms of their mandate, composition, activities, and so on, but in all districts they did provide both a vehicle and a forum for working through how the district would approach this priority.

The same leadership team approach was replicated in every elementary school, again with flexibility as to who was included depending on school size and organization. The goal of these teams was not so much to implement the provincial strategy as it was to ensure regular and focused attention in each school on improved literacy and numeracy work. Just having these teams at each level marked an increase in capacity. An important element of the Ontario strategy was that each district and each school had at least some scope to find a way of improving that fit its history and culture, as long as it was working actively on the central challenge of improving student outcomes in a way consistent with research and evidence.

For the high school graduation initiative in Ontario, an analogous model was employed. However, instead of creating a special-purpose secretariat, the ministry funded a dedicated position in each school district for a Student Success Leader—a senior person with lead responsibility for the overall initiative. These leaders remained employees of the districts, not of the ministry, though the ministry worked closely and directly with the Student Success Leaders, bringing them together regularly, providing them with materials, and using them as a sounding board as the elements of the strategy were developed and implemented.

Student success used the same approach at the district and school level, with a leadership team established in every secondary school and every district. The high school leadership teams were often, but not always, led by vice-principals and included guidance counselors and student success teachers (a role described in chapter 2).

The impact of these leadership structures has been considerable, even startling. In many schools the existence of the leadership team has been the impetus for regular conversations about progress, success, and challenges—precisely the sorts of issues that somehow never got to the forefront of people's time in earlier years. There are good results simply from shining a light on an issue and putting a structure in place to give it attention.

The Ontario strategy was modeled on the English strategy, also outlined briefly in chapter 2. In England, the National Literacy and Numeracy strategy included the creation of ten regional teams across the country to provide direction and support to schools and local authorities for implementation of the strategy. Somewhat later in the process another regional team was added to work with teacher-training institutions to align their work with the strategies. In addition, more than 600 positions were created across England for literacy and numeracy consultant teachers, who were to provide direct support to teachers and schools around changed literacy practices, such as implementation of the Literacy Hour with its three-part lesson structure. Schools were also asked, if not required, to designate leaders or coordinators for each strategy.

Resources and materials are an important part of capacity-building, but insufficient on their own. Certainly schools and teachers need good curriculum documents, lesson plans, and teaching strategy ideas. Most jurisdictions working on change will put this element in place. Ontario supported its strategies with resource books, new curriculum materials, webcasts, and other kinds of resources. So did England as part of its Literacy and Numeracy strategy. Major U.S. initiatives have also almost always involved some resources for schools and teachers of this kind—for example, the creation of new curricula in Boston to support the "Focus on Children" plan.

Resources alone, however, will not change social practices. Teachers need to see not only what they might do differently but how they could do it in the reality of their classrooms. The key to this developing understanding is ongoing work with colleagues—seeing others carry out new practices with students like yours and having others help you learn to do these new practices. That means personal contact with colleagues, in the school setting.

School-based learning can be supported through several means. One is the use of learning communities, discussed further later in this book. People like to learn from colleagues engaged in similar work, and effective schools virtually always exhibit a strong sense of community in which teachers work together, exchange ideas, and support and teach one another. There are many things schools and school systems can do to support collegial learning, from policies to resources to leadership, all of which are part of the infrastructure for improvement.

Learning communities may, and often do, require outside assistance as well. Sometimes the people in the organization simply do not have the skills or knowledge to improve themselves. They need somebody who knows more to show them what they could do differently. This is where such roles as coaches or lead teachers come into play. Sometimes learning communities can get caught up in self-satisfaction ("we're doing fine"), blame ("if only we had better students or parents"), or internal politics ("I don't respect that person so I'm not going to pay attention to anything he says"). An outsider may be in position to uncover and challenge those patterns, pushing the team to a deeper level of learning.

Many schools and systems are increasingly interested in roles such as coaches or instructional leaders. Boston is one example of a district that made use of coaches and school leadership teams. The Boston strategy involved extensive use of school-based coaches to support the new curriculum and teaching expectations, coupled with an instructional leadership team in each school. Working with local colleges and universities, Boston also developed programs for alternative certification and a leadership development institute to support new principals. As a related important element, Boston built a common web-based system, giving all schools access to current data on achievement and attendance of all students.

These new roles are another good example of infrastructure that supports capacity-building and change. Having the roles is not sufficient, though. Processes need to be in place to support the roles. If there is no acknowledged time for literacy coaches to do their work or for teachers to work with new resource materials, then change is less likely. If the proposed changes are never discussed at staff meetings or other school events, change is less likely. If they are not communicated and reinforced internally and externally, then change is less likely. If there are no data on either the changes or their results for students, success is less likely.

Ontario has also used community-building strategies extensively to support local capacity. Many Ontario districts were already engaged in some kind of learning-community initiative prior to 2004; the introduction of the new strategies simply provided a sharper focus for their work. However, many other districts began or extended their use of learning community models, often supported with provincial funds, as part of their capacity-building for the strategies. The networks of district leaders that the ministry created for each strategy can also be seen as learning communities. In 2006 Ontario invited the superintendents of some of its most challenged districts, along with a few from the most successful districts, to create a learning network that would help all districts do better. Every single invited superintendent took an active part in this network. Similarly, the ministry supported networks of principals and held many events that allowed teachers to meet across districts.

Effective use of data and research can also be important. Research that supports changes in practice and local data that show that current practices are not working are both powerful levers for getting people to try something different.

Many different kinds of data and approaches to gathering it can be useful. For example, school walk-throughs, used extensively in San Diego, can be powerful aids to learning about good—and not so good—practice. Another good example of the impact of data is the widespread use of "data walls" in Ontario elementary schools. A data wall is a means of displaying the status and progress of each student on some important common measure such as reading skills. Typically the reading status of every child in the school is displayed (in a private place, of course, such as a staff room) in a way that allows everyone to see which individuals and groups are making more or less progress. Often data walls use different colored Post-It notes to show different groups or classes of students, so anyone looking immediately gets a sense of what is happening group by group and in the school as a whole. Data walls are great vehicles for creating discussion among staff about the reasons for particular patterns, leading—if the school atmosphere is right—to good discussions about what might be done differently to improve students' performance. An analogous approach can be used by districts or states for the same purpose. The point is not to have winners and losers but to push everyone to consider how performance overall can be improved. If data walls or any similar tool is used for individual rewards, then they will soon lose any value or legitimacy as a school improvement device.

It is possible, as the examples indicate, to organize supports for change in many useful ways. The specifics should be tailored to each context. As long as the essentials of dedicated structures and roles, supportive processes, and evidence of use and impact are included, increased capacity is like to result.

**CONCLUSION**

This chapter may have begun as a depressing list of reasons as to why things go wrong. To be sure, we have many examples of ineffective or even quite negative changes in education. Yet there are grounds for optimism as well. Remember Higdon's Law:

1. Good judgment comes from experience.
2. Experience comes from bad judgment.

We will inevitably make mistakes in any important endeavor. The question is whether we learn from those mistakes so that our subsequent performance improves. We have made many mistakes in education in the last two decades, but we have also learned a great deal. We know much more about the challenges to implementation and how we can address them. We also know much more about which changes matter most, the subject of the next chapter.

# 5

# An Agenda for Improving
# Teaching and Learning

Creating and maintaining meaningful school improvement is difficult, but we have also been learning a great deal in the last few decades both about what needs to be done and how to do it. Although the barriers, as described in the previous chapter, are significant, educators are in a better position than ever before—at least from the standpoint of knowledge—to achieve better results for our students. There are two sets of factors that require attention.

The most important elements of improvement involve strengthening teaching and learning practices and adult-student relationships across all classrooms and teachers in a school or system. Our knowledge about effective practice, though still quite incomplete, has increased dramatically and continues to improve; there is no excuse for retaining practices that are less effective. These practices are the subject of this chapter.

Changing instructional and related practices, however, will only take place in the right school and system context. Without the right supporting organizational elements, improved teaching and learning either will not occur or will not last. These supporting conditions are discussed in the next chapter.

## NINE ESSENTIAL PRACTICES
## FOR IMPROVED OUTCOMES

Let us turn our attention to teaching and learning, which lie, after all, at the heart of the schooling enterprise. Many authors have produced lists of priorities for school improvement, and most reform plans also contain a statement of priorities (see box 5.1). Borrowing from these and many other similar lists, the essential practices for improved outcomes proposed in this volume include nine elements, as follows:

1. High expectations for all students
2. Strong personal connections between students and adults
3. Greater student engagement and motivation
4. A rich and engaging formal and informal curriculum
5. Effective teaching practices in all classrooms on a daily basis
6. Effective use of data and feedback by students and staff to improve learning
7. Early support with minimum disruption for students in need
8. Strong positive relationships with parents
9. Effective engagement of the broader community

There is obviously quite a bit of overlap in these lists, although there are also significant differences among them. None of the proponents of any particular list would claim that theirs is the only reasonable for-

---

**BOX 5.1**
**Improvement Priorities of Selected Reform Plans**

Marzano's frequently cited review (Marzano 2003) includes the following:

- School level—guaranteed and viable curriculum
- Challenging goals and effective feedback
- Parent and community involvement
- Safe and orderly environment
- Collegiality and professionalism

---

- Teacher-instructional strategies
- Classroom management
- Classroom curriculum design
- Student-home atmosphere
- Learned intelligence and background knowledge
- Motivation

Working from a somewhat different perspective, Fullan, Hill, and Crevola (2006) focus on three instructional needs:

- Transforming classroom instruction
- Creating expert instructional systems
- Building a critical-learning instructional path

Here are two examples drawn from important recent efforts to improve student outcomes in major U.S. cities. The Boston Public Schools' "Focus on Children" Plan, 2001 (Aspen Institute 2006), prioritized:

- Clear expectations for what students should learn
- Rigorous, consistent curriculum
- Expectations about instructional practice
- Support for teachers through professional development
- Appropriate formative and summative assessment

And Philadelphia's Children Achieving Plan from 1995 listed ten strategic elements (Christman, Corcoran, and Corcoran 2002):

1. High expectations for all students
2. Standards to measure the results of reforms
3. Shrink the central bureaucracy
4. Intensive, sustained training for staff
5. All students healthy and ready to learn
6. Community support and service for students
7. Up-to-date technology
8. Public engagement
9. Adequate resources
10. Address all priorities together, at once, starting now

mulation, and readers may well want to construct their own list with some different elements. However, it is likely that any thoughtful list would contain many elements in common. Indeed, there is considerable consensus about the importance of improved daily instruction, engaged students, effective use of data, and so on. The issue is not putting together the right list. The real challenge is making these things happen in a school or district or state, so the focus of this chapter is less on providing lists of things to do and more on thinking about how these elements fit together and can be moved forward.

It is also important to keep in mind any list like this is "a meal, not a menu," meaning that one cannot just pick a few items and ignore the rest; all the items on the list must be addressed to some degree. One can put more or less emphasis on particular items at any given time. Some can be given more importance than others. The particular form that each takes will depend at least to some degree on the context of the school or system. Secondary schools have some additional complexities that require different change strategies—for example, due to specialization of courses and teachers. Small schools might address some of the priorities differently from large schools. Many of the issues play out differently in rural settings than they do in urban communities. But all nine elements will have to be taken seriously by every school at some point in any serious effort to improve student outcomes.

### High expectations for all students

If we don't believe students can achieve, then they are highly unlikely to do so. It's really as simple as that. As discussed earlier, we have lots of evidence, historical and current, to show that despite all the rhetoric about high expectations, in practice we often underestimate students' potential. This is true both for individual students and for groups or communities. There is nothing new about the call for high expectations, or the mantra that "all children can learn." The challenge is to move from "high expectations for all" as a slogan—where it is already common—to its being truly grounded in daily practice in schools—which is much less common.

So many adults and young people can tell stories about teachers who said they would not amount to anything, about guidance counselors who urged them to take an easier program and lower their horizons, about schools that did not really seem to care if they were there or not. Any educator can tell such stories. One is the story of Arne Boldt, a Manitoban with one leg who learned to high-jump 6 feet, 9 inches. Videos of this amazing feat can be found today on YouTube even though it was done some thirty years ago. Boldt learned to achieve this astounding physical and psychological feat because of his own indomitable will but also because he had people who supported and believed in him; he certainly did not fit anyone's preconceived idea of a successful high jumper!

Consider some further examples. Last year I had the opportunity to interview for admission to a top Ivy League university a young man in Toronto named Mark. He is the first in his family to undertake postsecondary education; he already has a business diploma from a community college and now wants to do a business degree at a top university. This is a young man who at age 12 was 100 pounds overweight and a victim of bullying, and was told by a teacher that he was a disgrace to his family who would never amount to anything! Luckily, Mark had a family and other teachers who believed in him. At age 13 he took up martial arts, earned two black belts, lost 100 pounds, and went from being a student who could barely read to honors list in high school and in each year of college. At least one teacher certainly got his potential wrong, though luckily some others saw more in him.

As deputy minister of education I visited many schools and heard many moving stories from students whose lives had been changed by the actions of a teacher. One that sticks out in my mind was in a school in a small Ontario city in the fall of 2006. At an event where the minister of education was recognizing the school's efforts to increase student success, a young woman got up and talked about how, a year earlier, she had a serious drug problem, had been suspended several times, was in trouble with the law, and saw no future for herself. But the school's guidance counselor, she said, refused to give up on her even when she had given up on herself. With this teacher's support and that of family and friends, she had turned her life around, was close to graduating from high school, and saw her future completely differently. As she told the story she was in tears, and so, of course, was the audience.

Such stories are easy to find. Thousands of students have their lives changed for the better every day by the actions and concern of teachers. But there are still too many students for whom this does not happen. And that is why a focus on high expectations for all students must be at the very top of our list of valuable teaching and learning practices.

Although it's important to talk about high expectations, changing the way things are on the ground does happens not by rhetoric or goal statements but through the other items on this list. Educators, like parents, must not only understand what they should do but see *how* they can do it within what they understand as the real constraints and conditions of their situation.

### Strong personal connections between students and adults

All the studies of dropouts tell us that the strongest single factor in students' leaving or staying is their feeling that someone in the school knows who they are and truly cares about their future. In 2004 the Ontario Ministry of Education commissioned a study of school dropouts in which the researchers interviewed several hundred young men and women. Some had left school, some were still in school despite disliking it, and others found schooling to their liking. Universally these young people, successful or not, said that the most important factor for them was whether anyone in the school seemed to know who they were or care about what happened to them. Over and over, dropouts reported that nobody seemed to care if they stayed or not.

So often, even one caring adult can make a big difference in a student's life. A young teacher named Amanda Cooper, very involved in the Ontario Student Success initiatives in her district and also a doctoral student at the Ontario Institute for Studies in Education, concluded after conversation with her colleagues that quite often it took less than 20 minutes of real, supportive, one-on-one time with a student to change the student's course or trajectory in the school from negative to positive. Twenty minutes! Motivation researcher Susan Nolen tells of asking teachers working with her to spend 30 minutes getting to know a student with whom they currently do not relate very well, and having them tell her that this simple step changed not only their view of the student but often dramatically altered the way the student behaved and engaged in their class. Getting to know students as people is the strongest single factor in raising our expectations as to what they can do.

Many innovations have been adopted by schools and districts to try to build better adult-student relationships, especially in high schools. These include house systems, student advisory groups, home room advisor systems, and others. The most notable recently is the small schools initiative, strongly supported by the Gates Foundation. But personal relationships cannot be built by changing structures; they require—well, personal relationships. They are much more a matter of culture than structure, as evaluations of the small schools initiatives have found (David 2008; Evan et al. 2006). In the 1990s Ontario attempted to create a Teacher Advisor Program in which each teacher would work with and get to know a small group of high school students. The program failed in most schools because teachers were so put off by the government's overall agenda of funding cuts, disrespect for collective agreements, and increased workload that many would not engage with this new process even though it made sense to them conceptually.

On the other hand, the introduction in Ontario high schools in 2005 of Student Success Teachers has had a very positive impact, as described in chapter 2. It may be necessary to make some structural or operational changes in a school to support better relationships, but nobody should think that better relationships will flow just from changes in school structures.

So what do we do to support better adult-student relationships in schools? One part of it is the overall climate in the organization. Where educators and support staff believe in their work, feel they are respected, and see their mission as both important and supported, overall human relationships will be better, with spillover to teacher-student relationships. That is not enough either, however. The best strategy schools can use is to take advantage of and support the positive relationships that occur naturally between staff and students. Some of these are between athletes and coaches, musicians and their directors, students and favorite teachers. There is much merit in letting both students and adults find the people with whom they relate well, since no adult will be equally effective with all young people, and each student has her or his own character that needs a somewhat kindred spirit. If a relatively open process of connecting people is coupled with a strong safety net for students in difficulty, as described later, the results are likely to be good.

### Greater student engagement and motivation

Increasing student motivation to learn is the single most powerful thing schools could do to improve results. We all know the difference motivation makes for performance. It is almost impossible to prevent motivated students from doing well (not that anybody would try!), and it is just about as difficult to help unmotivated students succeed. The interesting thing is that a great deal is known about human motivation in schools and elsewhere (Marzano 2003; McCombs and Whistler 1997; Kohn 1999). Unfortunately, the motivation research has never been strongly connected to the education policy literature despite the obvious importance of doing so.

A substantial research literature in psychology tells us that students at school and adults in their work or personal lives are motivated largely by the same things. We want tasks that we find meaningful in some way. We wish for some autonomy in how we do the work we undertake. We want supportive feedback that helps us improve our performance and gentle assistance if we get stuck. We want good colleagues to work with, meaning people we respect and who respect us. And we want a sense that the work is of some genuine consequence to someone, whether it be a craft project, a musical performance, a piece of writing, or a science assignment.

In principle these conditions ought to be manageable in most classrooms, and indeed good teachers put them into practice daily. Such practices as choice in assignments, clear standards for good work, the opportunity to revise and improve work, opportunities to work with peers, and supportive assistance when performance is not yet good are all under the control of teachers. Yet boredom and lack of engagement remain endemic in schools around the world, and seemingly unmotivated students are a main complaint of teachers. In discussion it sometimes turns out that what educators may mean by engaged and motivated students is that the students do what we want obediently and without complaint. That is not, however, how most adults would think about motivation and engagement in our own lives. It is important to recognize that motivation is situational, not an unchanging character trait. The same students who appear to be totally unmotivated in class may be quite willing to spend endless hours of their own time rebuilding a car engine or learning a new video game or sewing something they want to wear. Greater engagement is a vehicle that improves students' work and makes teachers' lives easier as well.

It is important for schools and districts to know how their students are experiencing their education. Just as principals tend to be more positive about school conditions than are teachers, so teachers are often more sanguine about student attitudes than students themselves report. Schools and districts that collect regular data from students on their attitudes toward school and learning are better positioned to take the necessary steps to improve motivation in ways that are entirely consistent with the other items on this agenda. The development of new, simple online surveys, as one example (such as Tell Them from Me, *www.thelearningbar.com/ttfm/who.php*), makes it easy as well as useful for any school to keep track of student attitudes and perspectives. More importantly, this is an area in which significant change can be brought about relatively easily, without requiring new programs or additional staff, and with results that are positive for teachers as well as students, since increased student motivation is very positive for teachers' experience of their work.

## A rich and engaging formal and informal curriculum

Curriculum is often described as a central element for school improvement. My perspective is different; I put teaching and learning practices far ahead of curriculum as a means of improving student outcomes, and believe that the emphasis on curriculum in many places has not been the best priority for limited time, energy, and resources.

For one thing, curriculum, no matter how good, is often not used, or not used fully by teachers and schools. Curriculum documents almost inevitably end up with too much material in them so that teachers feel compelled to race through large numbers of topics rather than focusing on quality teaching and learning in a more limited number of areas. Or the curricula are written by—and for—highly expert teachers and are not manageable for the large number of teachers who do not have the same depth of knowledge and background. The Ontario elementary school curriculum, as an example, has more than 3000 separate objectives in it—amounting to nearly two per day for 200 days a year for 8 years. This is simply not sensible. Yet efforts to simplify curricula often end up having exactly the opposite effect, as all sorts of groups seek to have their own particular preferences inserted into curriculum documents and governments find it impossible to resist the pressures on them to add more goals. After all, don't we want all students to know the names and birthplaces of all the presidents, or the capitals of all the countries, or the names of all the elements and their places on the periodic table, or any number of other facts and skills? The fact that most of us do not remember most of our school curricula even a few months, let alone decades, later does not prevent efforts to add steadily more content to school programs. As the humorous graduation greeting card says, "As you graduate from high school it's very important to keep one thing in mind. . . . Because it would be a shame to forget everything!" Writing new curricula or writing performance objectives is not a good way to use teachers' time in comparison with improving daily student assessment practices or learning new pedagogical practices.

That being said, schools that want to engage students fully do pay attention to having a broad range of programs and activities, whether curricular or extracurricular. This is less a matter of curriculum content than of having a range of areas of study and activities within those areas that can appeal to the great diversity of student aptitudes and interests, since it is very important that all students find at least some part of their school day appealing to them. Activities such as music, drama, and sports often provide opportunities for students who are not as interested in the standard academic work to demonstrate their skills and find a place in the school. The same is true for community engagement activities such as outreach or volunteer or community service programs. Even in the more traditional school subjects, such as language or science, ways can be found for students to explore different kinds of skills and talents, whether these involve writing, speaking, organizing, leading, supporting others, and so on.

Curriculum organization is more significant at the secondary level, where schools struggle, as they always have, with the problem of finding ways to address the interests of diverse students while avoiding the common pitfall of a status hierarchy of courses and programs in which some come to be seen as places for "less capable" students. Secondary school systems around the world have tried various ways of addressing this problem, but with limited success. The seemingly inevitable preference in secondary schools for university preparation almost always leads to any other program or track having lower status and being filled primarily with students who cannot or will not do the "real thing," which is academic courses. At the same time, parental and student expectations for participation in postsecondary education have been rising, so there is increasing resistance to having students in any program that does not allow access to postsecondary study. That preference is, it must be noted, well grounded in the evidence that shows that tracking and streaming in secondary schools around the world is related to less interesting instruction, less student engagement, and, most importantly, poorer outcomes. Moreover, as discussed earlier, it appears that many people can master more demanding content if they have the right supports and the right motivation. Yet efforts to have a single, primarily academic, curriculum for all secondary students seem to fly in the face of what we know about how many students find this approach uninteresting, and in the face of evidence that many students will either not go on to postsecondary education or will not complete their postsecondary programs.

There is no evident resolution to this problem, although there are some pointers that take us in good directions. Given how many young people change their plans, or have their plans changed for them by life circumstances, our systems should provide maximum ability for people to move from one life track to another at any point in their life. Primarily, this means giving young people many different avenues to point themselves toward higher education or more advanced skills, during or after their time in high school. For high schools and school systems it means trying to stay away from dead-end curriculum tracks that are not linked to any real and useful credentials, such as vocational education has often been.

Most important, it is a mistake to see the answer to the problems of student diversity in secondary school as residing in more—or less— course choices by students. Student success depends much less on curriculum than it does on good teaching and strong interpersonal relationships. Many years ago, as a new university student myself, I spent a couple of months talking with seniors in high school, especially in small and rural schools, about going to the university. One piece of advice I used to give, and still believe, is that if you scout out the best professors, their courses will be interesting even if you start out not caring about the subject. The same is true in schools; curriculum matters less than quality of teaching, as shown by the very significant differences in student achievement from one teacher to another in the same course or curriculum. The whole "small schools" movement is driven by the idea that having many courses to choose from is less important than having good teaching and good relationships in whatever courses students do choose. That is the direction for schools.

At the same time, to reinforce a theme raised earlier, schools should be slower to assume we know what a student's potential is and quicker to offer students opportunities to demonstrate their ability to do more demanding work. However, this should not be done by insisting that all students take courses or study material that we already know most of them do not find interesting, challenging, or useful. It's a tough balancing act that depends on the right combination of course choices and pedagogical practices.

### Effective teaching practices in all classrooms on a daily basis

Improving daily instruction is the elephant in the room of school improvement. Sometimes governments or districts try to tackle this by imposing particular instructional practices, such as has happened in many U.S. school districts. For reasons discussed elsewhere in this book, imposed instructional practices are almost certain to fall short of expectations if not to fail outright. Yet we know that there is plenty of room to improve teaching routines based on experience from many schools that have done so, with striking results for students. Teachers need and deserve a significant degree of autonomy in their work (recall that this is critical to building and maintaining motivation), but there can be no professional autonomy that protects the use of practices known to be ineffective, such as using grades to punish behavior or belittling students' work or character.

Think of teaching practice as analogous to other professional practices such as medicine or engineering or nursing. Surgeons doubtless have their own styles and preferences, but they also have agreed routines and standard procedures that they all use. I can't decide that I prefer to remove an appendix via the lungs, no matter how autonomous I feel as a surgeon. Nurses work differently with each patient, but they also have standard routines for many practices, such as putting on or removing bandages, or giving injections. Airplane pilots don't decide to change the way they do takeoffs or landings to suit their own styles. Yet none of these professionals sees these standard practices as impinging on their autonomy or taking away their professionalism. Quite the opposite—standard practices help them do their jobs well by improving the likelihood of quality work and reducing the need to make an impossible number of individual judgments in one's work. Effective routines are central to good practice in every profession, including teaching.

Teaching has very few similar standard practices when it comes to actual instruction. Creating more such practices is quite possible. Indeed, it is precisely what happens as schools and systems work on effectiveness. It happens not through mandates but through carefully organized social processes that build understanding of the practices, awareness of their value, capacity to implement them, and pressure to use them. When teachers work together to share practices, including with expert coaches—because we do not want the sharing of ineffective practices—and with support from administrators and supervisors to learn to use them, it is possible to see quite remarkable changes in instruction over relatively short periods of time. Moreover, when done well these changes get firmly embedded in teachers' work such that they will persist even if the supports and pressures are reduced. This is precisely the kind of approach described by Fullan, Hill, and Crevola (2006). It is about shared practice based on results and a constant quest for improvement, an approach that energizes teachers while helping students.

There is a tendency to see such routines, standards, and structures as somehow inconsistent with freedom and autonomy, an argument often advanced in education. However as Joseph Campbell pointed out in his analysis of cultures (1972), structures can actually be supports for creativity and innovation, not just barriers to them. Campbell used the example of the sonnet in poetry as a highly restrictive form that created the possibility of some of the most beautiful poetry in the English language. Japanese haiku would be a similar example— the rules actually create opportunities for new forms of artistic expression. The same would be true of sports; Campbell uses the pole vault as an instance of another highly structured activity that produces great beauty and expression when carried out well.

Consider, at a somewhat more mundane level, the increasing convergence in reading instruction in Ontario elementary schools over the last few years. The Ontario government did not mandate any particular reading instruction. Instead, the ministry through the Literacy and Numeracy Secretariat, in cooperation with school districts, provided teachers with examples of good practice and the skills to use those practices. Professional development, resources, coaches, learning communities, and other strategies were used toward this end. As a result, practices such as guided reading, shared reading, data walls, classroom libraries of leveled books, word walls, and shared writing are now ubiquitous in Ontario primary classrooms. Teachers do not see these as imposed practices but instead as methods that produce better results for students and are therefore to be supported and welcomed by teachers.

To take one example, as deputy minister in Ontario I visited a number of schools that had been involved in our Turnaround Schools program (described earlier). In one particular school, by no means unique, I met with the staff working with the 300 or so high-needs students. Three years earlier this school had had fewer than 20 percent of its students reaching the provincial standard in reading at grade 6, and now it was over 70 percent. The teachers, fiercely proud (and rightly so) of what they had achieved, said several interesting and important things about their journey.

First, they said at the start they did not believe their students were capable of such improvement. Now they realized, they told me, that any school could do something similar, since there was nothing, they felt, particularly remarkable about them as a group of educators. They had truly embodied the power of high expectations.

Second, they said that they used to feel that the students' personal problems required attention before things like reading could be taught. The school had had a large number of behavior problems. They had learned, though, that as more kids learned to read and were successful, behavior problems declined precipitously. They said that good teaching was the best strategy to improve student behavior.

Third, they said that external support from a literacy coach and a skilled diagnostician as well as the development of a strong internal community among them were critical factors. They had to learn new teaching practices, which they did together. Three years later they owned those practices. They continued to support each other daily, and not only had their students improved tremendously, but these teachers found their work more satisfying and rewarding. That is the journey of pedagogical improvement we should be seeking for all schools; not imposed practices, but collective ownership by educators of the practices that we know work for more students.

### Effective use of data and feedback by students and staff to improve learning

So much has been written recently about using data to support both teacher and student learning that little needs to be said here beyond recognizing and reinforcing that movement. In order to improve, people need honest and supportive feedback that helps them see where their current performance falls short—and where it is already strong. Assessment for learning (e.g., Earl 2003; Bernhardt 2003) works for adults and children. The key elements of effective assessment practice in classrooms are quite well described—clear standards for good work through vehicles such as rubrics or exemplars; opportunity to revise and improve one's work; grades based on final level of performance rather than averaging across the term or year; and the separation of grading of academic work from judgments about motivation or behavior.

Schools and districts are also advised, if not hectored, to make better use of data on student achievement, and many places are taking this injunction seriously. In some places schools are awash in data about student achievement. These data can help us know more about what is happening. Teachers tend to be acutely aware of the performance of each individual in their class but much less aware of patterns of achievement over time, such as whether students tend to struggle more with expository versus fictional writing or with fractions in comparison to decimals. Identifying these patterns in data is important to understanding the key areas for intervention or further attention.

Having data, however, is not at all the same as knowing how to interpret or use the data, and we are learning that the latter requires careful, sustained attention. Teachers, principals, superintendents, and parents need to learn more about how to analyze data, what are the key questions to ask, and what cautions to apply to data—for example, that student and classroom achievement tends to be unstable from class to class and year to year, so that judgments should not be based on single data points. As Garmston and Wellman (1999) have pointed out as well, data analysis is not just a technical process but can be a highly emotive one. Analysis of data is bound up with questions about individual and collective performance, judgment and blame, feelings of inadequacy or superiority. These emotional issues require attention as well, or they will overwhelm any thoughtful data analysis. Ontario has built a good student information system that provides schools and districts with high-quality current data on students. Just as importantly, the ministry invested significantly in helping district leaders, principals, and teachers learn more about analyzing data and using it to inform school policies and practices, an investment that will need to continue—and will pay dividends—long after the information system itself is accepted as a commonplace.

A further important caution is that assessment and data do not tell people what to do next. It is important to know, say, that our fourth graders are not doing well in expository writing, but that does not tell the staff what to do to generate improvement. The latter requires work to review the research, share and test new practices, and help teachers integrate better practice into their classrooms in a sustainable way. Data can only help if they are linked to the other items discussed in this chapter, and in particular to changed instructional practices.

### Early support with minimum disruption for students in need

Huge amounts of money are spent every year in our schools trying to repair problems that might well have been prevented. Think of the cost of having students repeat a year of school, and how much additional support and tutoring that money would have bought if spent on preventing failure instead of treating it—and in this case often treating it unsuccessfully, since one of the strongest findings in education research is that retention in grade is an ineffective practice (Hong and Raudenbush 2007).

More successful schools and school systems give priority to early intervention for students who are struggling. Moreover, they do so in ways that do not generate labels for students, do not stigmatize students, do not involve long processes of "identifying" problems, and are minimally disruptive of the regular school experiences of the students and their classroom teachers. For example, many years of research on so-called withdrawal programs shows their very limited effectiveness (Knapp, Shields, and Turnbull 1995; Anderson and Pelliger 1990). On the other hand, intensive one-on-one support for students very early in their school careers has been shown to be effective in many cases, especially if it is matched with ongoing changes in regular classroom practice to support students' emerging skills, particularly if students then get ongoing support in regular classrooms to maintain their gains. Improved outcomes are not like a vaccination that cures the disease and prevents recurrence; the problems that gave rise to the initial lack of achievement likely still remain in the student's life, so require ongoing attention even if not to the same degree as the initial intervention.

In general our schools are set up relatively poorly to provide this kind of non-invasive early support. We devote far more resources to separate special-education programs, most of which require time-consuming and laborious identification processes, than we do to quick catch-up efforts. The enormous emphasis on "identification" of students' problems in terms of some arbitrary set of categories mostly related to funding is a large barrier to doing better. Assessment and identification of a learning problem only makes sense if we know what to do with the problem to get better results. Currently, school systems devote large amounts of time and money to putting students into categories often without any clear idea of what to do to help them get out of the category!

Early intervention is not just an issue in primary grades, either. In secondary schools we know that students who fail one or more courses in their first year of high school have a much lower probability of graduation. Measures in high schools to help students stay on or get back on track are as important as early reading interventions in primary grades.

An example of how early intervention can work in high schools comes from the Ontario Student Success Strategy, described more fully earlier. In most high schools significant numbers of students—perhaps

30 percent or even more—fail at least one course, resulting in more years of having to be in school and lower graduation rates. The Ontario goal was to increase the number of students who were able to complete all their courses successfully, especially in grades 9 and 10.

The first step in doing so was for schools to know, relatively early in the term, which students were at risk of failing. The ministry introduced, as one of its secondary school performance indicators, data on credit accumulation. Each school was expected to keep track of the number and proportion of students who were achieving all eight credits in grade 9 and another eight in grade 10. As schools began to gather and analyze these data, they became much more aware of how much failure there was, which courses presented the greatest difficulty, and which students required additional support.

As noted just earlier, having the data does not in itself provide a solution to an identified problem. In Ontario a number of high schools were already doing something called "credit recovery" to assist failing students. Students were enrolled in a low-enrollment course with a teacher, where they worked on gaining the credits for courses they had failed in the previous semester by completing or upgrading their work. Typically, students had successfully completed some parts of the course already but then had either stopped attending, stopped handing in assignments, or encountered some units within a course with which they had real difficulty. A teacher worked with eight or ten students, on a range of different courses, to help them complete their work so that their original teacher could now recognize that they had done what they needed to pass the course and get their credit. Credit recovery, however, was not a recognized course in the Ontario system, so schools using it had to "bend" the rules around course designation and student assignment. Moreover, credit recovery practices were quite inconsistent across schools and districts. For example, some schools would only award a grade of 51 for any credit recovery work, while others would provide a grade that recognized appropriately the work students had, in the end, accomplished.

Starting in 2005, the ministry recognized credit recovery as a legitimate academic activity in high schools. The Student Success Commission, an organization set up by Minister Kennedy at the start of the Student Success initiative to bring together school districts and the high school teacher unions as well as the ministry, issued guidelines for credit recovery programs that were acceptable to all parties and brought a greater degree of commonality of approach. Student Success teachers often either organized or even taught credit recovery classes.

Credit recovery, along with other measures such as improved "early warning" systems, better course selection, and better student-teacher relationships, is part of the reason that course failure rates in Ontario high schools are declining noticeably and graduation rates are rising. When students see that a mistake early in their high school career does not doom them to an entire extra year, they have renewed confidence and focus and are more likely to stay engaged in their schooling. Early intervention even in grades 9 and 10 can be just as important as in grades 1 and 2.

### Strong positive relationships with parents

The education literature is full of injunctions about the importance of parent and community engagement to school success. It is a truism to say that parents are their children's first and most important teachers. Although the empirical evidence on the effects of parent involvement on student outcomes is not as strong as is sometimes made out (Corter and Pelletier 2005; Jeynes 2007), it is hard to see how a school could be successful without strong parental support. We do know that children do better in school if they live in households where there is more active support for learning.

Educators often blame students' failings on their parents and families; it remains common to hear teachers talk about how they can't expect more from children given the problems in their families. While this is an understandable view from teachers who are frustrated by their inability to make progress against the challenges children bring with them, it is also an entirely unhelpful perspective. Research on parental involvement indicates that teachers and parents tend to have negative stereotypes about each other (Eulina and de Carvalho 2001).

Teachers, especially in high-poverty or high-minority schools, often see parents as uninterested in their children, if not actively negative influences. Yet parents overwhelmingly report high aspirations for their children and a strong desire to help their kids succeed. On the other hand, while teachers feel they are working hard for students, many parents see teachers and schools as dismissive of their concerns and uninterested in the knowledge they have. They feel that once the school has a view of their children, it is unchangeable even if incorrect.

For many years in the 1970s and 1980s, and even into the 1990s, the focus on parents was around governance—trying to involve parents in school councils or other bodies that would have either advisory or, in some cases such as England or New Zealand or Chicago, significant decisionmaking powers. On the whole these efforts produced rather marginal returns. Initial surges of interest in these new governing bodies were followed by diminished interest and often difficulty in recruiting enough people to fill the available spaces. Contested elections turned into acclamations or even vacancies.

We have learned gradually that parents' real interest, at least for the vast majority of parents, is not in running the school system but in doing what they can to assist their children in being successful. This is both easier and more powerful for schools. The steps that can be taken to help parents help their children are generally less contentious than governance issues, often involving simply the provision of appropriate information and resources or more frequent contact with teachers around academic issues. So there is a happy coincidence here, even if it is not universal, of what parents mostly want to do, what schools mostly want them to do, and what is relatively easy to accomplish.

An important caveat, though, is that supporting achievement does not necessarily mean that parents should be taking on instructional roles around homework or reinforcing the rules and policies of the school. It does mean doing the things parents see as their role—setting expectations, helping children navigate difficult relationships, providing a good learning environment, and, yes, advocating for their children with the school.

A great deal has also been learned about how to engage parents more effectively. Some particularly interesting work has been done about finding ways to engage parents in academic work other than through standard homework—for example, fun activities that parents and children can do together that reinforce learning in various areas (Merttens and Newland 1996; Sheldon and Epstein 2005). A new review of evidence from New Zealand (Robinson et al. 2008) shows powerful potential effects on achievement from well-crafted literacy programs that are effectively shared between schools and families, with appropriate supports for families.

Schools find some parents more difficult to reach, perhaps because of language barriers, perhaps because of parents' own bad experiences with the school system, or simply because many parents, in the face of economic hardship or personal issues, are working two jobs and facing their own challenges in the struggle to have a decent life. Yet we have more and more evidence that patience, persistence, and respect for parents' situations can improve school-home connections, often dramatically. Visits to homes, provision of good news about students, translation and interpretation services, and understanding of different cultural practices around education are all important elements that help build bridges with parents. Most important is a genuine commitment to partnership coupled with respect and ongoing effort to create dialogue and mutual understanding.

Yet schools and districts often struggle to make real progress, and dissatisfaction with the nature and extent of parent involvement continues to be common. One reason is that building relationships with parents takes real time and effort, which cannot simply be added to all the other responsibilities of teachers. Few schools or systems devote significant resources to parent relationships despite all the talk, so in practice efforts fall short of what is needed. Usually contact with parents is expected to be done by teachers and principals on top of everything else they do. A few school districts have created positions for staff whose role is to build parent engagement or community involvement, but these are relatively uncommon and are usually dependent on project or other funds that may disappear, and with them the related positions. Given the potential impact of parents on their students' motivation and attitude as well as skills, parent engagement would seem to be a cost-effective area in which to invest more resources.

Resources are not the only barrier to more effective parent involvement. There is an inevitable tension between the professional world of the school and parents' necessary advocacy for their own children. Both are legitimate points of view. Still, in all too many cases parents feel that they are only wanted when they support what the school is already doing. As soon as they raise concerns or questions, they feel shut out. One area of leadership development that needs more attention, in fact, is around conflict management so that schools are able to manage more effectively the inevitable conflicts that will arise with parents and community groups, especially in areas or among populations that feel they have been underserved or marginalized. This issue is discussed further later.

### Effective engagement of the broader community

Parents are only part of the larger community, albeit an important and often the most vocal part. Communities are vital elements in the story of student success and can have an important influence beyond the characteristics of the children or families who live there. For example, communities with high poverty levels tend to produce worse education outcomes even among children of similar background and ability (Nettles, Caughy, and O'Campo 2008).

Still, every community, no matter how poor, has resources it can bring to bear to support success for students. Any community, no matter how much it is struggling, has people in it who can be mentors and role models for students, whether in the school or beyond. Indeed, community support may be most important in those areas where there is the least community infrastructure and where schools most feel its lack. Interesting recent work on community development (Kretzmann and McKnight 1999) maps the resources that exist even in quite poor communities, some of which could be brought to bear in support of effective education. These include churches, youth organizations, ethnic groups, sports groups, and others. Most communities also have some local people taking on vital leadership roles, who could be important resources for schools. The important research on resilience (Ungar 2004) shows that even under quite adverse circumstances, a few strong and positive relationships can change a young person's trajectory in a good direction. Teachers can play this role, but so can mentors from the broader community.

As with parent engagement, building strong community links is real work that cannot be done in the spare time of busy people. While everyday interactions with the community are very important, as discussed in chapter 7, schools and districts also need to plan for community engagement.

As one example, William Whyte Community School is in one of the poorest neighborhoods in all of Canada and has a population that is overwhelmingly Aboriginal. The community suffers from high unemployment, poor housing, and lack of local infrastructure and exhibits many of the typical inner-city problems of low educational attainment, high levels of substance abuse, and violence. Yet over a number of years, due to determined efforts by the staff and community and using well-known principles of community development, William Whyte was able to implement a range of activities that helped build community capacity and self-reliance (Hunter 2000). The school either supported or spearheaded the development of many initiatives. A food co-op branch in the school became a vehicle for adult literacy and improved nutrition for children. A women's organization began to provide catering at local events, including school events, and to make and sell crafts, bringing not only additional income but also increasing pride and self-confidence among members of the community. The school used some of its funds to hire more local people as aides and then to support some of them as they entered university teacher-education programs. These efforts did not turn William Whyte into a middle-class community or school, but they did help the children and the school in important ways.

William Whyte is not unique. Many efforts have been made to improve schools through building the political capacity of local communities (e.g., Shirley 1997 and Cross-City Campaign 2005), and a recent report by the Ford Foundation (Petrovich 2008) reinforces the importance of these strategies. Like parent involvement, though, community-building initiatives tend to be afterthoughts in the education improvement efforts of most school systems.

A challenging area for community engagement in Ontario has been around Aboriginal education (referring to people described in the United States as "American Indians" and in some other places as "indigenous"). In Ontario the Aboriginal population, because it constitutes less than 2 percent of the total, tends to be overshadowed in policy discussions by the much larger population of recent immigrants and visible minorities. Yet Aboriginal student achievement lags badly behind provincial and national averages, as it does across Canada. And although Canada's First Nations (Indians) now run their own school systems on most reserves, the great majority of Aboriginal children are not living on reserves, so they are attending regular public schools.

For more than a century in Canada non-Aboriginals have determined what is best for Aboriginal people, without much success. So any initiative to improve Aboriginal education has to be consultative with and respectful of Aboriginal families, communities, and organizations. Over a two-year period, Ontario built an Aboriginal Education branch in the ministry, built good relationships with provincial and local Aboriginal organizations, created after extensive consultation an Aboriginal Education Policy Framework that is widely applauded by Aboriginal groups, galvanized a group of school districts with significant Aboriginal enrollments to pay more attention to this issue, created new resources and funds for improvement in this area, strengthened professional development for teachers, and generally changed the climate around Aboriginal education to one that is much more optimistic than was the case only a few years ago. The key to the entire process was a commitment to do better by working in partnership with those who were most involved—Aboriginal families and communities.

## PUTTING IT ALL TOGETHER

The outline of important areas of improvement may seem a daunting if not impossible task to many educators. How is it possible to develop all these areas at the same time, given how difficult it is to implement even a single change in curriculum or instruction in a school?

The challenge is by no means a simple one. But there are things that can be done to make the task more manageable. Some of these are general change strategies described at various points in this book, while others are more closely connected to the instructional nature of the points in this chapter.

The first thing to note is that the nine areas are complementary, if not synergistic. Changing assessment practices is one way of improving student engagement. Effective use of data supports early intervention with minimal disruption. Parent and community engagement are closely linked, and so on. A school or district does not need, or want, nine separate initiatives; indeed, that would be a really bad way to proceed, as it would drown the organization.

Although all nine points are important, not all nine require the same attention with the same intensity. Where to start, and what to emphasize, should be based on the criteria outlined in chapter 4—that is, Which measures have the greatest potential to improve results compared with the amount of effort they will require? This may look different in each school or district depending on local circumstances. Where is there already a base of success from which to start? Where are there local champions? In what areas is the staff most receptive? Where can one find support from the wider community? In some schools one would want to begin with an emphasis on internal work, in others with community-building.

It is particularly important to look for local champions to support, if not lead, various initiatives. Every school or district has these people, who already know quite a bit about a particular area and would welcome the opportunity to assist in an area of concern to them.

A multi-element strategy is also, inevitably, a multi-year strategy. Not everything can be done at once, and the effort to try to do so is self-defeating. To say this does not mean accepting lack of progress or setting a slow pace. The challenge is to keep the organization working at its full capacity for change—no more or less than that. The research on stress shows that both too much and too little are bad for us. The school community will provide guidance on this point. If there are simultaneous complaints—presumably from different people—that too much is happening and also that things are taking too long, then it's likely that the balance is about right.

A school or district's ability to develop and manage an agenda like this is dependent on the right supporting organizational conditions, which are the subject of the next chapter.

# 6

## Organizational Supports
## for an Education Agenda

The previous chapter outlined a set of educational priorities and practices that are essential to improved student achievement. Improvement in these areas must be the heart of any school improvement plan, since these are the factors that can change student outcomes.

To make these improvements possible, however, and especially to do so across large numbers of schools and classrooms, requires a broader strategy. As the earlier discussion pointed out, having the right reforms is not enough; it is also necessary to have the right political and organizational strategy to support those reforms.

A new principal or superintendent is unlikely to have success just by insisting from the outset that instruction must be improved. When I became deputy minister in Ontario, I joked that we would improve results easily; I would write a letter to all teachers in the province telling them to teach better, starting next week (or, if I were in a good mood, "please teach better starting next week"). Obviously, talking about instructional change is not enough; the climate to support instructional change has to be built as well. This chapter looks at the organizational structures and processes that are necessary to foster and support good teaching and learning practices and therefore requisite to any real and lasting change.

These conditions are not the purpose of an improvement initiative, which is why they are not included in chapter 5 as essential requirements for improving student outcomes. But without them, the true drivers of improvement cannot be put in place or sustained. In many discussions of education improvement, either the two are confused or the latter set is ignored. An example of the first situation—confusing supporting conditions with central elements of improvement—is when the first call in any change is for more resources, or when professional learning communities are seen as the goal rather than as a means to ensure good instructional practice. As for the second situation, all too often the school improvement literature gives little or no attention to the importance of supportive system policies or appropriate allocation of resources (which is, as we will see, quite different from just asking for more resources).

### FOUR KEY ORGANIZATION SUPPORTS FOR CHANGE

Based on my experience and reading of the research, I have defined four key organization supports for change. Others might organize the factors somewhat differently, but many of the basic elements will be the same.

- Engagement and commitment by the adults in the system
- Effective collective processes for educators to continue to improve their practices (often referred to as professional learning communities)
- Aligned, coherent, and supportive system policies and practices
- Appropriate allocation of resources

### Engagement and commitment by the adults in the system

Psychological commitment is necessary because education is always a mindful matter. Education as an enterprise depends for its success on the hearts and minds of its participants—teachers, to be sure, but also system leaders, parents, and students. For learning to happen, learners and teachers must be engaged and care about what they do. Just as

120

teachers cannot succeed if students do not commit themselves to learning, so schools cannot succeed unless teachers and other staff are committed to doing whatever they can to support student success.

Learning cannot be mandated from above, nor can good teaching. Creating commitment is in part a matter of setting a clear, compelling vision that engages people's hearts and minds. Educators are overwhelmingly idealists, who took up their careers because they wanted to help improve students' lives. That idealism has to be tapped by leaders. That is why goal or mission statements do have a role to play in educational improvement. Commitments to higher levels of success for students, or to stronger and more caring school communities, have great appeal to many educators.

But ambitious goals in rhetoric are not enough. Goals have to be matched by real actions. Without specific approaches and practices that promote and sustain the appropriate attitudes, commitment will not last—in fact, will turn into cynicism as the reality fails to match people's hopes. All too many organizations invest a great deal of time in developing an ambitious mission statement or goal statement with little or no follow-up action due to the problems of insufficient political support and inadequate implementation discussed earlier.

The first requirement to build commitment and engagement is mutual respect and trust among all the partners in a school or system, including teaching staff, support staff, students, and parents. Isn't it obvious that people will feel better, work harder, and be more productive if they feel they are valued by the organization? And who, after all, would be in favor of disrespectful practices? Yet so often practice does not live up to the intent. Surveys of workers in most large organizations show that they often do not perceive their workplaces as embodying these features. The larger the organization, the more likely it is to revert to depersonalized communication and reliance—wrongly and ineffectively—on orders and policies. Scott Adams, creator of *Dilbert*, says that almost all his ideas for cartoons about dysfunctional organizations come from real incidents sent to him by readers.

Despite all the literature advocating respectful practices in organizations, many schools and school systems still retain many features of hierarchical organizations in which there is a widespread belief that subordinates should do what they are told. Superintendents want principals to follow directions, which principals likewise want from teachers, and teachers from students. Many people like having power and being able to use their authority over others. As a senior manager in government, I ran across so many situations in which teachers spoke of the lack of respect they felt they received from management. I also saw such incidents. Very early in my work in Ontario, I visited a large secondary school. The principal was showing me around the school, during the course of which we interrupted several classes. Teachers appeared not to know why we were there, but the principal never introduced me or explained my presence. We would go into a class, he would explain something, and we would leave again, without a word either to teacher or students. This certainly felt like a disrespectful practice to me!

Sometimes the problem is simply one of time. The pressures of the moment get in the way of our informing others, or inviting their input. People will forgive the occasional failure of this kind if the overall atmosphere in the organization is one of respect, but leaders also need to remember that what saves a few minutes now could end up costing many hours later in dealing with the effects of resentment that could easily have been prevented. In the Ontario Ministry of Education, we had an endless struggle to keep communication with staff active and open in the face of competing pressures on people's time. Often we fell short and ended up with problems of poor understanding or false rumors that we could have prevented fairly easily.

It would also seem self-evident that organizations should have good data on attitudes and feelings of engagement from staff and stakeholders. Yet such is not the case. Very few schools and school systems have organized processes for gathering opinions from any of these groups, although that proportion does seem to be increasing now. Instead, input comes either informally through staff meetings or committees, parent councils' comments, or is sought when particular issues arise. On issues that are absolutely critical to school performance, such as students' sense of engagement with school or parents' satisfaction with communication from the school, most schools have little or no information beyond the anecdotal. Schools and school systems should be doing regular surveys of the attitudes and experiences of staff, students, and parents in order to know whether the organization is communicating the appropriate stance to its people.

Gathering opinion is the easy part, even if it is not common practice. It is much harder to show that input is being taken seriously, since there will inevitably be at least some conflict among the parties in their preferences and wishes, and just as likely disagreement within groups such as parents or teachers or students.

One reason that respectful practice is not as common as we might want in our organizations is because it is hard to maintain. It takes time and it means resolving disagreement through discussion rather than fiat. What happens when people have deep disagreements that cannot easily be bridged? How much consultation and discussion can any organization manage without bringing its decisionmaking processes to a standstill? These are not questions that have easy answers. It is naïve to think that all disagreements can be resolved through communication, certainly in the time that most active organizations like schools have available. It's so much easier just to insist that people do what they are told, to invoke authority, or to threaten consequences for resistance. These practices require us to pay careful attention to people we may think misinformed or misguided. They require lots of compromise yet remain essential.

The simple fact is that schools cannot succeed unless we have good teachers who want to be there. In their study of education reform in a number of large U.S. cities, Danielson and Hochschild (1998) conclude:

> These case studies teach us, over and over, that the people who operate the educational system will not be reorganized, decentralized, priced, privatized, or otherwise reformed out of the picture. Someone has to run whatever system operates public education, and lots of someones have to teach our children every day, starting tomorrow. (292)

When the government for which I was working in Manitoba came to office in 2000, they introduced legislation to remove limitations on the scope of collective bargaining for teachers that had been put in place by the previous government. This legislation was quite strongly opposed by Manitoba school boards; their association even took out a full-page advertisement in the newspaper stating their opposition to these measures and their concern that it would impose additional costs that they could not afford.

Many school boards, as well as teacher organizations and individuals, appeared before the committee of the legislature that reviewed this bill. The various school boards read nearly identical briefs about the challenges of the bill and the importance of local autonomy. Apparently, the irony of identical briefs all extolling, in the same words, the importance of local autonomy failed to register with most boards! At one point in the hearings, Minister Drew Caldwell asked the representatives of the provincial school boards organization whether they had taken out similar advertisements against government policy when the previous government had cut their funding several years in a row. They had not, reinforcing the view in the government that many school boards viewed teachers' rights to bargain collectively with disfavor.

The current push in the United States toward merit pay is a good example of the wrong policy solution in regard to teachers. It assumes that the only problem in education is one of motivation, whereas the argument in this book is that both *will* and *skill* matter. Aside from the fact that most teachers do not like merit pay, there are very considerable practical difficulties in determining what "merit" is and how it can be determined—which is the main reason teachers do not like it. Proposals for merit pay for teachers also ignore—in fact sometimes assert the opposite—that the vast bulk of the workforce in modern economies is not paid on the basis of merit. Doctors don't earn more for being better diagnosticians. Airplane pilots don't earn more for making nicer landings. Security guards—one of the largest employment groups in the United States—do not earn more when there are fewer security incidents. Most service and retail workers, the largest single occupational group in modern service economics, do not get paid by performance. Even for corporate executives, data show only a very weak link between their pay and the long-term performance of their companies (Pfeffer and Sutton 2006).

Working conditions for teachers provide an area of particular potential for taking steps that both satisfy teachers and have the potential to improve student outcomes. Some of the provisions built into Ontario's 2005 collective agreements, such as the creation of the position of Student Success Teacher or the increase in specialists in the arts in elementary schools, met provincial policy interests while also being welcomed by the unions. These steps were fundamental to being able to get agreements all across the province with essentially no disruption.

Leithwood's review of research on working conditions and their relationship to student outcomes (2006) shows how many of the working conditions that matter most to teachers, and to their organizations, are also highly related to what we know about effective schools. Leithwood's careful review of the evidence shows that teachers' engagement and satisfaction are related to their sense of both individual and collective efficacy. These, in turn, are supported by conditions such as effective leadership, good opportunities to continue to learn, and opportunities to work closely with colleagues. All these ought also to be central, as outlined in the previous chapter, to any school improvement initiative. There is a real opportunity here for a coincidence of interests and a move away from polarized labor relationships. As Leithwood (2006) puts it: "Although most contemporary efforts to improve student learning have targeted teachers' motivations and capacities, inadequate working conditions seriously undermine any potential these efforts may have" (5–6).

### Effective collective processes for educators to continue to improve their practices

The most important single support for all the practices discussed in chapter 4 is ongoing training in the context of people's real work settings. While education has a long history of professional development work, there has never been a high degree of satisfaction with how this work is done or what it produces. For at least thirty years, critiques of professional development have described its lack of impact on subsequent practice. Elmore (2002) maintains that professional development should be constructed as a "collective good rather than a private or individual good, and its value should be judged by what it contributes to the individual's capacity to improve the quality of instruction in the school and school system" (14). Given how critical effective professional learning is, and how much time and other resources PD involves, we cannot continue to support activities that do not produce significant results.

Fortunately, over the last decade or so, interesting new models of training have been developed in schools and in other sectors. Unlike the usual professional development events that happen once and mainly involve sitting and listening, effective training is rooted in actual classroom practice and involves groups of teachers working together. These efforts may be, and often are, supported with materials such as lesson plans, but the focus has shifted from the materials to creating the social conditions under which they are likely to be used. Learning is not just a matter of gathering together but of engaging with real ideas and practices, supported by friendly yet incisive critique of current practice.

Effective learning to support better teaching and learning requires what several writers have called the "deprivatization of teaching"— moving away from teachers doing what they individually think best or simply are used to doing in their classrooms to practices grounded in evidence and shared across a school or district. Shared practice is important because it is more likely to be effective as each person learns from the experience of colleagues, and it helps build the sense of community and common purpose that is vital to maintaining engagement. Clearly, this sort of learning is central to the development of agreed practices by the profession, as discussed in the previous chapter.

Although nervous at first about others watching them, teachers overwhelmingly find that strong, supportive learning communities energize their teaching. An excellent literature has emerged around learning communities (e.g., DuFour et al. 2005; Stoll et al. 2006) that can guide schools and districts in adopting these practices.

Just creating learning communities, though, is not enough. Structures are also needed to make these communities real and to ensure they do the intended work of instructional improvement. The main danger to learning communities is that they fail to focus on working steadily to improve daily teaching practices. It's very easy for a "learning community" to pay attention to everything but the real work of looking at and improving everyone's daily instructional practices. People love talking with colleagues, but there is no guarantee that the talk will be about what matters; it's so easy to spend time talking about all the problems that are due to actions of others—complaining about students, parents, or administrators, for example. Real improvement through learning communities means spending time on things like student assessment practices, organization of lessons, common reviews of student work, and other real practices.

The developing role of "coach" or "lead teacher" is another manifestation of the new approach to supporting instructional change and one that supports mutual learning. The idea is to free some time for a teacher to work with other teachers around instructional practice. There is not yet much evidence on this strategy, but it is clear that it looks quite different in different settings and that it has potential but also raises some difficult issues. For example, coaches can have more or less formal roles, and working with them can be more or less voluntary on the part of other teachers. Where high levels of collegiality and openness exist or can be built, and where teacher leaders have the trust and confidence of other teachers, a coaching approach can work very effectively. Where those conditions do not exist, this strategy runs into difficulty.

## Aligned, coherent, and supportive system policies and practices

Vision statements and organizational culture are important, but they are not enough. We also know from bitter experience that even the highest level of commitment is rarely impervious to a stupid system. In schools and school systems, we face the difficult yet important challenge of aligning the various elements of the system. When rules and procedures don't line up with what people believe to be good practice, trouble results—with, as the song says, a capital *T*. As is the case with respect, just discussed, many organizations, including many schools and districts, simply do not practice what they preach in terms of alignment. They talk about valuing initiative but require everything to be approved in advance. They talk about creative teaching but evaluate based on narrow criteria. They talk about teamwork but mostly issue orders. And so on.

Think about all the routines and practices in a school or district that can either support or detract from the key priorities just mentioned. A prime example is evaluation practices. If teacher and principal evaluation procedures do not reinforce the organization's goals and missions—and so very often they do not—then there will be a powerful negative dissonance. Many other routines could also be mentioned, however:

- Do staff meetings focus on goals and priorities, or are they taken up with administrative matters?
- Is instructional time in the school protected, or is it constantly interrupted for less important matters?
- Is conversation in hallways and staffrooms focused on priorities, or is it about everything else?
- Are routine reporting requirements—for example, on budgets or attendance—given more importance than time for teaching and learning discussions?
- Do school and district communications, both internal to staff and external to the community, reinforce the school's priorities and goals?
- Is hiring and placement of new staff consistent with priorities? Are the best staff placed in environments where they are most needed?
- Are evaluation practices for staff and students consistent with the school's goals and priorities? Or do they lead people to be defensive and to focus on avoiding mistakes instead of learning new skills?

The mundane elements of school operations must line up with the dynamic goals of improvement if there is to be any chance of success.

A friend of mine became principal of a large high school and noticed that despite a stated interest in encouraging active learning, very few field trips were being taken in the school. When he inquired, teachers told him that it was so much trouble to organize a field trip because of transportation, conflicts with other class schedules, permission forms, and collection of money that they just did not bother. This is a perfect example of how great intentions can be foiled by administrative requirements, and it is an example all too familiar to many educators. My friend was able to remedy this by setting aside particular days in the school calendar for field trips and simplifying many of the other elements, with the result that the number of field trips rose significantly.

To judge the extent to which your system actually supports the requirements of good instructional practice, ask yourself this question: Who will get into more difficulty in a school—a great teacher who does not always do the paperwork or follow all the policies, or a mediocre teacher who always complies with the rules? Who is more likely to get promoted—a principal who attends all the meetings, does all the required work, and creates no problems but is unable to generate real enthusiasm and energy in a school, or the opposite? Do we reward people who work tirelessly on behalf of students but who sometimes bend the rules on budget, or the opposite? Then ask the same question about students: Who will get into more trouble, an obedient student who consistently does acceptable but mediocre work, or a challenging student, who does very good work but is always challenging the boundaries of the system? All too often our organizations reward compliance rather than accomplishment, creating exactly the wrong effects in terms of our goal of improvement.

Large bureaucracies such as departments of education are particularly susceptible to this problem. In most government departments, a large amount of time and energy goes into administrative functions that have very little relationship to the organization's ability to help schools improve. It is a constant struggle in any organization for managers to make sure that people get to spend their time on what matters, instead of on administrative work that may be necessary but has little added value.

One of the big mistakes many organizations make when they embark on reforms is to combine reform with major changes in the structure of the organization. Quite often districts or state departments or national ministries believe that improvement also requires a reorganization. They set about changing roles, structures, and reporting relationships. That is almost always a mistake, as structural reorganizations take a great deal of time, engender a great deal of uncertainty among staff, and rarely result in significant improvements in the way the organization works. Time that should be spent on education change is instead used to write new job descriptions or reorganize office space. People are distracted from their real work by worries about changing jobs, titles, and reporting relationships. An organization should try to make its existing structure work if it possibly can. Then, as time shows that some changes may be needed to support improvement more effectively, these changes can be made gradually and with greater staff acceptance.

### COMMUNICATIONS

Alignment and coherence are matters of practice but also matters of communication. People in an organization need to hear constantly from management about the big picture in a way that allows them to understand what the organization is doing and how their particular work fits into the larger plan.

Many years ago I heard a talk on classroom management by a researcher named Walter Doyle. As I recall it, Professor Doyle said that in working with young children it was important to remember that until the children knew where to put their lunch and where the bathrooms were, they would not hear anything else that was said to them. The same is true of adults. People need to see how they fit into the bigger picture and how their work makes a contribution. Once they see this, they are vastly more likely to support and contribute to organizational purposes.

In most organizations, including in education, this internal communication around strategy and alignment is insufficient or nonexistent, especially with front-line staff. For example, in most organizations there is little or no communication on organizational purpose to people like secretaries, even though they do much of the work of direct public contact and have an important impact on how the public sees the organization (discussed further in chapter 7). And even teachers typically do not get reliable information on district or school initiatives, so instead all sorts of rumors spread.

Communication requires repetition. Many organizations think that creating a plan and sending it out means that everyone understands it. That's as fallacious as a teacher assuming that once a concept has been explained, all the students understand it. Communication requires both refinement and repetition—frequent restatements of core messages directed to different audiences and with different emphases. It's only repetition that establishes a message as something to be taken seriously.

Communication in organizations is not only a matter of telling staff what is happening and why, although that is important and not done enough. It's also a matter of hearing from people so as to understand how they see their work, the organization, and their place in it. The importance of gathering regular data on staff attitudes and morale has already been discussed. But communication has to be thought of, not just in terms of a few specific actions, but as an important activity for the entire organization.

The Ontario Ministry of Education is a large organization, with about 2000 staff, half of whom are involved in providing direct service to students through a number of provincial schools that serve students with severe disabilities. The other half are involved in the ordinary work of a ministry—developing and implementing policy, providing funding, organizing accountability, and so on.

During my time as deputy minister in Ontario we implemented a variety of practices to improve internal communications. These included:

+ Providing extensive and regular e-mail updates from the deputy to all staff with news on achievements, priorities, upcoming events, and updates on our main strategies and other important issues. Toward the end of my tenure I also created a blog on our internal website where I could post more frequent and shorter comments.

- Organizing ministry-wide open events that any interested staff could attend to learn more and provide input on our major priorities and strategies. These events regularly attracted 100–200 people.
- Holding twice-yearly open meetings of the senior management team with all staff to update on priorities, achievements, and challenges.
- Creating cross-boundary teams that brought people from various parts of the organization together with strong leadership and a clear mandate to tackle an important issue.
- Authorizing and promoting freer exchange of information within the organization to reduce the "silo" effect.
- Doing "walkarounds" in which I would randomly visit parts of the organization without notice and just chat with staff about what they were doing and thinking. These had in themselves quite a powerful positive effect, as people were not at all used to seeing senior management in informal settings.
- Promoting greater coherence in external communications to the education sector through better cooperation across ministry branches.

These practices take time, to be sure, but they have powerful and important effects on staff understanding, commitment and morale that make them highly cost-effective. In large part it's the whole set of practices that matter, as any particular one will only reach some people and can be dismissed as token. They are as important as any other element in creating organizations that can understand, foster, and sustain effective change.

## ALLOCATING RESOURCES

Any call for reform in education will be accompanied by a demand for more resources. Schools, like other human service organizations, are always under pressure to do more things, which requires more resources. Most books on education change have very little to say about resources, yet resource issues are at the very center of practitioners' work. There is only space in this book for a very brief discussion of the issue, important though it is.

The first point is that providing high-quality education to large numbers of young people takes a lot of money. OECD countries spend on average more than $7000 per student per year for this purpose (OECD 2007). Because there are large numbers of young people between 6 and 18, the totals get awfully big very quickly. For example, total U.S. education spending in 2004–5 was about $536 billion (*www.ed.gov/about/ overview/fed/10facts/index.html*)—a large amount although only about 4.7 percent of the total U.S. economy. Ontario is spending some $19 billion on K–12 education in 2008–9, out of an economy worth about $600 billion.

Still, thought of in other ways, the total amount spent on public education is not that huge. In 2007 Americans spent $740 billion—quite a bit more—on travel (*www.tia.org/pubs/pubs.asp?PublicationID=33*). To make another comparison, about $10,000 per student per year translates into about $55 per day, or about $11 per hour per student, which is about what many people would pay for a babysitter. So how big the amount looks depends an awful lot on your standard of comparison. And when we consider the benefits that education delivers, as shown in box 6.1, the money seems well spent.

The general stance in the education sector is that any new initiative requires new and additional resources. It's not hard to understand this claim; change is generally easier with new resources. It is probably necessary to add some resources to support change, if only to give people a sense of optimism about the future. The old slogan about "doing more with less" has long lost any luster it may have had (and it probably never had much to begin with). New resources also support the emphasis in this book on building commitment to change at all levels of the organization. Reformers who think that they can change a system for the better without any new money are probably deluding themselves. Moving the machinery of a big system usually requires some lubrication, and money is that lubrication.

Money works as a lever for change in that a relatively small amount of money, if used well, can generate a substantial amount of change.

**BOX 6.1**
**The Benefits of Education**

Benefits to individuals:

- More education is associated with better employment outcomes, higher incomes, and more job satisfaction (OECD 2007: 6; Vila 2005).
- Education is strongly linked to better health and welfare outcomes. People with more education tend to live longer (Lleras-Muney 2005), be healthier (Arkes 2004; Spasojevic 2003), and experience less stress and more life satisfaction (Helliwell 2002).
- Education is linked to citizenship. People with more education are more likely to vote (Campbell 2006; Wolfinger and Rosenstone 1980), to be informed about public issues (Campbell 2006), to volunteer in their communities (Dye 1980), and less likely to commit crimes (Witte 1997).
- More education is linked to greater tolerance and respect for diversity (Vila 2005).
- Children's success in schools is itself linked to their parents' education, with mothers' education level being an especially important predictor of children's success (Feinstein et al. 2004). This means that an improvement in educational outcomes has multigenerational effects.
- There are also benefits at the national level. Countries with higher levels of education (and, notably, lower levels of educational inequalities) tend to have better economic growth, lower levels of unemployment, less crime, less corruption, and more public confidence in public institutions. As one simple illustration, a sophisticated analysis of various economic and social indicators in many countries over many years, put together by Swedish professor Hans Rosling at gapminder.org, shows a powerful relationship between years of education and the size of the national economy. The relationship between median years of education and size of the economy is very strong all across the world and across many decades.

In short, better education is associated with just about everything human beings value. This is why public education is such a big part of overall public spending and employment around the world.

Because schools see themselves as having very little flexible money, even a few thousand dollars in a school can sometimes support a lot of improvement. A school with 40 or 50 staff and a budget of millions of dollars will often work hard on a project that is bringing in $50,000— less than one additional salary. The trick, as always, is to use the money for things that matter instead of having it spread around among lots of areas with no real impact.

Ontario, as an example, added a significant amount of money to its education system from 2004 to 2007. Funding rose by some 25 percent over those four years; even more on a per-pupil basis, as enrollment was declining at the same time. As already described elsewhere, most of these additional funds were carefully allocated to such priority areas as more teachers in key areas, high-quality professional development, and infrastructure supporting improvement. And salary increases for teachers were part of a recognized need to improve morale in a system that had felt battered and under attack. England's Department for Children, Families and Schools also increased funding significantly while implementing its Literacy and Numeracy strategy.

Also insufficiently recognized is the room that exists in every organization, including schools, to make better use of existing resources. A full discussion of this issue is beyond the scope of this book, though some good ideas can be found in Odden and Archibald (2001) or in Levin and Naylor (2007). Since the vast bulk of spending goes to pay salaries, the most important resource decisions concern who is employed, and how staff use their time, neither of which gets adequate attention in most school reform efforts. Some of the possibilities for improving outcomes by reallocating existing resources include:

♦ *Improving teachers' skills.* If each teacher, or even most teachers, were able to learn and implement even a few improved practices in a year along the lines described earlier, the potential efficiency improvement in schools could be very considerable.

♦ *Reallocating staff assignments.* Years ago Karen Miles (1995) showed how many teaching positions in the Boston schools were not assigned to direct work with students, and how much class sizes could be reduced if more positions were reallocated to direct work with students. More recently, Odden and Busch (1998) have made the same point.

+ *Addressing imbalances in staffing.* The balance in staffing between classroom teachers, specialist teachers, teacher assistants, and other staff is rarely discussed explicitly in schools but should be. In many systems, the number of teacher assistants has been growing faster than any other staffing category despite a lack of evidence that these roles have any positive effect on student achievement. Whether the answer is fewer assistants or better training and clearer role definition is debatable, but it is increasingly clear that spending more money in this area does not help bring about better student outcomes.

+ *Reducing failure and grade repetition.* As described earlier, retention in grade and course failure in secondary school are highly ineffective and very expensive practices. Money used to correct failure would be much better used to prevent it in the first place through earlier and better supports to students.

+ *Reducing staff attrition and absence.* Absenteeism rates among teachers and support staff vary greatly from one school and district to another. So do teacher attrition rates. Both absence and attrition impose substantial costs on organizations in terms of productivity as well as money. An estimate by the National Commission on Teaching and America's Future reported that teacher turnover cost U.S. schools more than $7 billion in the 2003–4 school year. The commission also calculated that it costs schools anywhere between $4,366 and $17,872 to replace a teacher, not including lost productivity (*www.nctaf.org/resources/demonstration_projects/turnover/Teacher TurnoverCostStudy.htm*). Attrition and absenteeism can be reduced through good human resources practices, yielding significant benefits to schools and districts, but few organizations give this issue much attention. Good working conditions, discussed earlier, are of course central to reducing absenteeism and attrition.

+ *Reconsidering special-education practices.* Special education has consumed a growing portion of education budgets, much of which goes to practices such as withdrawal programs or self-contained classes that do not seem to produce benefits for students. The entire process of identification in special education is enormously expensive in terms of time while generating little value, especially when assessment cannot be linked to effective programming. In Ontario, reducing paperwork for special education in 2004 and 2005 freed the equivalent of several hundred person years across the system for more productive activity.

- *Improving "back office" administrative functions.* School systems are large businesses, as already noted, but they tend, rightly, to be much more focused on education than on the administrative parts of their operations. Also, school systems almost everywhere are managed by educators, which means that they do not always have the business or administrative expertise they need. Ontario's school districts are among the biggest employers, purchasers of services, property managers, and transportation agencies in the entire province, yet few of them have the level of professional expertise in these areas that a comparable company devoted specifically to those activities would have. So costs for activities such as constructing new schools, managing existing schools, or transporting pupils vary hugely across districts. Some districts, for example, spent twice as much as others per square foot for new buildings. While it is not at all exciting work, helping districts improve these functions through shared services, setting service standards, and providing short-term expertise can free significant amounts of money while also improving services.

These are only instances; the key point to remember is that there is always room to improve efficiency in our organizations. Quite often the steps needed to make these improvements are very consistent with the education agenda outlined in this chapter, so are helpful in their own right in addition to freeing resources for more strategic uses.

## CONCLUSION

It is vital to have an education improvement agenda well grounded in research and evidence as well as carefully considered in regard to implementation. But the right education strategy is not enough. Unless the issues in this chapter are also addressed, educational priorities are likely to remain underdeveloped, and staff will feel torn because of multiple demands, insufficient supports, and lack of prioritization. The work of school improvement requires both a strong focus on a few key activities *and* sufficient attention to the broader context and demands to enable everyone to have and maintain that focus. It's a paradox, to be sure, but one that people in our successful schools and systems balance successfully every day.

# 7

## Building Public Confidence in Public Education

### WHY PUBLIC CONFIDENCE MATTERS

Public confidence in and support for public schools is essential to any effort to improve schooling on a sustainable basis. Indeed, it is fundamental to the survival of public education. As former Ontario education minister Gerard Kennedy often said, "We only get to do in schools what the public is willing to support." Educators, like other professionals, sometimes forget this truth because of our deeper knowledge of schools and the very natural feeling that our expertise ought to be given precedence over public opinion.

The importance of public opinion is clear if one considers how many desirable reforms in education have failed because they have not been able to generate support from the public, or how many ineffective policies have been put in place because they did have substantial public support. Examples of both come readily to mind. In some settings, efforts to reform grading and student-assessment practices have failed because parents and others, including students, are so familiar with traditional numerical grading systems, even though we have substantial evidence of the advantages of "assessment for learning" (Earl 2003). The same difficulties have arisen around changes in teaching and learning in areas such as reading and elementary mathematics. Retention in grade is another example of an ineffective practice that is hard to change because it seems common sense to many people. Many jurisdictions in the U.S., and some elsewhere, have adopted such policies as "ending social promotion" or "naming failing schools" because these are seen to have public support. Ontario endured years of conflict in education in the 1990s because governments felt there was public support for an approach that attacked teachers as lazy.

In other cases, advocates of policies seen by educators as highly undesirable have been able to convince voters that they are "common sense." Examples would include the focus on testing and accountability as a main driver of school improvement, the idea that choice and competition are essential to better education, or the idea that merit pay for teachers will improve student outcomes. Although none of these ideas has much empirical support in research, they are believed by many people and so have a real influence on education policy choices.

Yet the opposite can also be the case. Where relationships are good and trust has been built, community supporters can provide important positive assistance and, just as importantly, help buffer the school system from short-term pressures that might otherwise badly derail an improvement agenda. In Ontario in the last few years, in England during the first Blair term, or in many other instances that could be cited, support from important political actors was absolutely necessary to secure not only the resources but also the attention and protection from extraneous pressures that allowed real improvement to take place.

## WHY CITIZENS MATTER MORE THAN EXPERTS

The political process must and does depend on the views of average citizens. As Gary Doer, Manitoba's popular premier for the last ten years, once said to me when as deputy minister of education I was trying to make a point about expert opinion on an issue: "Ben, that may be true, but it's not what people believe." In the political world, public opinion is king, whether well informed or not.

Educators often seem bemused by how little the public knows about how education works. Citizens are often quite ignorant about how our systems work, not only in education but in every area of public policy. Research in political science (e.g., Lapia and McCubbins 1998) has shown that people may hold strong views based on little or no knowledge—for example, the belief that students need to be drilled on spelling or that advanced mathematics is fundamental to success. People can also want incompatible things at the same time—such as schools that promote both obedience and critical thinking, or highly qualified teachers who work for very low wages, or high levels of support for students coupled with very strict disciplinary practices. Do people want more public services or lower taxes? The answer is, "Yes." Years ago, economist Kenneth Arrow (1951) showed that it was nearly impossible to aggregate public preferences; that people could prefer Option A over Option B, Option B over Option C, but also Option C over Option A. Politics rarely works on careful calculus of preferences, since these tend to be unstable and inconsistent.

Educators may make the mistake of thinking that if we just explain what we are doing and why, people will support it. But that is not necessarily so. People's core beliefs are highly resistant to change even in the face of strong contrary evidence, as for example people who still do not believe that smoking is a health hazard or that bicycle and motorcycle helmets save lives. What everyone "knows to be true" also affects individual beliefs. You cannot change people's minds through "brute rationality," although over time evidence does affect public opinion and the climate of ideas, as it has in the case of smoking and drunk driving.

At the same time, most beliefs that people have are not so deeply held and are subject to fairly sudden shifts as new evidence emerges or circumstances change. Consider our approach to diet, where people change their buying and eating habits rapidly on the basis of newspaper reports of research, so that foods move rapidly in and out of popular favor. Think of changing attitudes toward staples like eggs or butter, or luxuries like wine or chocolate, all of which were once thought bad for you and now are considered quite okay. (The food debate is also an interesting example of the impact of research, and the reporting of research, on public attitudes and behavior.) The same can apply to some areas of education, so that if people see or hear that a particular school or school system is doing well or badly, or that a particular program works well, they tend to believe it, but could be persuaded otherwise with some effort.

If public knowledge is limited, and public attitudes often fickle, why not just let experts make the decisions, as many educators argue? The simple answer is that is not the way democracies work, not only in education but in other fields. Although we want expertise to triumph in our own area of knowledge, we are not so ready for this to be the case in other areas where we are the "public" and others, with whom we disagree, are the experts. Presumably, generals feel they should make the military decisions, doctors and nurses want to make the key decisions about health care, engineers about highways, naturalists about parks, foresters about lumbering, and so on. In each area experts believe, naturally enough, that they know best. Yet in every one of these cases the judgment of experts is regularly overridden by public opinion that is running in a different direction, whether well informed or not, and often for good reason.

The reality is that most of us have quite strong opinions on many issues about which we know relatively little. Indeed, it could hardly be otherwise given how many issues are on the public agenda at any given time. One can only have expertise in a very few areas. Where we are not expert, though, we may still have forceful views, and we would not at all appreciate our elected leaders telling us that whatever we think, they are going to have the courage to do what the experts say. That is why educational goals and targets get set at levels that educators may find unrealistic, if not laughable, such as all students achieving proficiency. Ontario's 85 percent target for high school graduation is seen as very challenging by educators, but most of the public would favor a target close to 100 percent.

Those who work in education tend to think that more decisions should be left to the experts, but it's important to keep in mind that experts can be, and often have been, wrong. Knowing the most is not the same thing as knowing what is best. Think of the constantly changing news about which foods are good or not good to eat, which exercises are better for us, or what is happening to our climate. Expertise is never absolute. Knowledge grows, situations change, and today's truth becomes tomorrow's myth. Just about every practice in the list at the start of chapter 4 was recommended by at least some experts. Only a few years ago, technology experts wanted all children to learn to program computers in Basic as a skill that would be fundamental to their futures. Other experts agreed, a few decades ago, that children with serious disabilities should not be educated in local schools. Experts have also at one time or another advocated sterilization of mentally handicapped people, lobotomies, institutionalization of handicapped children, and so on.

Moreover, on many and even most issues in education, experts do not agree. The heated debates among researchers and educators on matters such as how best to teach reading or which programs produce the best results are clear evidence that experts are not of one mind, which makes it harder for them to gain public trust. School systems also adopt quite different policies on issues such as retention in grade or special-education strategies, further confusing people as to what is "known." No wonder the public is uncertain about what to believe.

So while expertise is essential, it is not everything. On the other hand, one cannot put an unqualified faith in public opinion, either. We do not demand that people be knowledgeable when they vote, and it is highly unlikely we could agree on what knowledge would be necessary if we did want such a criterion. In diverse societies, people can and will disagree on many issues of public import. Politics is the main way we resolve those differences without violence. It is an example of what Lindblom (1990) called "interaction" as a way of making decisions rather than "cogitation," which is the idea of expertise, also represented in the legal and court system. Evidence and professional expertise can be and often are important parts of both the political and the legal process, but they are not determinative. Making public decisions about public policy and institutions is a very imperfect enterprise, but it's the best we have.

One frequent response to frustration with public opinion is to call on politicians to "have the political will" to do what is right, whether popular or not. That's a comforting idea that invokes images of heroism, but it faces some big challenges. These challenges apply not just to elected officials but also to other system leaders. Everything in the next few pages will be familiar to most principals and superintendents, who are also regularly asked to make unpopular decisions that somebody considers to be the right thing to do.

All too often, what is meant by "political will" is that something should be done that *we* approve of but many other people oppose—for example, that politicians should increase taxes to provide more funds for schools. While that strategy may make sense to people who work in the school system, leaders need to think about the whole range of pressures and issues facing them, not only the needs of any one part of it. Although polling may show that people are prepared to pay more for education, more complete polling might show that they are prepared to pay more for a number of public services, provided that their overall taxes do not rise! In government and politics the choices are always trade-offs—more of one thing means less of another. Polls rarely ask people what they are prepared to give up in order to pay for their priorities, but people who spend time in politics will tell you that most of the time people say they want more but are seldom truly ready to give up anything in its place. Mostly what people want is to have more of their own preferences while somebody else gets less of their preferences, a solution that carries considerable political risk.

Doing what is unpopular is unlikely in any electoral system. This is not because politicians lack courage but because voters punish politicians who do unpopular things by removing them from office. We don't really want politicians to do unpopular things; we elect them for precisely the opposite reason—to do the things that most of us support.

Moreover, even where there is a sense that a particular action may be popular and expedient but misguided, just opposing it is not necessarily the best strategy, either. At any given moment a school or system is managing a wide array of issues. It is not possible to stand on principle on every single matter, especially because many educational issues are genuinely contentious. Though some of us may feel we know what is best, people with differing views will have exactly the same conviction.

Taking bold action can even turn out to be counterproductive in the long term if it is too far from the public mood. Politicians can then lose the next election, often resulting in the reversal of their policy, and sometimes much worse than just its reversal. For example, the Ontario government in the early 1990s put in place many policies around greater equity in education, sometimes in the face of considerable opposition. When that government was defeated and replaced by a new government, all these policies and programs were eliminated, and the word *equity* was taken out of Ministry of Education policy documents, leaving things worse than they had been in the first place. The same can be true at the district level. A board that decides to make hard choices can find itself defeated and its policies reversed. The wrong decision by a principal can alienate staff with long-term consequences for the school's larger goals. In every setting, difficult political calculations have to be made as to whether one can and should fight for any given issue as a matter of principle. It may be that giving some ground to a strong alternative view is the best outcome that can be obtained at a particular point in time, and that further resistance may actually lead to a worse outcome.

## WHO IS "THE PUBLIC"?

The term "public support" is a bit misleading, since it implies that the public is a homogeneous entity. When we say "the public," what do we mean? School systems tend to conflate "the public" with "parents" and to focus their communication toward parents. However, the proportion of the population with children in schools is declining in many, if not most, developed countries. Typically, only one-fourth to one-third of the population has a direct connection to schools through their children. A broader understanding of who the public is and why their views matter is therefore important.

Political theorists have long debated the question of "the public" and how citizen views shape political decisions. This is not the place to restate a vigorous and complex debate on the nature of politics, but it can be said that while views on this question differ among scholars, just about everyone recognizes that it is inaccurate to think about the public as a collection of autonomous individuals, each of whom has equal voice. Polling reinforces that perspective because each individual respondent counts equally. But individual opinions are not the primary force in politics at any level. Although opinion polling is important, political people know that it's not only what people think that matters, but how strongly they hold those views and whether they are prepared to take action to support them, because it is action that drives the political process. The same is true in any organization; some people's opinions carry more sway than others, and it's not always those who are most knowledgeable, either!

People form their views primarily through social interaction— through their discussions and contact with others—as well as through the knowledge they get from their own experience and from the media. Individual views are substantially shaped by social forces. For this reason, political debates and decisions tend to be driven much more by organized groups and interests than by the opinions of masses of individuals.

A good example is the process of public consultations. Schools and school systems, like other public institutions, do a great deal of consulting the public on many issues. Indeed, public consultation in education, as in other fields, has been increasing steadily for at least a couple of decades. Typically, though, these processes engage only a relatively small number of people, and predominantly those who are already organized, such as teacher groups or parent groups or external interest groups. The "public," in the sense of ordinary citizens, rarely participates.

The lack of citizen participation is not surprising, considering how many public issues are under discussion at any given time. At one point while I was deputy minister in Manitoba, I asked my staff how many public consultations were underway in the province and was told after some inquiry that at that particular time the government of Manitoba alone had more than 100 public consultation processes going on in areas ranging from education to parks to highways to health to environment. It would be impossible for most citizens to participate in more than a very few such processes simply on the grounds of time, let alone of knowledge and interest. People take part where they have very strong views, are very directly affected, or are represented by an organization that has the time and staff to participate in these various processes. Again, some voices matter more than others, or as George Orwell put it, "All animals are equal, but some animals are more equal than others."

From a political perspective, the "public" is really made up of an array of groups and organizations. Individuals may belong to or affiliate with several different groups and therefore may have conflicting views on issues depending on which of their affiliations is being invoked at any particular time. Groups and organizations will have differing levels of political power and impact, with, as in every society, some interests carrying more weight than others, although these relationships also change over time.

Since pressures and decisions in education are shaped largely by organized groups, it is important for school leaders to think about and understand the interest groups in their community. A little thought shows that there are many, many groups that may have an interest in education. The enormous number of community organizations in so many fields, including education, is one indication of how many groups do play a role in what is called "civil society."

Parent organizations are at the top of the list because parents have the deepest interest in the schools. Parent organizations at the school level are highly variable in their membership and efficacy, ranging from quite weak to quite powerful. (More is said on this point in chapter 9.) In addition to parent organizations in schools, however, parents are involved in a wide range of other organizations, whether or not connected to education. Parents may belong to more than one parent organization connected to education—for example, a special-education interest group or an arts group as well as a local parent council—as well as to other community groups.

In addition to the range of organizations with direct school interests, other local groups such as faith organizations, youth agencies, or local charities can have important constituencies around schooling matters. Ethnic associations can be very important vehicles for reaching—and hearing from—people who may otherwise have relatively few direct links to schools, such as newcomers who do not speak the majority language. Sports, recreation, and arts organizations often see students in a very different and more positive light from schools. Business and labor organizations almost always have views about educational issues; the views of business organizations such as chambers of commerce or employer councils have been highly influential in many jurisdictions. Many of these organizations have both a local presence in a school or district and a broader presence at a regional or national level.

The challenge for schools and school systems is to develop a better understanding of who is in their community, and to find ways to reach out both to established groups and even more to people who do not already have the means to make their views known. An informal survey of community organizations and their leaders is a good start and generally fairly easy to do, since students will be able to identify many or most such groups. Another useful approach is asset mapping—locating on a map such community assets as churches, youth agencies, libraries, sports organizations, and others that are potential sources of support. Then, gradually and over time, the school can build contacts and relationships with these organizations through the principles of good communications discussed at various points in this book.

## WHAT LEVEL OF PUBLIC CONFIDENCE
## DO WE HAVE AND NEED?

What can we say about the current level of public support for our schools? One often cited finding is that people are much more supportive in polling of their local schools than they are of the education system generally. The feeling seems to be that while public education is a mess, the local school is pretty good. This finding, by the way, is highly consistent across countries (Loveless 1997), and not only for schools but also for other public services such as health care as well.

The more direct knowledge people have about schools, the more positive their views seem to be. Almost half (46 percent) of Ontarians award their local community schools either an A or B grade; most others award a C. These ratings are similar to grades offered both by the Canadian public as a whole and have changed very little over the past 20 years (Hart and Livingstone 2007: 2).

Canadian results on this question (48 percent A or B) are also very similar to those in the annual Phi Delta Kappan poll in the United States (49 percent A or B). A comparison of Canadian and U.S. polling data also shows that public grades for local schools have risen slightly in the United States over the past 20 years, whereas in Canada they have remained stable (Hart and Livingstone 2007: 7).

While it is true that people are generally more positive about their local schools than about schools generally, polling also shows that overall confidence in schools, as in other public institutions, has been declining in most Western countries for several decades. Loveless (1997) cites recent studies which "indicate that Americans have lost faith in public schools" (127) and provides polling data over two decades to that effect. Other data show a similar decline in confidence in other public institutions (Newton and Norris 2000).

Analysts disagree as to the reasons for this decline. One possible reason is higher levels of education, which tend to make people more critical. (When educators stressed the importance of critical thinking as a goal of education, we did not think it would be used on us!) Another is the influence of the media in exposing problems and weaknesses of public institutions. While this kind of reporting is vital to a democracy, over the long term if it is primarily negative and not balanced it can also have a corrosive effect on levels of public trust in all institutions.

Schools are not alone in facing these challenges. All public institutions have the same pressures. The increasingly difficult mood was captured by a Bruce Kaplan cartoon showing a young girl tugging on her mother and asking, "When will I be old enough to sue people?" Doctors now face patients armed with reports from the Internet about the latest medical research. Patients want public information on each surgeon's success record. Medical licensing bodies are under pressure to publicly post all complaints about doctors. Nurses get criticized if someone has a long wait in an emergency ward. To take another example, the police face much tougher scrutiny of all their practices. Any untoward incident is likely to yield a review of what happened, usually by an independent body, even though police officers regularly have to make very difficult decisions instantaneously and under enormous pressure. And does anyone want to speak up to defend politicians? We absolutely need good people in elected office, yet we make their work almost impossible to do by scrutinizing not only their public decisions but every aspect of their personal lives and character. Education faces increased public scrutiny, but so do all other professions and many occupations.

Difficult as it may be for the work of professionals, there are good sides to this more critical environment too. On the plus side, it is harder now for public institutions—and private ones too, for that matter—to get away with poor performance than it used to be. Institutions must be more aware of their responsibilities to their clients. Schools can't so easily dismiss parent concerns or treat students the way we sometimes did a generation ago. People want higher standards, better outcomes, and more information. They want more say, and they want their concerns taken seriously. All that is good in the long run, even if it does produce some real strain on the system. These tendencies also make it so important for every public institution to do whatever it can to build public confidence.

To answer the question in the title of this section, how much public confidence do we need, the answer must be "as much as we can generate." Powerful forces are pushing increased skepticism if not cynicism. Active engagement in responsible efforts to increase public understanding for public schools is essential. If public confidence is so vitally important, what do schools and school systems need to do to help build and sustain it?

## WHAT CREATES PUBLIC CONFIDENCE?

Educators often feel—and complain—that their hard work is unappreciated by the public. A frequent comment at education events when public attitudes come up is that "we need to get our story out and tell about our successes." If only people really knew about the schools, the feeling seems to be, schools would get much more praise, or at least understanding, and a lot less criticism. The polling data on local schools tends to support that view.

It is understandable, but mistaken, to think that generating public support for schools is primarily a matter of giving people more information. How the public understands educational issues and how that understanding gets translated into decisions are complex processes shaped by much more than school communication efforts, although these are important and currently quite inadequate in most places.

Although public education has a legacy that provides much to be proud of, it is not by any means a perfect or unblemished record—nor could any universal public program ever achieve a state of perfection. We need also to be aware of some of the reservations about the positive results of education.

First, increasing levels of education have not always reduced broader social inequalities. A society can provide more education for everyone without reducing the gap between the top and bottom of the outcomes distribution. Indeed, rising overall levels of education in a state or country can be associated with increasing inequality as those who have more get more, leading to wider gaps in outcomes—the "Matthew effect." If educational qualifications are not equitably available, they can be used to cover up other kinds of discrimination. If some groups fall behind in educational attainment, that gap can be used as an excuse for shutting them out of labor market or other opportunities as well, even if their lesser educational attainment is essentially the result of social forces beyond their control. That is why we need to be concerned not just about good outcomes overall but also about good outcomes for all students and all population groups.

Second, more education can be used as a way for employers to avoid their obligation to provide training and learning opportunities for their workers. If the public sector is expected to provide all the skills people require for work, then the expenses required to create profits by giving workers skills can be shifted to the public sector while the profits themselves remain private. OECD data show that countries vary widely in the degree to which their employers support skill development of workers (Giguere 2008). In many European countries, workforce preparation is explicitly seen as the responsibility of employers, whereas in North America this responsibility tends to be given to public institutions. Employers can blame the deficiencies of their workers on the public education system rather than assuming responsibility themselves for development of human capital. If the taxation that pays for public education is also inequitable, then even greater inequity may result as those who benefit most do not pay their fare share.

Finally, more education can create tensions for individuals, families, or communities as it may lead young people to reject traditional values or existing practices, as described by philosopher Nick Burbules in "The Tragic Sense of Education" (1990). While assimilation of immigrant children into the mainstream is a policy goal in many if not all countries, it does not come without some cost, because it can alienate students from their families. Over many generations immigrant families across the world have worked hard to educate their children, but often the result is family strife as children adopt very different values from those of their parents, such as rejecting their parents' religious beliefs or cultural identities. Similarly, more education for women can threaten power structures in patriarchal families or communities, leading to marriage breakdown and sometimes violence against women. Schools see the results of these tensions in the strained relations between students, parents, and the school.

These concerns need to be taken seriously. They are cautions on how to make improvements in public education, not reasons to avoid improvement, but they do remind us that more or better education does not solve all problems.

Many educators immediately jump to the influence of the media as being a primary factor in negative public attitudes. Media reporting does matter, and we will return to it shortly. However, in schools as for other public institutions, the most important single factor in shaping public attitudes is the daily interaction people have with schools. The key implication for school systems is to remember that in everything we do, building public support must be an important consideration.

Every day millions of people have contact with schools, primarily through their children or their contact with other people who have children in school. Schools are not businesses in the usual sense, and the relationship with students and parents is not one of business and customer. That is a mistaken way of thinking about the nature of education, which is not a service or commodity. Still, it is the case that daily relationships, like those in business, do matter to the way people think about the education system.

The daily interactions of children, parents, and other people—whether with teachers, principals, secretaries, or bus drivers—all shape their perceptions of how good our schools are. Every time someone is abrupt to a caller on the phone, or when a parent's concern is not heard, or when a student feels she or he has been treated unfairly (justifiably or not), public confidence in schools is affected.

All this means that schools must pay attention to personal contacts and relationships just as any other organization does. How we greet people, whether phone calls are answered or quickly returned, whether people feel their concerns are really heard—all of these have an impact on how people feel about schools. Each individual incident is probably fairly trivial, but they do cumulate.

Moreover, the impact of direct contact is not restricted to what happens in the school. Unlike what happens for most businesses, people's view of schools is also affected by what students do out of school. When students are rowdy in public, toss trash on the streets, or vandalism occurs—or even when students dress in unconventional ways and are normally boisterous—some people will blame the schools. This may be unfair, but it's reality.

These interactions do not just affect the people to whom they occur, because people talk to one another. A common saying in business is that each unhappy customer tells ten others. The same is likely true in education. Parents talk among themselves, extended families talk about schools, and people in the community talk to one another. Bad news travels fast, and people pay much more attention to what is unusual and threatening than they do to what is frequent and positive. Following Gresham's Rule ("bad money drives out good"), negative incidents have, unfortunately, a much more powerful impact on people's attitudes than do positive incidents. One street robbery will have a much deeper effect on people's ideas about safety than hundreds or thousands of safe events. One accident will have a more powerful impact than tens of thousands of uneventful trips. Even an offhand negative remark by an educator can have much more lasting effects than was ever intended. Human cognition works against people having an appropriately positive view of what schools do.

## MEDIA AND COMMUNICATIONS

The focus on direct personal experience does not mean that other factors are unimportant. Media coverage does matter. Most people get most of their knowledge about public affairs from the media, especially television. Constant coverage in the media of something like poor standards or violence in schools does affect public attitudes and is part of the reason that people have more negative opinions about schools in general than they do about their own local schools.

It's all too easy to complain about the media and its weaknesses, many of which are all too evident. Coverage of many issues is superficial and tends to focus on negatives or on conflict. Reporters often do not know all that much about the issue they are covering, and so can get facts wrong and miss important nuances. Fundamental issues may not get much attention while minor matters do. The particular notion of balanced reporting held by many media means that even views held by very few people or with no empirical support can get reported as "the other side of the issue." The constant desire for novelty in the news means that what is vitally important today drops totally out of sight in a few months. Think about international events such as wars or famines that can dominate our conversation for days or even weeks and then disappear entirely very soon after. Education, on the other hand, gets relatively little coverage considering how big a share of our national economy and public effort it is.

Media coverage of education is also difficult in that the issues that often get the most attention are not those that research suggests are most helpful to improving student outcomes. Chapters 5 and 6 outlined a set of policies and approaches that have a strong warrant from education research as being important for effective education. Yet most of these are difficult to explain to the public and lack the immediate attention-grabbing qualities that put issues in the public eye. Think for a moment about the media and public interest in the following pairs of issues:

- Building teacher capacity for effective instruction with diverse learners *or*
- School boards overspending on travel and entertainment

Here's a second pair:

- Building a climate of respect for all learners *or*
- A student being beaten or stabbed in or near a school

Of course the first item in each pair is much more important for building long-term quality education. Yet it is the second in each pair that will get much more public and media attention. Even when the discussion is not about a specific incident but about an educational issue, the framing of the issue often works against a deep understanding. A discussion of the merits of social promotion will get more attention than a discussion of how to improve daily teaching practices to reduce failure in the first place. A discussion of anti-bullying or zero tolerance measures will get more attention than a discussion of building a school and community climate of respect for all learners.

Even though everyone has gone to school and most people feel they know quite a bit about effective education, the reality is that few people have enough sense of schools as complex social institutions to be able to understand the requirements for lasting and sustainable change. The same applies to the way education is covered by the mass media. Much of what is proposed in this book as sound strategy would simply not be of interest to reporters even though it is vital to students.

Educational leaders know this problem instinctively. How many school boards complain that they get many more parents coming to a meeting on bus routes than to a meeting on reading instruction? It's easy to get people worked up about things like tax rates or allegedly unfair treatment of one neighborhood or group against another. It's much harder to galvanize people around the steps that are needed to build lasting improvement.

A good example occurred in Ontario in late 2005 when the government announced its Student Success Strategy. A first announcement was made outlining the overall program and all the components, described in chapter 2, that would help improve high school graduation rates. This announcement got virtually no media attention. A week later Minister Kennedy announced the legislation that would require young people who had not graduated to remain in school or some other appropriate learning setting. He also said that students who did not do this would be unable to apply for or receive a driver's license. This latter announcement got an enormous amount of media coverage, almost all of it around the driver's license issue, which brought out strong feelings both for and against. Kennedy had predicted exactly this, saying that the driver's license debate would be the vehicle to draw public attention to the importance of the high school graduation issue and to all the steps the government was taking, announced but ignored, to help schools and students do better. This proved to be entirely correct. Although the government eventually withdrew the driver's license proposal, its purpose had been achieved in that there was much more public awareness of and interest in the larger issue.

Without defending the media, which certainly has its weaknesses, it is only fair to point out that covering public affairs for a newspaper, radio, or television station is difficult work. Many of the issues are quite complicated, yet there are, as in politics, too many issues at any one time to give any combination of them the attention they might require. While as consumers we want better media coverage, it is not so clear that we are willing to pay for it in higher prices. And if the media are prone to sound bites and short stories, it is perhaps because that is what readers and viewers watch and read. If *Survivor* gets twenty times as many viewers as a special on global warming, should we be surprised that the former gets more hours of television coverage than the latter? How many of us regularly read long feature articles or view in-depth documentaries on public issues? How many of us read only the head-line or first paragraph of a newspaper story and then skip to the next item? The same dynamics work here as in politics. If people really read or watched more in-depth coverage, the media would be much more likely to provide it. To make this point is not to attack citizens for their weaknesses either, since there are always many more issues to think about than there is time to consider them.

The limitations of the media are real and endemic. Like the other important barriers and constraints in this book, they must be under-stood, and educators need to think about how to compensate for them, since they are not going to go away. And there are steps schools and, even more, school systems can take to combat some of these tendencies and their negative effects. As mentioned already, the most important is to build strong, positive daily interactions with students, parents, and community members. This is not only good public relations, it is also good education.

### School communications

Schools' own communication activities are important and often under-valued. The most powerful of these, school newsletters and websites, are rarely done well. Most school newsletters are full of news about events, awards, and administrative matters, but they give parents and other readers very little information about the bigger picture of the system's goals, accomplishments, and challenges. Many studies show that parents want to know more about the instructional program of the school, but schools often don't tell them much. While not all parents have web access, especially in low-income communities, more and more do, and the web used with e-mail offers tremendous possibilities for making important and meaningful school information readily available to parents with a small expenditure of effort.

Many communities also have media that schools can use to provide a more positive message, such as local newspapers, typically weekly, or local cable television channels. These outlets are generally more open to telling positive stories than are the major media. They are often read or watched by many more people that one might think and can thus be very useful communication vehicles for schools. So are other local media efforts such as leaving copies of school reports or newsletters for pickup or casual reading in local businesses where people other than parents might see them.

Most educational organizations continue to rely heavily on print communications—letters, newsletters, and the like. The media world is changing. Newspapers in most places are losing circulation, and so is network television. Communication, especially among the young, is increasingly electronic. Cable television, broadcasting on demand, listservs, RSS, podcasts, the blogosphere, and the amazing multiplicity of websites on every topic one could imagine (and quite a few that most of us would not have imagined . . .) are increasing their share of public attention as a source of information, especially among young people. YouTube gets more viewers than network news. Facebook and MySpace are primary vehicles for sharing information—and misinformation. Nobody knows how this world will develop in the next decades or what it will mean for civic knowledge and participation, but multiple media channels certainly open up new possibilities for the education system to communicate with its varied publics, including getting more response.

Harried school administrators will rightly respond that they do not have the time to devote to school newsletters or to create fancy websites, let alone to having a presence in the world of blogs, podcasts, and online video. Even school newsletters are often thrown together at the last minute or delegated to someone on the staff. Part of the answer lies in teamwork and delegation, as discussed later. Another part lies with students, who in many schools already have primary responsibility for website creation and maintenance, and are more knowledgeable about and more interested in many of the new media. Learning about school issues and public relations by putting together communications vehicles would seem to be an entirely worthwhile educational activity for students, even in elementary school. The point is not to be fancy, either, but to provide simple, useful information that will help readers and viewers in the community better understand what schools are doing and why.

Schools should not have to do this work alone, either. Districts or states could assist schools by providing information on curriculum, effective teaching, student assessment, and other such issues in formats especially for parents and the public. Many parents would read and use this kind of information if it were made readily available to them in various forms. Universities and other policy or research organizations, which are in the business of public communication, could also provide useful supports to local school efforts. Many universities, for example, have publications and web presences designed to provide broad public information, yet few of them think of partnering with schools and districts as a primary distribution vehicle even though that would be cost-effective for all parties.

Communication is a vital activity for all educational organizations. To be effective it needs a reasonable infrastructure and level of support, which it currently rarely gets. The net result of all these efforts would be increased public knowledge of and, very likely, public support for what schools are doing, often with a very modest investment of effort.

### Telling the real story

In looking at these communications channels, it is important to resist the temptation in most organizations to make all communications positive, to talk only about successes. This is a natural tendency but a mistaken one. The public is too smart to take this kind of unending good news seriously. However positive people are about our schools, they know the system is not perfect! The challenge in communications is to combine a positive overall message with a realistic assessment of limitations and challenges.

This is admittedly difficult. No organization wants to expose its limitations in public, just as none of us individually likes to stand up and proclaim our faults. We have a strong suspicion that any admitted weaknesses will be used against us by the media or others who see themselves in opposition. And as media attention and political debate can often focus on relatively trivial matters—such as putting a bottle of wine on an expense claim—instead of on the outcomes for children in our schools, admitting problems is a high risk. Many politicians have learned the hard way that admitting anything negative leave you open to all sorts of abuse.

Even success can produce a bad result. Consider the promise by English minister David Blunkett in 1997 that by 2002, 80 percent of students would reach the government's achievement target. In fact, in 2002 the result was about 78 percent, an impressive gain over the 55 percent or so who had reached the same level a few years earlier. But because the target had been set at 80 percent, and so much had been staked on it, the 78 percent result was widely reported in the media as a failure rather than as a very significant improvement.

The result is that school systems and governments can become excessively cautious about sharing information, even when it is largely positive. To take just one example, in 2006 the Ontario Ministry of Education commissioned independent evaluations of our two key strategies—elementary literacy/numeracy and high school student success leading to higher graduation rates. These evaluations were contracted to well-known independent organizations. In addition to giving the ministry valuable feedback on our progress, we also hoped to have initial results available before the 2007 provincial election, so that the government would have independent evidence to present to voters regarding the success of these initiatives. We were, it can be added, quite confident that the initiatives were having positive results, as outlined earlier in this book.

The first round of reports were indeed completed prior to the 2007 election, and they were, as expected, strongly positive in their assessment of the reforms. Of course, they also identified areas where more needed to be done or where particular aspects had not yet fully taken hold—entirely to be expected only one to two years into such large-scale efforts. The government, however, nervous at that time about its reelection prospects, decided not to release the reports because they were not 100 percent positive. The irony is that nobody would believe a report that had only positive findings! In short, even when the news is good, there can be strong disincentives for sharing it. As a minister once said to me years ago about her lack of desire to release reports done by the department, "Ben, you don't ask a dog to fetch the stick that will be used to beat it."

Still, for school systems there does not seem to be any option other than to share information openly, since everyone knows that all our institutions do have flaws and difficulties. Nobody is graduating 100 percent of their students or achieving all the goals people want from schools—which is almost certainly an impossible task in the first place. The challenge is how to position communications in a way that is fair and open without laying oneself open to unreasonable criticism.

## HOW SHOULD THE PUBLIC JUDGE THE PERFORMANCE OF EDUCATION SYSTEMS?

An important element in sustaining public confidence in education has to do with the need to provide a range of objective information about the system's performance. This brings us squarely to the issue of testing and test scores as measures of system performance. Educators often complain that they are judged only by the results of system–wide tests, which are at best an incomplete accounting of everything the school tries to do. This is a valid criticism. It is easy to see how much damage can be and has been caused by a reliance on results of a single test to make highly consequential decisions about children and schools and to provide the sole means through which the public is expected to judge the work of the education system. This situation persists in many places even though public opinion data show that most people believe that a single test is not a valid basis for judging the performance of students or schools (Hart and Livingstone 2007; Daggett 2007).

There are some positive signs that the testing mania is waning, at least somewhat. Wales abolished much of its universal testing a few years ago. Finland, the highest-ranking country in student achievement in three successive rounds of PISA testing, has very little national testing. England has moved away from universal testing of eight-year-olds. While I was deputy minister in Manitoba, the government replaced the grade 3 provincial assessment in language and mathematics with a quick checklist of key math and language skills that would go to parents early in the third grade. Ontario has quite limited provincial testing—grades 3 and 6 language and math are the only ones in elementary school, along with a grade 9 mathematics test and a grade 10 literacy test. Despite these examples, achievement tests and examinations remain powerful forces in many education systems, most notably in the United States, which has the additional challenge of having tests that in many places are not linked to curriculum.

In thinking about the prevalence and persistence of large-scale testing, the question that comes to mind is why these programs were put in place and persist. If single tests are not good measures of performance, why are they used so often? There are several answers to this question, but the most important one is that the public wants evidence on system performance. Tests are seen as one—though not the only—legitimate indicator, with few alternative sources of judgment available.

People are in favor of testing and public results of testing because they want to know how well our schools are doing, how well we are looking after their children and spending their money. This is an entirely legitimate desire in a democratic society. And here is the key point—in many places the large-scale tests are virtually the only information the public has about system performance. It's not as if in earlier years, before the increase in testing, schools were providing a broad range of useful public information about their performance and results, now displaced by narrow testing data. Although there was nothing to prevent schools and school systems from reporting publicly on indicators they considered more meaningful, the education system did not do so and still does not do so in most places. Had school systems been reporting publicly basic performance information such as high school graduation rates, suspension and expulsion rates, retention in grade in elementary schools, or special-education referral rates, there would have been less demand for test data. Reporting performance data of various kinds is one of the things that would make school newsletters and websites more powerful and interesting. In the absence of any countering information, people are open to believing the charge that results are poor and that the system is covering up its inadequacies, leading to the supposed solution of national, state, or local tests.

Some would argue that all public indicators are limited and potentially misleading. That is true. No single indicator, or even a set of indicators, will cover the whole range of goals people think are important for our schools to address. But the absence of perfect information cannot be a reason to have no information. If school systems did more reporting of their own performance indicators, it would provide some balance to the heavy focus in the media and elsewhere on test results.

In every field of public discussion, a few key indicators come to dominate public debate even though they are recognized as inadequate. In the private sector, one reads regular laments about the reliance on quarterly earnings and share prices, sometimes at the expense of long-term company health. In the economy, changes in gross domestic product (GDP) or unemployment rates or housing prices are powerful indicators. More recently, the world price of oil has been cited as a kind of shorthand for the overall state of the economy.

In all these cases, and in many others one might cite, those working closely with the data know that each indicator is only approximate, and there are usually vigorous debates about how each indicator should be calculated. For example, GDP only values activities that are expressed monetarily, therefore ignoring vital functions such as unpaid household work and valuing positively activities that produce pollution or even destruction. War is good for the GDP! Despite these flaws, it is likely impossible to avoid entirely a situation in which a small number of indicators are at the forefront of debate.

In the current climate of declining public confidence in all institutions, pleas by educators that testing should be replaced by independent teacher evaluation or by trust in the profession will prove fruitless. These pleas are seen as a way of hiding poor performance—which, we should remind ourselves, has been the case in some schools and systems, to the detriment of many students. Some schools and systems just do not generate good or excellent results. This may well be due to all kinds of factors beyond the school's control, but data are a way to illuminate the problem so that action can be taken.

Schools and school systems could, though, be proactive in broadening the public discussion by providing public information on performance using better indicators, presented in more nuanced ways than is typically done with test scores. Give people more and better ways of judging how things are going by including some indicators on the aspects of education that are most often ignored by tests. Systems could report on progress through the grades, participation in extracurricular activities, volunteer work, and post-high school activities to give a broader sense of valued outcomes. Much of this information is already available in system records and could be reported, even on a sample basis, relatively easily.

As one example, Ontario put in place in 2002 a grade 10 literacy test as a requirement for high school graduation. The test was unpopular with students and teachers but quite popular with the public according to polls, in part because there were no other indicators of the performance of the high school system. As recently as 2003, Ontario was unable to report a provincial high school graduation rate, and most schools and districts also could not report a graduation rate. Nor does Ontario have provincial examinations at the end of high school like many Canadian provinces, and other countries, do. No surprise that the results of the literacy test became a de facto indicator about the high school system.

By 2007 that situation had changed entirely. As part of the focus on improving high school outcomes, the province was reporting a graduation rate annually, districts and schools were increasingly doing the same, and all districts were also gathering and reporting the proportion of students who were on track to graduate by completing the appropriate number of courses in grades nine and ten. As a consequence of reporting these richer and more important indicators, public and media attention on the results of the literacy test dropped quite substantially.

Many other indicators could be gathered and reported publicly while also providing useful information for school improvement. One instance would be student and staff engagement and satisfaction. A major complaint about test scores is that they set up unfair comparisons between schools where there is parental choice. This is a valid concern. The research on school choice shows that parents do not want to choose schools solely on the basis of test performance (Woods, Bagley, and Glatter 1998; Fuller, Elmore, and Orfield 1996). They also want a school where their child will fit in and be cared for. But there is rarely any public information available on these latter points, so test results may be the only data parents have. Staff and student engagement levels are also important from a management perspective in keeping schools healthy places to be. School districts and schools ought to compile and publish data on these issues.

Starting with one or two additional indicators that are meaningful and readily available is probably more important than trying to work out a complete list. Adding more data to the public debate will be helpful. It will not remove the impact of test scores, but even small improvements in reporting can, over time, reduce the reliance on tests as the single indicator of school outcomes. The point is to think about public reporting in ways that deepen public understanding of educational issues and challenges.

## PUBLIC DEBATE

As an important social policy issue, education will always be a subject of public debate. Educators should welcome debate because it can bring constructive public attention to real educational issues, such as the gap in achievement related to poverty or the difficulties in having enough high-quality teachers. Districts, for example, can face very difficult choices around keeping small schools open, locating special programs, or differential resource allocation to high-need schools. These are issues on which people can have quite legitimate differences of opinion, and the discussion about them can be a healthy part of democratic dialogue, essential to good public policy. The challenge is to have public debate that is constructive, deepens public understanding of educational issues, and builds public support for schools.

This is not easy to do, as many forces push in other directions. For one thing, the issues that are most often in the public eye related to education are not necessarily about educational matters. More often they are about money, blame, or both.

Let's start with money. Governments and school systems love announcing how much money they are spending on an initiative while critics are constantly complaining that there is not enough money or that it is being used for the wrong things. The debate over whether or not there is enough money is often unhelpful to building public confidence because it does not focus attention on the work that schools really do or how they do it. Instead, arguments turn on amounts of money, and often amounts that are so large as to be pretty much meaningless to most citizens, for whom the distinction between spending $200 million or $210 million on something is not at all evident. Of course money matters, as discussed in the previous chapter, but it matters because it is used for a particular purpose or achieves a particular result, and these issues are often obscured in the discussion about quantity unrelated to any particular use.

Public debates about education also have a tendency to turn into blame exercises, with governments blaming schools or teachers, and schools blaming parents or governments. The current mania to determine who is "accountable" really seems to mean most of the time deciding who will be blamed and punished, a highly negative approach that will not build the kind of openness and commitment needed in our public organizations. Meanwhile, citizens are often left wishing that people would stop trying to blame someone else and get on with doing something to create improvement.

People have the right and the obligation to express their views and to criticize education policies or decisions. And of course educators will, and should, continue to argue for more spending on schools. Complaints and blame exercises also have their place; sometimes conditions are bad and those problems need to be brought to public attention. The challenge for those working in the system is to weigh carefully—more carefully than we often do—the potentially negative effect of our criticisms on public perceptions, since those negative perceptions may result in less public support, less funding, and a worsening rather than an improvement in conditions. We do not want people concluding that the public schools are in such bad shape that they ought to send their children to private schools or work in favor of voucher systems.

Even the conversations that teachers have with one another or with parents in their non-school lives have impacts on public perceptions of schools. When educators complain publicly about school conditions, or kids, or standards, they reinforce negative perceptions among the public, even if their concerns are entirely justifiable. This is not to say that people should stifle legitimate concerns, but rather to point out that public strife over schooling can have negative effects on public support.

The Ontario story of People for Education is a good illustration of the challenge of balancing critique and support. People for Education (*www.peopleforeducation.com*) was created in 1996 by a small group of parents—mostly mothers—who were concerned about the education policies and budget cuts of the Ontario government that was elected in 1995. Through a combination of hard work by volunteers and very good political skills, People for Education gradually became an important presence in the public debate about education in Ontario. They launched an annual survey of school programs that was, for quite a few years, the only reasonably reliable source of information on the impact of budget cuts on school staffing and programs. For example, they were able to document an increase in class sizes and decline in support personnel.

The organization also did a lot of work to engage the media. They were careful not to take partisan political positions but to stick to supporting the need for a strong public education system. Since they were a group of parents, and since they had compelling data as well as stories to offer, they became a "go to" source for the media and one of the most quoted organizations on education in the province.

The election of a new government in 2003 and the development of a very different education agenda presented a real challenge to People for Education. How should they now present themselves? Should they continue to be highly critical of the problems that remain, or should they be more positive about the many steps the new government was taking that did address their concerns? If they are too positive, they risk losing media attention, and some of their supporters would see them as being too easy on the government. However, if they are too negative, they run the risk of continuing to erode public confidence in education ("it's never good enough"), precisely the problem they set out to address. Over the last few years, People for Education has moderated its critique in many ways, has tried to acknowledge the evident progress that has been made, yet has also continued to identify areas it sees as weaknesses and to focus particularly on its belief that the school system in Ontario needs more money. This is an uneasy balancing act with which the organization continues to struggle. The role that brought it to prominence no longer exists in the same way, yet after so much work and success, and with the education system certainly nowhere near perfection, the leaders are reluctant to abandon or even dramatically alter their work.

This challenge facing People for Education is not unique; many organizations in the education sector have struggled with the challenge of how much to recognize and support progress, when it is often much easier to continue to be highly critical.

## CONCLUSION

As public institutions, schools are dependent on citizens' willingness to send us their children and give us their money. Neither of these can be taken for granted, and in the emerging world of greater skepticism about all institutions, public support requires explicit attention. Although there are negative pressures from various sources, such as the media, there are also many things schools and school systems can do to improve public knowledge and understanding of the work that schools do and the challenges with which educators struggle. Some of these things are quite simple to do. In the long run, the credibility of any institution depends primarily on what people in that institution do, because over time citizens will recognize and respond to quality. Public confidence is not just a matter of people's opinions, either. As Matthews (2008) points out,

> Typical public engagement campaigns tend to rely on external persuasion, which doesn't produce the same intensity of political will. A persuaded populace isn't the same as a committed citizenry. Being sold on what others have decided does not create reservoirs of political will. (561)

That belief is both encouraging and daunting. It puts the future of schools largely in the hands of those in the education system but raises the constant possibility that, as Pogo put it so many years ago, "We have met the enemy and he is us."

# 8

# Leadership for Improvement

Leadership has been written about as much or more than any other topic in the whole literature of education. Rooms could be filled—indeed, many bookshelves have been filled—with books on education leadership, with new ones appearing faster than anyone can keep track, let alone read them. Just about every adjective imaginable has been used in front of the word "leadership" in a book or journal article title. There are myriad definitions of the term, and just as many lists of characteristics that leaders should have.

Two questions immediately arise. First, why is there so much writing about leadership, and second, why hasn't this work resolved all the issues by telling people in leadership roles what they need to know and do?

The answers to those two questions have much to do with the content of this chapter and the next one. Leadership is one of those things we know is vitally important, yet it is very hard to describe in any way that actually helps people know how to do it in particular circumstances. As the protagonist in *Zen and the Art of Motorcycle Maintenance* said about quality, "We may not know how to define it, but we all know it when we see it" (Pirsig 1974). Further, knowing the importance of leadership does not necessarily help us know how to do it ourselves or to create the conditions that foster and support its existence. People continue to write about good leadership because we know it is important yet find it very hard to discern how to have more of it.

Leadership, however, is not just, or even mainly, a property of individuals. Individuals are only able to exercise their skills fully in the right context. Just as teacher learning is as much a matter of the right structures and culture in a school, so leadership is strongly related to the structures and cultures of districts, states, and countries, a fact that is often not given enough attention in discussions of leadership. The latter part of this chapter discusses the steps education systems need to take to attract, develop, and retain capable leaders.

A central challenge to effective leadership has already been mentioned a couple of times in this book—that is, the problem of balancing the need for change with the need to manage effectively all the necessary ongoing functions of an organization. Both aspects are critical, but they turn out to be conflicting, in that the more one does one, the less one seems to be able to do the other. Leaders are typically exhorted in books such as this, or in workshops and professional development or even in graduate programs, to be change agents. They then go back to their districts and discover that the press of the immediate or routine seems to make the work of change impossible.

This dilemma is both acute and real, and it is the reason that there are two chapters on leadership in this book. This chapter is about leading for improvement, which must be a central concern of every educational leader. The next chapter is about how to reconcile the press for change and improvement with the ongoing work of running a school or school system and with the inevitable political pressures, while living to tell the tale!

Both chapters are intended to help people in leadership roles understand how they can actually do the work of leadership in a satisfactory way given the many conflicting tasks they are asked to achieve. The discussion is not about new metaphors or conceptualizations of leading; instead, it tries to provide practical guidance on a manageable number of things that leaders in education at all levels need to make the focus of their attention. My goal is to lay out a set of priorities and plan of action that a reasonably competent and committed person—that is, most of us—could actually put into action.

The nature of the challenge is clear if one looks at any of the existing sets of leadership standards. As one example, box 8.1 lists expectations for education leaders drawn from one of the six ISLLC standards in the United States. As one looks at these, or any of the many other similar lists, the inescapable conclusion is that we need, or want, or expect our leaders to be perfect. Taken as a whole, any such set of practices or skills describes something that no real person could ever attain. It's doubtful if there has ever been a single person who could meet everything that is in any set of leadership standards. Nobody is good at everything. Real people have faults and weaknesses along with their strengths.

As long as our leadership models suggest that leaders can somehow embody all, or even most, of these qualities, we will be disappointed by the results, just as we expect our political leaders to be superhuman and then are disappointed when they turn out not to be so. Peter Drucker (1986) wrote that

> Whenever a job defeats two people in a row, who in their earlier assignments had performed well, a company has a widow-maker on its hands. When this happens, a responsible executive should not ask the headhunter for a universal genius. Instead abolish the job. Any job that ordinarily competent people cannot perform is a job that cannot be staffed. Unless changed, it will predictably defeat the third appointee the way it defeated the first two. (127)

## LEADING IMPROVEMENT

As an alternative to the long lists of standards or competencies, some writers on leadership have proposed conceptualizations of a smaller number of main tasks of education leadership. The idea is to give leaders a list that looks more manageable to them. The similarities in these various approaches can be seen by looking at three important current formulations.

Leithwood et al. (2006) produced a synthesis of the leadership research for the National College for School Leadership in England. Their "Seven Strong Claims about School Leadership" are:

**BOX 8.1**

**ISLLC Standard 2**

A school administrator is an education leader who promotes the success of all students by advocating, nurturing, and sustaining a school culture and instructional program conducive to student learning and staff professional growth.

The administrator has knowledge and understanding of:

- student growth and development
- applied learning theories
- applied motivational theories
- curriculum design, implementation, evaluation, and refinement
- principles of effective instruction
- measurement, evaluation, and assessment strategies
- diversity and its meaning for educational programs
- adult learning and professional development models
- the change process for systems, organizations, and individuals
- the role of technology in promoting student learning and professional growth
- school cultures

The administrator believes in, values, and is committed to:

- student learning as the fundamental purpose of schooling
- the proposition that all students can learn
- the variety of ways in which students can learn
- lifelong learning for self and others
- professional development as an integral part of school improvement
- the benefits that diversity brings to the school community
- a safe and supportive learning environment
- preparing students to be contributing members of society

The administrator facilitates processes and engages in activities ensuring that:

- all individuals are treated with fairness, dignity, and respect
- professional development promotes a focus on student learning consistent with the school vision and goals
- students and staff feel valued and important
- the responsibilities and contributions of each individual are acknowledged
- barriers to student learning are identified, clarified, and addressed
- diversity is considered in developing learning experiences
- lifelong learning is encouraged and modeled
- there is a culture of high expectations for self, student, and staff performance
- technologies are used in teaching and learning
- student and staff accomplishments are recognized and celebrated
- multiple opportunities to learn are available to all students
- the school is organized and aligned for success
- curricular, co-curricular, and extra-curricular programs are designed, implemented, evaluated, and refined
- curriculum decisions are based on research, expertise of teachers, and the recommendations of learned societies
- the school culture and climate are assessed on a regular basis
- a variety of sources of information is used to make decisions
- student learning is assessed using a variety of techniques
- multiple sources of information regarding performance are used by staff and students
- a variety of supervisory and evaluation models are employed
- pupil personnel programs are developed to meet the needs of students and their families

1. School leadership is second only to classroom teaching as an influence on pupil learning.
2. Almost all successful leaders draw on the same repertoire of basic leadership practices.
    a. Building vision and setting directions
    b. Understanding and developing people
    c. Redesigning the organization
    d. Managing the teaching and learning programme
3. The ways in which leaders apply these basic leadership practices—not the practices themselves—demonstrate responsiveness to, rather than dictation by, the contexts in which they work.
4. School leaders improve teaching and learning indirectly and most powerfully through their influence on staff motivation, commitment and working conditions.
5. School leadership has a greater influence on schools and students when it is widely distributed.
6. Some patterns of distribution are more effective than others.
7. A small handful of personal traits explain a high proportion of the variation in leadership effectiveness. (Leithwood et al. 2006)

Michael Fullan has been one of the most influential writers about leadership. His most recent book (Fullan 2008) identifies "Six Secrets of Change":

1. Love your employees.
2. Connect peers with purpose.
3. Capacity building prevails.
4. Learning is the work.
5. Transparency rules.
6. Systems learn.

A third new and important formulation comes from the New Zealand Best Evidence Synthesis program (*www.educationcounts.govt.nz/ themes/iterative_bes*), an effort of the New Zealand Ministry of Education to produce syntheses of knowledge on important education issues with a strong focus on practical implications as well as quality of evidence. A new publication by Viviane Robinson and colleagues (2008) identifies and describes in detail five characteristics of school leadership that make a difference to students:

+ Dimension One: Establishing goals and expectations
+ Dimension Two: Strategic resourcing
+ Dimension Three: Planning, coordinating and evaluating teaching and the curriculum
+ Dimension Four: Promoting and participating in teacher learning and development
+ Dimension Five: Ensuring an orderly and supportive environment

Each of these lists provides useful ideas both about what leaders should do and how they should do it, although overall there is more of the former than the latter. Drawing from these and other writings and from the ideas developed earlier in this book, I propose my own list of seven practicalities that all leaders need to manage if they are to lead improvement in student outcomes:

1. Establishing a vision and goals
2. Building a strong team
3. Creating and supporting the right culture
4. Communicating vision, direction, and accomplishment
5. Recruiting, developing and retaining leaders
6. Building internal and external support
7. Maintaining the focus on teaching and learning

The first five of these tasks are discussed in this chapter, while the next chapter addresses the final two in discussing problems of managing all the other things that get in the way of improvement.

## Establishing a Vision and Goals

Just about every book on leadership says that leaders either set or support the setting of an organizational vision and obtain widespread support for that vision. But how does one actually do that? Given what's already been said about how divided communities and school systems can be on many issues, commitment to common goals is not an easy thing to create or maintain. From observation, three points seem important to keep in mind in goal-setting work.

First, goals should be few in number and easy to understand and remember. One of the big mistakes in many such exercises is trying to include everyone's area or interest in a goal statement. But as argued throughout this book, an organization, no matter how big, can only concentrate on a very small number of things with any degree of focus—probably no more than three or four. So trying to be inclusive can result in the dispersion of effort and attention. If everything is important, then nothing is really important.

Of course, limiting the number of goals can create conflict. That's why the central goals have to command widespread support in any school or district, and with parents and the public. Recall that Ontario had three goals: improving outcomes, reducing inequities in outcomes, and improving public confidence in public education. Moreover, there were only a few main initiatives in support of those goals, the most important of which were improving elementary school literacy and numeracy and increasing high school graduation rates. While there were other initiatives and issues, as there must be in any school system, the core of the work could be put on a single piece of paper or even a single transparency. This made it easy to remember. And these were goals that were easy for most people to support and, conversely, hard to oppose. Most people in the organization could see how their own work would contribute to and support the main goals. So instead of being divisive, the goals became an overarching framework for people all across the organization—in school districts as well as in the Ministry of Education—to understand how what they did mattered.

A second mistake often made in goal-setting and visioning exercises is to try to be clear about what everything means and how everything will happen. Lots of time can be spent considering hypothetical situations and weighing alternatives that will never be real. As Reeves (2006) puts it, the quality of the planning document may be inversely related to the success of the plan. Sometimes the effort to have clarity gets in the way and creates unnecessary conflict. In politics you often hear about a "big tent" in which many different people can be comfortable. Goal setting is similar. Keeping goals fairly general allows different people to see their way to supporting them and also allows things to evolve as the situation changes, as it inevitably will.

A corollary of both the above points is to avoid spending too much time engaging people in writing goal or vision statements, with the inevitable tendency to have long discussions of the wording. This is unproductive, even counterproductive. The whole process of establishing a vision and goals should not take too long or consume too much energy, since the real and more difficult work is putting the vision into practice. The goal is to keep everyone focused on actions, not words. We are all familiar with the vision statement produced after a year of meetings involving hundreds of people that then has no effect on what the organization does.

There must, of course, be regular feedback on progress, which may lead occasionally to revising the goals, but we learn more about our goals from trying to achieve them than from trying to write them down in the first place.

These ideas informed the approach that we took to develop a common sense of direction in the Ontario Ministry of Education. The Ontario ministry, like any large organization, faces constant challenges in building that common purpose given its large size, the hierarchical character of government leading to limited horizontal communication, and the specialized nature of the work that most people do. All these militate against common purpose, yet it was critical to have all elements of the ministry moving in the same direction if we were to be able to accomplish the government's important and ambitious goals.

The work of developing a set of common, broadly shared goals for the Ontario ministry began late in 2004. We called it our "strategic direction": "strategic" because it was intended to guide what we did for several years, and "direction" because it would inevitably change in its details and I did not want us to get trapped into spending huge amounts of time creating a document as opposed to developing some common understandings and approaches.

To achieve this purpose, we took a number of steps. First, the entire document was focused on the three clear and simple goals (better outcomes, reduced gaps in outcomes, increased public confidence), followed by a brief statement of key strategies for achieving those goals, and then by a list of actions supporting the key strategies. Each part of the organization should be able to see itself in at least some of the actions, thereby making a connection to the overall strategy and goals. At the same time, the overall document was kept brief (six pages) and also had a one-page summary version that was frequently referenced.

Since the document itself is not the point of the exercise, we gave careful attention to a process that would build understanding and support for the strategy all across the ministry and with our stakeholders. We used a highly participative process. There were several sessions for managers across the organization to discuss drafts. We also asked every unit of the ministry to hold a forum or meeting for all staff (including support staff) so that every individual in the organization had an opportunity to comment on the strategy. However because the document was seen as a "draft," people were encouraged to focus on the overall strategy and the supporting actions rather than on the wording of the document.

Although the process of creating the Strategic Direction was important, we also kept it short. The first draft was produced in November 2004, and by March 2005, four months later, we had a usable version with input from all across the ministry. Once the document was in reasonable form, we gave it life by referencing it constantly in ongoing internal communications, so that it became a living guide to what we did. For example, all managers knew that budget priorities would be set based on the Strategic Direction. We also shared it often and informally with stakeholder groups across the province so that everyone had the same understanding of our intentions.

Even though it never had a status beyond a draft, within six months the "strategic direction" became the guide to decisionmaking in the organization. It was spontaneously posted in many offices, frequently referenced in internal and external communications, and used by many branches of the ministry in their own operational planning. It had a powerful unifying and motivating effect on the organization. Its main elements, such as the three goals and key strategies, have also been widely adopted by Ontario school districts as organizers for their own planning.

About a year later we had a similar—though much less intensive—participative process in the ministry of revisiting and modifying the document in light of changing circumstances, which also served to remind everyone of the strategy and to renew commitment to it. When the government was reelected in the fall of 2007, they issued a new statement of intent that formalized the three goals and renewed the actions and strategies, so this process will guide Ontario education for six or seven years, giving consistent priorities and directions.

## Building a Strong Team

No leader, no matter how effective, can change an organization and maintain it in that changed state on her or his own. Organizations are about shared leadership and teamwork. Certainly we hear a great deal these days about the importance of what is called "shared" or "distributed" leadership in schools. As with so many ideas, it's not so clear what "distributed leadership" means or how to achieve it. Much of the literature on distributed leadership is quite vague as to what exactly is being distributed, and how this distribution works. One senses a quality of feeling good about sharing authority, a sense of virtue in this work, but not much clarity yet about how distributed leadership fits with such realities as designated signing authority, or individualized performance appraisal, or the legal authority and accountability vested in principals or superintendents. No matter how much leadership is distributed, an unhappy school board is likely to terminate their superintendent, not their distributed leadership group.

The term *teamwork* is, to this writer's mind, a better model or image than distributed leadership or shared leadership because most people know what a good team is and can recognize one when they see it. Good teamwork is much more than the sharing of authority or even "leadership." In a good team:

- People share a commitment to common goals.
- Members of the team all support one another in achieving those goals.
- Inside the team people may disagree about many aspects of what is being done, but they are united in working together on behalf of the whole organization.
- People contribute to the team in many different ways, with varying degrees of centrality.
- Making a contribution, even an important contribution, is not the same as having a leadership role.

The discussion of teamwork moves away from who has what authority or makes what decisions to who makes which contributions to the overall effort—which seems to be what many advocates of distributed leadership really have in mind.

The importance of teamwork is evident to all who have worked in schools. It involves not only common effort by the teaching staff but also the important contributions made by other members of the school community or team—support staff, parents, students, and others. A familiar comment among school leaders concerns the critical role that the secretary or head caretaker can play in a school, from being a critical positive force in the school community to quite the opposite. When I went to high school, admittedly a long time ago, the head secretary was probably the most important person in the school in terms of making things happen.

This is not so much a matter of "sharing leadership" with a secretary or caretaker but of inviting and allowing those persons to make the full contribution they can to the organization. In that sense, everyone in a school is, or could be, part of the team.

Building strong teams involves two main activities: bringing the right people into the organization and finding ways to strengthen the contributions that all team members can make.

*The right people.* When new leaders take over organizations, especially organizations that have been having performance problems, one of the first things that happens is turnover in staff. New leaders tend to create new teams around them, whether in schools, districts, or government agencies.

Some of this turnover is necessary and even desirable. Organizations can become ingrown. Many school systems seem to have a policy of hiring primarily or only from within, extending sometimes even to preferring to hire their own former students as teachers. People may get satisfied with a mediocre level of performance, or they have been using some inadequate ways of working for so long that they no longer see the deficiencies. New people bring different perspectives and new ideas about how things can be done differently and better. Every organization needs regular infusions of people with a different perspective. In my terms as deputy minister in both Manitoba and Ontario, new people played absolutely vital roles in helping to rejuvenate the organization and allow it to become more dynamic and effective.

Teams are more than collections of individuals, and building a strong team requires attention to the overall set of skills and personalities as much as it does to the individual team members. Sometimes the orientation toward a common mission and having everyone on board leads people to look for others who share, as much as possible, not only their values but their ways of working. This can be a mistake. Successful teams benefit from people who see the world differently, have different styles, and ask different sorts of questions. If one thinks of the analogy of a sports team or a theater group, a successful team has people who have diverse talents and contribute in different ways. Not everyone can be the star, and teams with too many stars sometimes struggle. It's just as important to have people who are effective and like being in supporting roles.

The same is true in school system leadership. Perhaps the principal or superintendent or state superintendent is a big-picture visionary, but she or he will need others on the team who worry about the details. If the leader is focused on instruction, somebody else has to look after other operational matters. If the leader spends a great deal of time on external relations, a vital area, then someone else has to do the internal work, or vice versa. As should be clear from reading this book, successful management of a school or system involves many different skills, from motivation, community relations, understanding instructional practice, and being able to build a timetable to managing the budget effectively. Nobody is good at all these things or would have time to do them all even if he or she had all the skills. Many years ago in the National Basketball Association, Nate Archibald led the league in both scoring and assists, the only time that has happened. When asked how he did it, Nate is supposed to have said that "we didn't have many good shooters to pass to, so I passed mostly to me." There is a good reason that assist leaders are not usually also top scorers.

As a deputy minister leading a large organization, I always sought to build a strong team with diverse people on it. I'm not a detail person, so I need some people on the team who do worry about details lest I get carried away by my enthusiasms. I tend to be impatient, so I need team members who are patient, who can remind us that sometimes it is worth taking a little longer to think something through or do it right. Even though those different perspectives sometimes annoyed me or made me impatient, I recognized the important role they played in making our organization stronger overall.

While some new energy is important, too many new and outside people can be a problem. Building the team is not just a matter of bringing in new talent. Inevitably, most of the people who will be relied on to improve any organization's performance are already working there. Although some jurisdictions do reconstitute schools with entirely new staff, this will always be a very exceptional circumstance; it simply is not feasible to do this in more than a handful of schools. Most of the time, we must seek improvement with the people who are already there. Some new energy can be an important step in boosting morale and confidence, but too much change, or a message that the existing folks are just not up to the task, is likely to be counterproductive. In particular, leaders who put too many people from their former jurisdiction into key roles in their new setting are likely to create a significant amount of unhappiness and resistance. It is vital to find the people in the existing organization whose talents and energies are not being fully utilized, and to provide them with opportunities to assume greater leadership and responsibility.

Building internal talent also takes time and attention. One of my former bosses and mentors, Ronald Duhamel, was a great developer of young people. He used to say that he looked for someone talented, gave them a job most people thought they weren't ready for yet, and watched them rise to the occasion. I saw this happen often.

But it's not just true of young people, either. Just as we have yet to tap the limits of most students' talent and potential, the same is true of adults. Most school systems have people whose abilities are significantly underutilized, for a whole range of reasons. Sometimes they just haven't been given a chance. Sometimes they are a bit unusual and so have been marginalized. Sometimes they are disenchanted and have given up. But in my years as a manager, I have been surprised over and over again by how much people can and will improve their performance when given the right encouragement and supports, and how people who have been typed as mediocre or problematic performers can become important positive contributors.

So much of the challenge here is matching people to the right work. Many organizations have a tendency to define a job and then try to make the people fit the description, when it would be better, wherever possible, to find more ways for people to use their skills and strengths. Early in my career as a manager I had asked one of my staff, a competent veteran, to do a particular task. He didn't do it despite several reminders. Eventually I asked him why it had not been done. I still remember his response: "Why don't you ask me to do what I'm good at?" He was entirely right. He taught me an important lesson for all managers, which is just as true for all teachers. If we can get people doing what they enjoy and are good at, we will improve performance and morale.

*Building a team environment across the organization.* Building a culture of teamwork in an organization is important but also intensely rewarding. As barriers to cooperation are removed and values of working together are reinforced, you can see the change in people's attitudes. Energy increases. People take more responsibility. They like their work environment more. The most talented people, especially, tend to like working in supportive team settings. An upward spiral develops.

The essential elements of strong teams are easy to state, although much harder to put in place.

First, building a strong team means giving many people real opportunity to share in developing and managing the strategy. The consequence is that not everything will be done in the way the leader her- or himself would do it. That grates on strong people, but there is no way around it, since the consequence of insisting on having everything done in one's own way is inevitably alienation of other people from the work. The leader's task is to make sure the focus and integrity of purpose are maintained rather than controlling every element of the work.

Another important cultural element is to have each leader feel a responsibility for the larger organization as a whole as well as to his or her own area of responsibility. In many organizations, managers are concerned only about their own area, and team meetings fail to generate lively debate. I once led an organization in which my predecessor had pushed the management group to compete with each other, resulting in a highly dysfunctional situation in which people would not cooperate on common goals. This approach is totally incompatible with success in complex organizations. For a system to succeed, every member of the team has to care about every part of the organization, no matter what their particular responsibilities are.

A corollary to the need for a holistic organizational perspective is that the leadership team should spend almost all its collective time on things that are important to the organization as a whole. Furthermore, every member of the team must feel both able and obligated to express views on all important issues, whether or not there is a direct connection to that person's immediate responsibilities. We do not want team members sitting quietly by in the face of proposals or decisions they regard as wrong. Leaders need to understand deeply that there is no value to having a strong unit in a weak organization or a strong department in a weak school or a strong school in a weak district. In the end, the entire organization must succeed or fail as a whole, which in turn requires that all team members feel responsible for the entire organization. This is one of the key messages leaders must not only communicate constantly but also put into practice.

When there are teams with varying personalities and skills, all of whom feel ownership for the broad agenda, there will be conflict among them. In a strong leadership team people can and will—indeed, should—disagree on important issues. Organizations want and need common vision, but that vision has to emerge from discussion and cannot be unilaterally imposed. A team can have vigorous, even heated debate. It must have such debates to build a real sense of common purpose. It could be said that the lemmings have a common vision—it's just the wrong one, and one wishes that some senior lemming at some point had spoken up about it! Shared leadership is not working, and real commitment cannot be built, if people have deep reservations that they do not express. This is a very difficult challenge given the normal inclination we all have to defer to "the boss," so it requires a particularly open approach by people in official leadership positions.

A true culture of teamwork also requires that all important information be shared as widely as possible. Instead of "need to know," use the principle that everyone should be able to know everything unless there is a compelling reason otherwise. Most organizations have far more secrecy than they need, with highly negative effects on trust and commitment. For example, everyone in the organization should have access to the budget in a way that allows them to see how finances are related to priorities. Everyone in the organization should have access to the main common databases and information analyses. People should be inclined to share information and ideas unless there is a good reason not to do so, in contrast to the situation in many organizations where the default position is "only share if you are given permission." When leaders act in these collaborative ways, it has a strong ripple effect on the rest of the organization as well.

### BUILDING THE RIGHT CULTURE

Strong teams are one important part of creating the kind of culture that can sustain an organization in achieving difficult things under pressure. But they are not enough. A vital organization, whether a classroom, school, district, or larger system, has to embody some other critical elements. Many books have been written on organization culture, in education and more broadly. Many useful lists of desirable cultural characteristics have been generated in this large literature. There is neither space nor a need to repeat those discussions here in any detail. The purpose in this chapter is to focus more on the "how" of creating culture in systems, so we can simply assume that we will want our schools and systems to have features such as the following:

- Focused on making progress on the key priorities that the organization has identified no matter what other demands and pressures may arise (this is the subject of the next chapter)
- Evidence-based, so that everyone in the organization understands the nature of current performance, the challenges to improvement, and is aware of research suggesting more productive or effective practices and strategies
- Open-minded and attuned to the views and needs of students and the community, so that there is a constant focus on what needs to be done instead of an assumption that present practices are already optimal
- Collegial, in that it is understood that improvement happens through everyone working together, and that every individual should be able and willing to explain and justify his or her choices and practices to colleagues (the points just made about teamwork apply not just to leaders but throughout the organization)
- Supportive of people as they experiment, learn, find individual ways forward, and sometimes fall short, yet always ambitious about what can and should be achieved, so unwilling to accept shortcomings
- Reliant on communication and persuasion to build commitment instead of authority. Educational organizations should be places in which anyone—whether students or staff—should reasonably

expect to be given good reasons to do things rather than simply being instructed to by a person in authority.

How does one build these, or similar, qualities in a system? Again, many books have been written on the matter. However, there are three basic things that leaders do to create organization culture. These are (1) to declare values (the easy part), (2) to model those values in practice (the very hard part), and (3) to gather feedback on how well one is doing and adjust accordingly.

1. *Declare values.* A first important step is to state, publicly and frequently, the values and qualities that the organization is attempting to exemplify. Many schools already do this through mission statements or value statements, but as we have already noted, these are often one-time efforts that are then forgotten. A surprising number of organizations do not consistently identify and promote in a public way, both internally and externally, the organizational characteristics they wish to embody. Declarations are not enough in themselves. It's easy to write values on a piece of paper with no follow-up, a situation that is likely to produce negative effects. But some clear statement of intent, repeated regularly in various ways, is a necessary first step.

2. *Model the qualities in practice by building them into systems and practices.* As Argyris and Schon demonstrated decades ago (1974), people can espouse the right values, but they find it difficult to behave consistently with those values. Because organizations are social settings, supporting the right behavior is not so much a matter of charisma or inspiration as it is of establishing and supporting the right systems and practices.

   It's often easy to get a sense of an organization's climate or culture just by spending a short time there. Do people seem easy and comfortable with one another? Is there a sense of purpose, energy, and accomplishment? Do people seem to enjoy being there? Do staff work well across organizational boundaries and roles? Although these are qualities everyone would like to have in their workplace, they are far from ubiquitous in school systems. These characteristics are not inherent; they are built through the work that leaders do, not just strategically, but in all their daily interactions.

Some important examples were discussed in chapter 6 in relation to supporting a focus on teaching and learning; those ideas are about organization culture. Every aspect of an organization, every process and structure, either supports appropriate culture or, whether intentionally or not, works against it. Many instances have already been mentioned, but it's worth reviewing these and adding others. For example:

- Are communications inviting rather than dictatorial? Consider the difference between a memo to staff that starts with "It has been decided that all schools will . . ." or "The district requires all teachers to . . ." compared with the same point being made as: "Through our discussions over the last few months, we agreed as a staff to . . ." The latter communicates respect and participation and builds support, while the former has exactly the opposite effect.
- Are meetings conducted in ways that legitimize and even invite diverse views to be expressed and debated? Or are dissenting or alternative views discouraged so that people remain silent if they have a contrary opinion?
- Are people encouraged to be interested in the work of the organization as a whole, or is the understanding that each organization unit or person "minds their own business," in which case the larger organizational interests will inevitably suffer?
- Is the budget shared openly, so that everyone in the organization understands how the priorities are turned into resources?
- Are cross-organization teams used regularly to develop and implement plans in important areas?
- Does the organization share research and data widely and invite people to discuss their import?
- Are staff at all levels encouraged to use their initiative consistent with the organization's goals, or does every decision require three or four levels of approval?

♦ Are people all across the organization recognized and thanked regularly for their contributions as a way of building a sense of efficacy and progress?

When put into these specific terms, the process of culture-building becomes easier for leaders to understand and support. It's less a matter of grand design and inspirational moments than of the many daily practices that tell people what kind of place their organization is. An organization can have all the ceremonies and rewards and symbols it likes, but if daily interaction is not positive and respectful, nobody will be taken in by the trappings.

3. *Monitor progress and make adjustments.* Staff engagement and morale (and, for schools, student commitment and satisfaction) are vital indicators of organization health and ability to improve. Just as data on student performance are essential in any effort to improve student outcomes, there is also no substitute for having data on student and staff perceptions of the organization if one wants to improve culture. As noted earlier, though, relatively few school systems gather such data on a regular or routine basis.

Many surveys of organization climate find that managers have a much rosier picture of the organization than do staff. Principals are more positive than teachers, and superintendents more positive than principals. This is not surprising. Typically managers are more heavily invested in the organization and are making judgments about their own actions rather than those of others. Surveys of staff morale in large organizations also show that it is extraordinarily difficult to get high satisfaction levels. These are additional reasons why education organizations should gather data on staff, student, and parent perceptions and attitudes—because one cannot rely on the perceptions of those who already have the greatest positive commitment, just as one cannot see how best to organize teaching by looking only at the work of the best students.

Gathering data on staff and student perceptions does not need to be laborious. One can use simple, readily available tools on an occasional basis to get a snapshot of people's feelings. A variety of quick online survey vehicles are now available, along with software that allows the tracking of attitudes in a way similar to rolling polls of political preferences. It's a matter of regular pulse-taking, with the results being shared and discussed as another way in which a school or system shows its belief in improvement through the use of evidence.

### COMMUNICATING STRATEGY AND ACCOMPLISHMENT

Much has been said in this book already about the importance of communications, and the degree to which that function is undervalued in education. Previous chapters had a considerable amount to say about the importance of internal staff, parent, and student communications and about public communications.

For most school leaders at all levels, communication is an activity to be done after everything else. Yet each time I go back to a management position, I spend more time on communications and give it higher priority, because school systems can only achieve their goals for students if there is widespread understanding of and support for those goals, and that support requires effective, two-way communications.

In most organizations people think of communication as a one-way flow of carefully screened information. Schools send newsletters to parents telling them how well everything is going. Governments issue press releases or white papers full of pious sentiments. Nobody believes these communications, which makes one wonder why organizations continue to spend so much time and money on them.

Instead, it's helpful to think of communication not just as an activity in its own right but also as embedded in almost everything that leaders do. Even the shortest conversations with staff, students, or parents, whether in hallways or classrooms or playgrounds, can be part of building organizational understanding and commitment to goals and strategies.

Communication has first to remind people constantly of the organization's goals and strategies—what it is that we are collectively trying to achieve. People inevitably get distracted by their own piece of the puzzle, so frequent reminders about how it all fits together, and of what the bigger picture is, are essential. That is, again, why goals have to be few, simple, and compelling, so that they can be repeated often. Effort depends on people seeing how their contributions matter, and how all the various parts add up to a desirable whole.

A second important task of communication for improvement is to build morale by constant reinforcement of positive elements—people's hard work and successes. Although much is said about the importance of celebrating accomplishment, it's still not all that frequent in most education organizations. Recognizing success does not require big ceremonies or fancy protocols, either. A short note to someone, a mention in a newsletter, and even a heartfelt stated thank-you in a short conversation—all these will have good effects. As long as the praise is authentic, there cannot be too much of it. Often the most effective people in a school are hardest on themselves, constantly focused on what has not been done and therefore most in need of reminding about how much has been achieved and of how talented they are. Success and positive external regard generate more effort, and leaders are key to the recognition of success. Of course, praise must be merited. People are acutely sensitive to being told things they believe to be untrue, but equally gratified to know that their hard work is being recognized. You cannot spoil good, talented people by telling them they are good and talented.

Effective communications for leadership must be two-directional. Two-way communication is vital both to the motivational work of building trust and to the substantive work of refining change so that it works most effectively. It's a matter not just of telling people but also of listening to their views and ideas—real, hard listening even to messages we do not want to hear, and with action following from what we hear.

No plan in the state department or board office or principal's office will ever turn out just as we imagined, which means adjustments will almost certainly be necessary. Feedback from participants is the best single means of finding out what is not working well so that it can be improved. Leaders absolutely need to be listening to what colleagues are saying about their realities, and we always need to take their concerns seriously. That does not mean always agreeing, or always doing what someone wants. It does mean acknowledging and respecting their views, and trying to find a way to accommodate concerns that they raise without losing the larger focus. Most of all, it means not being so caught up in our own egos that we are unable to recognize the merits of others' views, and to modify what we do in light of those. Indeed, making changes that respond to participant concerns is itself an important contribution to building trust.

## RECRUITING, DEVELOPING, AND RETAINING LEADERS

We hear frequently about the crisis of leadership in education, that we will not be able to find enough talented and qualified people to fill school principalships and superintendencies in the coming years because the jobs are getting too difficult. To be sure, educational leadership positions are challenging and are certainly not getting easier. All parties want more input and are less inclined simply to accept decisions made by leaders. Expectations for schools are high, and school leaders are seen to be critical to success.

By definition, there is never enough outstanding talent in any organization. Even if we were to use a military-style draft to bring talented people into teaching or school administration, we would likely not have all the talent we want. In every organization—not only schools—recruiting, developing, and retaining good people will always be among the most important organizational tasks. Although there has been more attention to these issues in education systems recently, on the whole they are still not carefully considered in most places.

Any organization that wants excellent leadership must pay attention to all three elements of recruitment, development, and retention. In many education organizations, too much emphasis has gone to recruitment, and the least to retention. It is always cheaper and more effective to develop and keep good people than it is to find and attract new talent.

## Recruitment

Some comments about recruitment were made earlier in the discussion of team-building. School systems must absolutely seek out the best people they can find, wherever those people are. While some—even most—promotions should certainly go to talented internal candidates, a system that rarely or never looks outside for new leadership will find itself beset with groupthink and will lack the diverse perspectives that drive change and improvement. It is no disrespect to the people in one's own organization to ask them to measure themselves against the best from elsewhere. Indeed, this is what good people will want to do.

At the same time, as already mentioned, most of the talent that will be key to improving any organization is already working in that organization. A sports team might be able to solve its problems by replacing its players, but a school system cannot. There are too many of them. Moreover, we also have to think about the system as a whole. If we improve some schools by taking the best teachers and leaders from other schools, what happens to those other systems? There are many accounts in the literature of innovative new schools where principals got to select a whole new staff from across a district. That's nice for the new school, but leaves all the other schools potentially worse off than before. Although each of us has primary responsibility for our own school or district or state, none of us should want to improve our own system by playing "beggar thy neighbor." Again, some mobility is good. Sometimes people need a new stage in order to reveal their true talents. Sometimes the fit between person and organization is wrong, just as a child having difficulty can often benefit from a new start in a new school where previous difficulties do not dog his or her future. But for individual schools and for large systems, developing one's current talent must be a key task.

## Development

Much interesting work is now being done on large-scale leadership development in education. A range of new training and development approaches, such as principal academies of various kinds, qualification systems for principals and superintendents, new graduate programs in universities, and so on, have accompanied the interest in leadership standards discussed in the previous chapter. The National College for School Leadership in England represents the most comprehensive approach anywhere, but many other interesting efforts are underway, such as New Leaders for New Schools (*www.nlns.org*), the NYC Leadership Academy (*www.nycleadershipacademy.org*), and a Master Principal Program in Arkansas (*www.arkleadership.org/master_principal.htm;* see also Wallace Foundation 2008). Although these strategies appear to be well grounded in the existing evidence, much more work needs to be done to learn which leadership development strategies seem most effective under which conditions (Leithwood and Levin 2005). However, some of the lessons from the broader training literature can be applied here.

As Leithwood et al. (2006) put it, the functions that leaders address are quite similar from one setting to another, but the ways they address those functions vary a good deal according to the context. For example, all good leaders pay attention to shaping organization goals, but that work may look quite different from one setting to another depending on culture, history, skills, and structures. In some settings a first requirement may be to focus on creating more commitment to a common direction, while in other cases creating a more optimistic culture may be more important to tackle first. A young staff will require different kinds of leadership and professional development than will a group of veterans. Leadership development, then, requires a combination of understanding the most important common tasks, such as those in this chapter, and thinking through their application in specific settings. The training literature in general shows that training and development abstracted from people's actual workplaces tends to have little impact on subsequent behavior (Hesketh 1997). Leadership development, therefore, has to have a strong local contextual element.

Current efforts to develop more mentorship and coaching models, more learning communities among leaders, and more feedback loops so that people can get more information on how their work is perceived in the organization all seem to be good directions. Leadership standards or qualifications can play a useful role, but only if they are the basis for application in specific settings. Otherwise they become a set of abstract formulations that are learned but not really applied, as is the case, sadly, for the way school curricula strike many students—and teachers.

At the same time, there is a constant danger in education that we are too taken with the local so that meaningful broader principles are neglected. As noted earlier in this book, not everything needs to be discovered anew in every school or district. Many good practices do travel well and should be adopted widely. We should be looking for more practices that have good evidence of effectiveness and then focusing on how, not whether, to use them in particular contexts. Several of the specifics already mentioned in this chapter, such as fewer and more effective meetings, are examples of practices that should be widely adopted without a great deal of local introspection, though they would need to be customized to the particulars of a given school or district.

### Retention

The most important task facing any organization is to keep its talent. Although this seems an obvious point, it's often neglected if not completely ignored. Many organizations seem to feel that their goal should be to squeeze as much work as possible from people while giving as little as possible in return. Many countries in the 1980s and 1990s tried to reduce spending on education by limiting wages and worsening working conditions. Then, a few years later, these same states and countries found—to their surprise—that they had a shortage of teachers. Like the stingy farmer who wanted to save by feeding his horse less and found that the horse died, school systems found that teachers left the profession, and in many places there was a scramble to find and train new ones and to improve pay and working conditions to attract and retain them. The net result was to have a less qualified, less experienced teaching staff with no real savings, when the entire mess could have been prevented if teachers had been treated better in the first place. Among the most heartening experiences I had as deputy minister in Ontario was meeting skilled teachers and principals who had decided to defer their retirement for a year or two because teaching was fun again.

We know what attracts and retains good people in teaching and school leadership. It is not primarily money, although educators want and deserve to earn a decent living for the work they do. Teaching is important work and should be paid at a level that attracts and keeps good people. However, pay is not the main determinant of satisfaction. People become educators because they believe their work will matter to students. We should want the same motivations to be the basis of interest in school leadership. Good people will stay in the profession if they feel supported in doing the work they care about—that they are treated fairly, have some autonomy in their work, have good colleagues to work with, have talented and supportive leadership, and have working conditions that make their jobs possible. These are entirely reasonable aspirations that every school system must try to support.

At the system level there are some inexpensive things that can be done to support both development and retention of good leaders. The qualities of a good culture, outlined in the previous chapter, and the organizational requisites outlined in chapter 6 are instances. A few of these are worth repeating because they are so important and so often violated.

First, don't waste people's time. Don't send them endless requests for information that is not really important or has already been provided in another format. Don't ask them to put paperwork ahead of students. Don't call unnecessary meetings. Just as schools help students and teachers focus on learning by avoiding too many announcements or other interruptions, so districts and larger systems should screen everything they ask of schools against the criterion of improving student outcomes. Anything that does not contribute directly to that purpose should be reduced or slowed down, if not entirely eliminated. A very high proportion of requests from governments to school systems, and from districts to schools, do not meet the test of real importance; having fewer such requests would in itself free substantial time for school leaders and simultaneously improve their morale.

Second, focus on the things that help people do their jobs. Give schools and leaders useful tools and resources—but only in amounts that a busy person is actually likely to use. Providing too many resources is almost as bad as too few, as recipients may feel overwhelmed by all the "help." Indeed, this is just what happened in both Manitoba and Ontario when the provincial ministries of education changed their main role from policing the system to supporting it. So anxious were ministry staff to help that they began to deluge districts and schools with that help in the form of resources, professional development events, funding opportunities, and pilot projects. In both provinces, superintendents of districts began to ask for less "help," or to have the assistance spread over more time.

In reality, people's beliefs and practices are more strongly affected by their personal connections and experiences than by what they read or hear. Because schooling is very much a print setting, we tend to want to produce publications, handbooks, resource manuals, and the like. But these are less powerful than bringing people together to talk about their work, with support from expert critical friends who respect their views but also push their thinking. There is nothing more important to learning than the chance to express and test one's ideas and practices in a supportive yet challenging setting.

This means reshaping meetings in most systems so that they are genuinely about learning how to do our most important work, not about sharing information (discussed earlier) or managing minor issues. Again, though seemingly common sense, this is often not the practice in large systems, where the bureaucratic needs of the organization somehow take over and drive what people do. Just ask most principals how many meetings they attend that are truly helpful to better outcomes for students.

As with any other important goal, leadership development and retention take thought and effort. A school or school system needs to spend some time thinking about these issues. They are not hard to understand, but they can be difficult to implement insofar as they run against current practice and people's habits. As noted earlier in this book, it is hard for people to change their habits or practices even when they know that the new practices are superior. This means that the system has to do more than exhort people to behave differently; the mechanics and incentives have to change. If people continue to be reprimanded for late submission of data but not for inability to get into classrooms, then they will continue to prioritize paperwork over teaching and learning.

Very few education systems have set out to improve leadership in a deliberate and sustained way, and even fewer have a plan that addresses all three elements of recruitment, development, and retention in a balanced way. Yet without careful attention to these issues, we will never have jobs that reasonably competent people can do well, or enough experienced and competent people to do the vital work of leading our school systems.

### CONCLUSION

There are many things about effective leadership for school improvement that we do not understand, but what we do know provides plenty of opportunity for improving current practices, especially across large numbers of schools and classrooms. Many of the suggestions in this chapter can be put in place fairly readily. Choosing the changes that produce the most value for the least effort is, as always, an essential first requirement.

Improving schools and student outcomes is not, however, the only thing leaders must do. Many other issues and activities also seem to demand their attention. The challenge of managing all those other areas is the focus of the next chapter.

# 9
——

# Managing the Distractions
# without Losing Focus

## THE CHALLENGE OF MAINTAINING FOCUS

A central argument of this book is that no organization can do every-thing at once at a high level, and that successful large-scale improvement requires identifying and focusing relentlessly on a small number of high-profile priorities which are most likely to improve student achievement. These priorities, as outlined in earlier chapters, should be around teach-ing and learning practices and community engagement, and around the organizational practices needed to support them.

Education leaders know and agree with this proposal. They know that it is essential to have a small number of key goals. No organization can do fifty things well all at the same time. There is a saying in the business liter-ature that "having more than two objectives is like having no objectives at all." As noted earlier in this book, reform works best and engages people most when substantial effort goes to a small number of easy to understand goals or strategies. Leadership books are full of the same advice—set out a clear vision and stick to it.

Yet all our experience shows that keeping focus over time is the single hardest thing to do in managing at any level, from a school to a national education system. When you try to follow the advice and to focus your school or system on a few key goals, such as improving early literacy or engaging parents more effectively, something surprising happens. All kinds of other pressures and demands arise, and leaders seem to find their time taken up with everything but the priorities on which they wanted to focus.

This is so even if most people in the organization have agreed to the priorities. A careful process of staff and stakeholder engagement, leading to agreement on priorities, while valuable in itself, is no guarantee that the very same people won't turn around the next day and demand action on a whole list of other issues. People do not need to be consistent and they often aren't.

As a result, education leaders at all levels constantly lament that their situations just do not permit them to do the things they know are important. Principals find they do not have time to visit classrooms or talk with teachers. Superintendents have the same problem in visiting schools or reaching out to the community. Elected political leaders, even when they have run on a clear set of priorities, find that the main pressures on them are not about those priorities, and they are constantly distracted by other matters.

Inevitably, focus suffers. The truly important is driven out by the urgent. The squeaky wheel gets the grease, even if the squeaky wheel is not the one that moves the bus. Not only do priorities get inadequate attention, but some of the most important ancillary functions of the organization also tend to get short shrift. A good example is communications, both internal and external. Constant communication to all important audiences is an essential element of any change and a major theme of this book, yet the time needed for communication is one of the first things to be cut back when leaders face a multitude of contending pressures.

## Why it's hard to stay focused

The problem of keeping a focus on priorities in the midst of other pressures is, like many others in this book, one that cannot be solved but can be managed. To know what to do about this situation, we first must understand why it happens.

The forces that make it so difficult to keep everyone in a large organization—or even in a small one—working on the same set of goals can be thought of as falling into two categories. One category could be described as *operational*. Setting a new direction does not eliminate the need to look after all the many existing needs and activities; the routine work of the organization still has to continue even in the midst of efforts at improvement. Moreover, both standard operations and change efforts are subject to unexpected changes in circumstances. Changing events and circumstances raise new issues and push attention in new directions. Surprise gets in the way, sometimes with devastating consequences.

The second set of distracters is best described as *political*. They arise from the fact that people in and around schools will always disagree at least to some extent on priorities and on how they are to be achieved. Schools and their surrounding communities are made up of many different people with different ideas and interests. On top of that, schools are expected to do many different things all at the same time so people in and around schools will inevitably have many differing ideas of what should be done and how.

To see how these factors operate, and can even create a "perfect storm" of problems, consider the example of the San Diego School District a decade or so ago (Hubbard, Mehan, and Stein 2006). In 1998 the team of Alan Bersin as superintendent and Anthony Alvarado as chief academic officer began their effort to change San Diego schools with great promise. Each was a talented, experienced leader. They had highly complementary skills, with Bersin leading the political side of the endeavor and Alvarado the academic side. They had a supportive community, including business leadership and significant additional funding from external foundations. They had support from the San Diego Education Association. They had a clear focus on changing instruction, particularly to improve literacy, using a plan that was well grounded in the research. According to the research on change, they were doing all the right things.

Changing instructional practices across a large district would have been daunting even with all those supports and skills. But the reforms in San Diego ran into both operational and political pressures. On the operational side, the new roles that were created, and the new responsibilities assigned to principals and others, did not always fit easily with the existing people and structures that the district had used. People did not always see how they could carry their existing work and the new agenda, and weren't always ready to give up past practice. The San Diego initiative was also hurt by some major unexpected events, most notably a large budget cut imposed by the state that threatened much of what the district was trying to do.

These operational challenges were exacerbated by various political pressures, including a badly divided school board and conflicting agendas on a variety of issues from various constituent groups, including different groups of parents with very different ideas about the reforms. Then, the San Diego Education Association, which had initially supported the new agenda, gradually changed its position and became a strong opponent of the plan. A small leadership team, no matter how talented, cannot maintain a strategy in the face of so many competing pressures. Conflict within the system itself contributed to unraveling of the initial base of support, so that within a few years much of the initiative appeared to have lost momentum; Alvarado left the district, followed a couple of years later by Bersin.

In light of this example, let's consider each of these categories more fully. These dynamics of operational needs, surprises, and differing political agendas are part of the human condition. They are not going to go away. This means that educational leaders must find ways to manage them.

### The importance of the routine

Reformers begin their work with an exciting new agenda—that is what reform means. But this new agenda arrives in an environment that usually is already full of activity. It's not that everyone has been sitting around doing nothing, waiting for a bold new vision. Classes have been running, extracurricular activities taking place, parent and community contacts ongoing. Schools are busy places, and even a well-functioning, highly successful school or district requires a lot of routine work.

James March pointed out many years ago (1984) that while change and innovation get the attention, much of the success of any organization rests on effective routines—timetables, bus schedules, maintenance, ordering of supplies, payroll, and handling of all the inevitable daily demands such as a sick child or a parent with a concern or an absent teacher. These things have to be looked after, no matter what exciting new vision is being offered. No vision, no matter how exciting, will mollify people whose paychecks have been lost or whose kids are not where they are supposed to be, when they are supposed to be.

The same is true at the state or national level. A new administration often believes that it will find substantial resources to reallocate by eliminating unproductive activities only to discover that most of what the bureaucracy does has to continue, or that the change needed to "free" resources will itself take substantial inputs of time and energy. Just as in a school, funds have to be allocated, reports produced, public inquiries answered, media interests dealt with, legislative committees informed, as so on. From the outside, every organization looks like it is engaged in a large number of unproductive activities, but from the inside it looks very different. Superintendents may criticize state or provincial departments of education for their ineffective work yet will staunchly defend their own district practices even when these are seen as equally ineffective by their principals. The same is true all up and down the system, because it is much easier for each of us to see the logic behind what we do compared with our perceptions of the practices of others.

Change advocates often underestimate just how much time and energy these routines take. The operational challenges are even greater in schools or districts facing more difficult circumstances such as high poverty levels or geographic isolation. Just where the need for a focus on student achievement is greatest, so are the distractions. Martin Thrupp's account of New Zealand schools (1999) shows how the schools with the greatest needs also have more disruptions, more absenteeism, more teacher turnover, often older buildings in worse condition, and so on. Even collecting money for a field trip can take much more time than in a more affluent setting. Where the routines are not currently effective, as will be the case in struggling schools or districts, improving them can itself be an important but time-consuming, and sometimes controversial, task. So immediately time and energy get diverted from big planned changes to handling the routines of organizational life.

### Surprise dominates

Israeli political scientist Yehezkel Dror's book *Governing Under Adversity* (1986) is one of the best discussions of the challenges of governing in modern societies. Among Dror's many insights is this remark: "At any given moment there is a high probability of low probability events. In other words, surprise dominates" (168). The reality is that many plans, even well-made plans, are undermined if not totally scuppered by completely unexpected developments.

It's easy to think of examples at every level. A school focused on changing instruction has a tragedy of some kind, such as a death. Or, more prosaically, a key person leaves the staff unexpectedly, perhaps because of a promotion or, worse, a serious illness. A skilled principal is moved to tackle the needs in another school. A safety incident distracts everyone from teaching and learning issues. A problem with the physical fabric of the building means that some space becomes unavailable. Even one incident such as this can set back a plan by months or even years.

The same distractions arise at district levels. An election brings new board members who may have different agendas. A key person retires or leaves for another district. The state or national government imposes new policy requirements or budget restrictions. Given the churn in education policy at many levels, these sorts of new requirements are all too common. It's no wonder that even strong school leaders are inclined to cringe when they hear about an impending new state, district, or national policy announcement.

To be fair to state and national governments, they face even more challenges in maintaining focus since there are usually more and stronger pressures pulling them in alternate directions. Think about a state or national government trying to maintain a supportive and effective education policy in the face of all the pressure to deal with other issues outside of education, not to mention the demands for quick fixes as just described. (These important dynamics of politics are described more fully in chapter 1 of my book *Governing Education* [2005].) And imagine what happens even to a carefully crafted strategy in the face of an emergency such as a natural disaster or emergency. How many plans and projects were swept aside by 9/11, the SARS epidemic, the Iraq invasion, or the subprime mortgage debacle?

Surprise has to be seen, paradoxically, as an inevitable part of the work of school improvement. The unexpected will happen, and it will get in the way of our plans. While we cannot be ready for any and every contingency—something we expect is by definition not a surprise—we can recognize the need to be prepared to deal with the unexpected without having to abandon our key goals.

### MAINTAINING THE FOCUS DESPITE DISTRACTIONS

How does one manage all the day-to-day demands *and* the surprises? There is no simple answer to this problem, which is faced not only by school leaders but by leaders in almost every organization in both the public and private sectors, all of whom feel diverted from their key tasks by other daily demands. The reality is that organization leaders will always have more things to do than they have time. Indeed, good leaders will partly create this problem for themselves because they will have a very long list of things they want to do and will push themselves to do more in order to achieve their goals. Still, there are several steps that can help address the challenges to focus. Some have to do with the way we think about the problems, and others are suggestions concerning actions to help manage them.

One of the first steps is to accept the reality of distraction. Although it is very tempting for leaders to treat these problems as nuisances—or at best as problems—no amount of arguing or convincing will make them go away. Any plan that assumes full-speed ahead without disruption is going to result, as my tenth-grade French teacher used to say, in "a rude awakening." The history of education reform is full of such instances, a number of which are described at various points in this book. If one anticipates difficulties, even if only in the most general way, one is better prepared to cope with them effectively.

The most critical resource available to leaders, just like teachers, is their time. The challenge is to use the time available for the things that matter most. There are two categories of things a leader can spend time on: (1) those necessary to the organization's success that only she or he can do and (2) everything else. For most of us, the latter tends to drive out the former, and the challenge is to reverse this situation. I don't advocate ruthlessness in leadership except in this one area; the ruthless management of time, others' as well as their own, is essential for every leader. One of the problems with the lists of leadership tasks or standards, as illustrated in the previous chapter, is that they do not help people differentiate or prioritize between what is good, what is important, and what is absolutely necessary.

The distinction does not come naturally to most of us, either. We tend to respond to what appears on our plate or to what others ask us to do even if those issues conflict with what we know to be really important. It's hard to say no to others' requests or to resist doing the task right in front of us. Better management of time and priorities will often feel counterintuitive, yet it is essential and therefore requires thoughtfulness.

Leaders in any organization should start by asking what things are vital and cannot be done by anyone else. When this question is put fairly, most of us will find that we spend far too much time on things that someone else could do, probably just as well as we could, or on things that are less than critical to the overall success of the organization. The key leadership functions described in the previous chapter, or some similar alternative list, are the vital tasks of leadership, which means that everything else is less important. That is often a hard truth to face, because it means we have to change long-held habits, but it is true nonetheless. In one of the Sherlock Holmes stories, Watson is surprised to learn that Holmes does not know that the earth revolves around the sun, whereas Holmes argue that since this does not matter to his ability to solve crimes, he pays no attention to it. Now that is focus!

In leadership it is also the case that "the best is the enemy of the good." When time is scarce, one has often to be satisfied with an adequate rather than an ideal response. Getting 80 percent of the result for 20 percent of the effort is a desirable approach when there are more things to do than there is time to do them. Many leaders have real trouble saying the words "good enough" and moving on.

What to do, then, about the very real pressures to spend time on all those other things? In a nutshell, resist it as much as possible. For example:

- *Schedule the most important things first, and in ways that are more likely to bind you.* Many principals complain they cannot get into classrooms because they are always doing something else. One solution is to schedule classroom or school visiting time in advance, make this known, and then try as hard as possible to protect it. You are likely to find that while you don't make all the planned visits, you actually do more school or classroom visits using this approach. You are especially likely to keep these appointments if other people know about them and are also participating. As a superintendent it's easy to put off a school visit to attend to something in the office, but if you've invited a colleague to go with you, you are more likely to keep the appointment. As a deputy minister I scheduled time to visit schools, told my secretary to protect that time from other meetings, and told the schools ahead of time that I would be visiting. This made it harder for me to cancel. Sometimes I would start out on a visit regretting the time because of so many other demands, but I always ended up happy that I had made the time. The same can be done by any principal or superintendent.
- *Reduce the number of meetings.* Most books on time management contain good suggestions on this issue. Most organizations have far too many meetings, many of which are not all that important. Yes, they are important to someone, but not to the organization's success. They happen because someone schedules them and everyone else goes along. Ask yourself, How many meetings are critical to getting my job done? If they aren't, don't attend, or attend only part of

them, or send someone on your behalf, or, if you are in charge of them, shorten them. Typically, meetings are scheduled for an hour, especially when done by electronic scheduling. Once the hour is booked, it tends to get used even if the work could be completed in less time. Do business by phone or e-mail or even five-minute hallway conversations. Always ask for an agenda in advance, and if there isn't an agenda, or the items are not all that important, then you have a perfect rationale not to participate or to arrive late or leave early. Many, many meetings are taken up with presentations of information that could be provided more efficiently and effectively on paper or e-mail. As a manager, my rule for staff meetings was no presentations of more than five minutes in any meeting. Anything longer was to be shared in advance in writing so we could spend our time debating important issues and making plans or decisions.

- *Budget your time.* Many school leaders see an open-door policy as important to creating visibility and openness. It's not. Efficiency suffers from frequent interruptions; you end up getting less overall work done without any compensating benefit. A leader can get the same or greater visibility by organizing walk-arounds and visits at times that work for you, instead of having your timetable dictated by other people. As a senior manager, I have always told my staff that they will get a much better response if they book time with me, or hold over issues until our regular meetings, than they will if they interrupt me when I am working on something else. I also responded very promptly to issues raised by my team members via e-mail. As a result, my staff felt they had very good access to me, but I was rarely interrupted when doing something important.

- *Delegate work to others—and trust them to do it.* Easy to say, this is very hard for most of us to do. To repeat, leaders have to do the things only they can do, and as few other things as possible. When I was appointed deputy minister in Ontario, pretty well all 72 school districts wanted to meet with me. I advised boards that given the focus we had on system-wide change, I would be unable to meet with individual districts on operational matters such as budgets, capital projects, or program needs. My senior managers would meet with them and would have the authority to respond appropriately. I would spend that time instead visiting schools and districts to get firsthand knowledge of the realities of our big strategies so that we could adjust them to be more effective. I would also be present at many provincial events where I could meet and talk with people from many districts. Not all districts liked this policy, but they all understood it as a reasonable way for me to allocate my time, and they did, in fact, see a lot of me, though not in regard to their individual district issues.

- *Don't be too deferential to the demands of the larger organization.* Principals, for example, will often complain about how much time they spend responding to information requests (really demands) from their district or state. The principle of ruthless prioritizing suggests that these ought to be low-priority tasks, delegated to others, done as quickly as possible, or deferred until more important tasks can be completed. If everyone responds to endless requests for information, the requests will continue to be made. This can be a difficult issue in organizations that are excessively hierarchical, in which case it has to be tackled collectively as a problem of organization culture. A colleague once asked at a district principals' meeting, where they were discussing reporting requirements, if the superintendent felt it was more important for him to do the reports or to be in classrooms. That put the culture issue squarely on the agenda! Senior leaders are more likely to reduce such demands if they know that their best people find them intrusive and unproductive. Sometimes being a good organization person means speaking up about undesirable practices and pointing out their costs in terms of the things the organization says it values, such as time in classrooms or with parents and students.

All this can be done in a positive way. One does not need to be belligerent, only persistent in noting one's intent to stay focused on the organization's stated priorities—to do the things that will actually have an impact on student outcomes. Most organizations can benefit from ongoing discussion of systematic steps that can be taken to make better use of the very scarce resource of leaders' time and energy.

◆ *Beware of the seduction of having more staff.* Every organization believes that if it only had more people, it could accomplish more. Schools are, it is true, administratively lean organizations, so there could be merit to having non-teaching staff dedicated to some support functions if it were clear that this resulted in a better use of professionals' time. However, that is not always the case. Adding staff means more supervision and HR support, which falls to school administrators. More people make the organization more complex, leading to more time for internal communications and—horrors—more meetings! The experience in England with adding additional support staff to reduce principal and teacher workload had very mixed results, with a leader in the organization of head teachers telling me that many principals felt that the additional staff actually increased rather than reduced their workload. An organization's first response to the demands of the work should be to try to improve its existing practices, not just to add more people.

## MANAGING ORGANIZATION POLITICS

The last part of this chapter is about managing political pressures within the education system. Few obstacles are more frustrating to education leaders than the problems of political opposition or distraction, partly because educators tend to see politics as an unnecessary interference with what they know to be right. I have argued throughout this book, however, that politics at all levels are an inescapable and necessary part of the education landscape. There will always be some degree of friction among actors who have different needs and, sometimes, different purposes. Managing the political agenda, then, must be a central part of any leader's work, whether in a school, district, or on a national stage.

In the 1990s a group of political scientists led by Clarence Stone studied education policy and progress in 11 major cities in the United States. Their analysis (Stone 1998) shows the many challenges in the broader context around creating and maintaining a coherent school improvement agenda. Efforts to improve schools in these cities ran into difficulties that included racial and ethnic tensions, defensive politics on the part of school administrators and employee groups, disorganized and competing parent groups, and badly split or weak school boards. Stone and his colleagues conclude that in their 11 cities—and in seven others examined in a subsequent book (2001)—school boards played a generally weak role. Even very strong superintendents could not create the necessary progress by themselves, and the ability of cities to put together and maintain community coalitions was very limited. Their review, consistent with examples already cited from various places, reminds us how important it is to attend to internal and community politics.

### Understanding interests

Our societies and schools are diverse. They are expected to do many different things. The people who make up our educational organizations, including students, parents, and other community members as well as teaching and non-teaching staff, are also diverse in their backgrounds, knowledge, interests, and perceptions. Even a small school has a total community numbering in the hundreds if not thousands. Any group that size will inevitably have and express a wide variety of views and concerns.

In the case of public education, we can think of concentric circles of interest. First and foremost, as suggested earlier in this book, should be students, although in practice they are typically seen as the objects of education or of reform, not as participants in its construction. Yet we know that if students are engaged and motivated, learning will follow no matter what else happens, and that the opposite is also true— practices that fail to engage and motivate students are unlikely to have good results. Because students are young and generally not well organized, they are often ignored and are not considered true partners in learning.

Parents are the next level, with the most direct interest in what happens in schools. It's not uncommon to see writers conflate "parents" with "the public," as if these were the same thing, but at any given time only about 30 percent of adult citizens will have children in school or about to enter school. Still, parents are the people with the most direct interest and likely to be the most vocal on education issues.

However, as mentioned earlier, just about every other organized group in society also has an interest in public education. Education is "everyone's business," which is part of the reason there are so many different points of view to be taken into account. The larger the scale of the organization, the more different players and agendas will exist. So a large district will have to take account of many actors and many different points of view, while at a state or national level the situation is even more complex. Yet even in very small communities, the politics of multiple agendas and interests can be difficult to manage.

The range of people and interests means that in any school or district—indeed, in any organization no matter how unified—there will always be some people who have priorities other than those chosen by the organization as a whole. Declaring literacy to be a priority will not stop music or physical education teachers from continuing to advocate the importance of their work. The school community may have set a priority on the arts, but some parents will want more attention on health or technology. However much consultation and involvement takes place, however inclusive the decisionmaking process, someone will always have a different view than the majority or consensus position.

Sometimes these different viewpoints are based on real disagreements about what is important. For example, teachers and parents who strongly value the arts may worry that a focus on literacy will narrow the curriculum. Special-education advocates may fear that accountability provisions will push their children's needs to the margins. Teacher organizations will be concerned that reform will turn into significantly more work for teachers without any additional remuneration. These differences may, of course, have an element, even a very strong element, of self-interest, but the boundary between principled concern and self-interest is often blurry since people connect their lives and work to the things they truly care about.

Sometimes people simply need to feel they have had some influence, regardless of the issue. They won't agree until they believe they have been heard. This is a legitimate human need for significance. I'm reminded of our oldest daughter when she was a very young child. There was a short period of time when we could not leave her with any babysitters, even her grandparents. We were entirely exasperated, but one evening we told her that we planned to go out, and her uncle and aunt would stay with her, but that we would not leave until she told us it was okay to go. A few minutes later she announced that we could go, and we never again had a problem leaving her with a sitter. Once she felt a part of the decision, she was content with it. This desire to have a voice is not confined to children; all of us feel it, and it should be taken seriously.

At other times opposition will be precisely that—opposition based on political differences rather than truly substantive differences in purpose. School boards may be split such that some members oppose the positions of others, no matter what they are, based on long-standing political differences. A teaching staff may have similar differences, so that what is supported by one group will automatically engender opposition from another group. Where labor relations have historically been poor, it must be expected that teacher and other staff unions will be suspicious of the authorities, whoever they are. Deeply rooted community differences, whether based on social class or ethnicity or geography, may also lead to automatic opposition to new proposals.

### The role of parents

Most school leaders with whom I talk, in many countries around the world, say that parents are becoming steadily less deferential, less respectful, and more demanding of schools. As we have seen, this is a trend that is not restricted to education. Physicians face patients armed with research from the Internet, demanding particular treatments. Just ask nurses or civil servants or lawyers, or any other occupational group, if they feel they are respected as they were 20 years ago; the answer will be a resounding "no."

People attribute this decline in deference to a variety of factors, from too much television to too much permissiveness to a general feeling that the next generation is coming to no good! The perceived decline in social cohesion from the "good old days" is also often blamed on schools. But is also reasonable to think that higher education levels in society have had an impact on declining deference, and that some of this change is actually a good thing. After all, we educate people in part so that they can understand their own and others' interests and advocate on their own behalf.

The increase in parental and community advocacy places new pressures and demands on schools at all levels. Individual parents can place enormous strain on teachers and principals, although it must be remembered that parents are also feeling the same pressure. It is, after all, parents' responsibility to advocate for their children. And sometimes they have legitimate complaints. There is plenty of evidence that schools sometimes do make incorrect or hasty judgments about children, or neglect to pay enough attention to parents' very deep knowledge of their children, and then are very reluctant to acknowledge the problem. Parents need to be assertive on these matters when they feel their children's interests are at stake.

The situation will be improved to the extent that schools can resist the temptation to see demanding parents as problems, and instead focus on ways to use conflict productively. A friend who was an experienced principal had a process she used with angry parents that involved beginning with an admission that the school was not always right; she wanted to understand the parents' views. Most of the time, she said, even a simple statement to this effect lowered the temperature very considerably and moved the discussion from one of blame to one of mutual problem-solving. Most of the time parents are well aware that their children have challenges, but they need the school to be a partner and ally, not an opponent who shuts them out of decisionmaking or does not recognize their knowledge of their children.

Principals, especially, need training in conflict resolution, as these are skills that can be learned. Protocols can be put in place to ensure parents' concerns are truly heard and conflicts get dealt with in ways that tend to reduce the tension. Since individual parents can consume huge amounts of time not only of school personnel but of district leaders as well, a small investment of time in conflict-resolution skills can yield big dividends in productivity, not to mention reduced conflict.

Parent organizations, both local and larger-scale, also can play an important role in shaping education policies and practices. Parent advocacy organizations have had important impacts in areas such as special education. Many of the changes in education policy around inclusion, for instance, have been driven by lawsuits and other pressures from parents or parent organizations. Here too, while schools often see parent organizations as a source of pressure or problems, they can also be a source of support, protecting schools from other political pressures. Smart principals and superintendents spend a lot of time building understanding and support from parent groups because that support is vital to any system's ability to sustain itself.

### Teachers and their unions

Teachers cannot be forced or bludgeoned into doing a better job. Experience in many places shows that education reforms that attack teachers do not work. To say it yet again, school performance depends fundamentally on having talented, skilled, and motivated teachers, and you can only get such people, especially in the very large numbers required for school systems, by providing them with reasonable pay and working conditions. Teaching, when done well, is hard work. Capable people will not take it on or stay in it if the conditions are poor, except in a relatively small number of cases where individual commitment to the work is extraordinarily strong. Even Catholic schools can no longer depend on nuns and priests for their teaching force.

Looking after teachers also means paying attention to teachers' professional organizations—their unions and associations. Teacher unions have gotten a bad rap in much of the discussion of reform, for reasons that often display a lack of understanding of the nature and role of these organizations. Many reformers seem to see teacher unions as an obstacle to reform; in the United States especially a number of commentators, particularly from certain foundations and think tanks, have been active in making this point. Some commentators take the view that the power of teacher unions should be curtailed substantially, if not eliminated outright. A number of jurisdictions—U.S. states, Canadian provinces, and several other countries—have sought to eliminate union resistance by changing laws governing teacher unions, such as removing the right to organize (in some U.S. states), removing the right to bargain collectively (as in England), or passing laws to limit the scope of collective bargaining or roll back wages and working conditions (as in many Canadian provinces in the 1990s).

Undoubtedly, teacher unions sometimes can and do get in the way of what management in a state or district or school wants to do. In a number of the cases examined for this book, opposition from unions played an important role in the foundering of a reform project, San Diego being one example. The same concerns were frequently heard during the recent reforms in Ontario, as school boards and school administrators often felt that Ontario teacher unions, which are quite powerful organizations with many thousands of members, were not always acting in ways consistent with the intent of the Ontario reforms.

The general stance in this book, however, is that opposition to change, whether from individuals or unions, needs to be understood and taken seriously, not removed by legal or other fiat.

The historical evidence is quite clear that teacher unions have been a main force for improving teachers' pay and working conditions. Where unions do not exist or have restricted bargaining rights, pay and working conditions for teachers tend to lag, and this will inevitably, over time, make it harder to recruit and retain talented people in large numbers. That is why it is a shortsighted strategy to try to reduce the influence of teacher unions. The reality is that excellent schools need strong teacher organizations.

To say that unions are important to the welfare of education does not mean that leaders in education should just accept whatever positions unions put forward. Unions can also be shortsighted and self-interested, sometimes even to the point of damaging their own members' futures by taking indefensible positions on important issues. Excessive attention to counting or calculating minutes or hours of work is an example of a wrong-headed approach because it diminishes the claim of teachers to be professionals. So is the claim that professional development ought to be the purview of each individual teacher, which flies in the face of what we know about effective organizational learning in schools and runs against teachers' preference for high-quality collective learning.

Some of the positions that unions take clearly do not embody the best available evidence around what is good for children. Often, however, these positions are a reaction to poor choices made by management in a few schools. For example, if teachers are consistently pushed to add additional tasks, they will eventually try to negotiate limits on hours of work. If teachers are forced to participate in professional development activities that they do not see as meaningful, they will eventually try to negotiate greater autonomy in this area. Many of the positions taken by unions could have been avoided had school management been more sensitive to creating the kind of workplace that good professionals want.

Be that as it may, that unions have limitations is not a reason to try to reduce or remove their influence any more than one should eliminate school boards because of their imperfections. Instead, constant effort is needed to engage teacher organizations and their leaders in dialogue, not only about the needs of their members but about the broader needs of the public education system. If public education declines, there will be fewer jobs for teachers and fewer members in teacher organizations. This is math that every union leader understands.

It would be naïve to think that one can create some golden era of harmony among system managers and union leaders such that there will be no more disputes. Many dynamics that are hard to change, such as union leadership and election structures, will make this relationship difficult and frustrating at least some of the time. However, to a considerable extent the responsibility for good labor relations rests with management, which means that a central task of managers and leaders of reform is to find ways to work productively with teacher organizations.

These issues were central to the negotiation of collective agreements in Ontario in 2005. In the ten years prior, Ontario had had very difficult labor relations, with many strikes and work-to-rule campaigns as well as grievances and general bad feelings. Although collective bargaining in Ontario is officially done at the district level, Minister Gerard Kennedy recognized that local bargaining, if left to the 72 districts, was likely to lead to further disruptions and would threaten the government's agenda around improved outcomes for students. Moreover, as the 100 percent funder of education, the provincial government was going to have to manage the results of all the settlements. Kennedy began a series of discussions with the provincial parties—the school boards and the teacher unions—with a view to seeing if there might be ground for a provincial "framework" that would set out the major elements under which local agreements could then be negotiated.

Kennedy realized that after so many years of conflict, it would not be easy to negotiate new agreements just because there was a new government with a different agenda. The old habits of conflict and negativity were still dominant in the organizations on both sides of the table. He also wanted to make sure the agreements reflected and supported the government's reform agenda. He therefore tabled proposals that would address many of the teachers' concerns while also supporting improved student achievement. Over several months of intense discussions, often lasting late into the night and personally managed by the minister and his young and brilliant chief of staff, Katie Telford, a set of general principles was agreed to among all parties that would allow them to negotiate local agreements with minimal difficulty. By the end of the summer of 2005, all Ontario teachers had new four-year collective agreements, an unprecedented step for collective bargaining in education in Ontario, and with essentially no disruption to the school system. It was an amazing feat of political effort and strategy, which a few months earlier virtually nobody in the province would have thought possible.

Among the main elements of this strategy were:

- having a student success teacher in every secondary school to support efforts to reduce failure rates, especially in grades 9 and 10;
- increasing preparation time for elementary teachers by adding more specialist teachers to support a well-rounded curriculum;
- building in more staffing to support the government's commitment to reduce class sizes in the primary grades.

These mechanisms gave the unions more members, but in ways that directly supported the government's improvement agenda. They were the key steps that allowed the parties to agree on other elements such as salaries. In addition, Kennedy put in place two other provincial structures, described a little later, to resolve disputes without resorting to formal grievance mechanisms and expensive arbitrations. They are an example of how a difficult situation can be turned around with clever strategy and determined effort.

Parents and teachers are not the only group whose views have to be taken into account. The same considerations apply to support staff in schools as well. Though teachers get the vast bulk of the attention—in part because so many education researchers and analysts are former teachers—the rest of the staff in schools also play important and often underappreciated roles. The fastest growth in school personnel in many countries has been in non-certified staff, especially teacher aides or paraprofessionals. But all support staff, from secretaries to bus drivers to caretakers, are also important to successful schooling. Just ask any successful school principal about how important it is to have good support staff!

### BUILDING SUPPORT WHILE MANAGING DIVERSE INTERESTS

How does one manage all the internal and external stakeholders whose ideas and interests require attention while still focusing on a well-grounded education agenda and its effective implementation? The strategies discussed earlier in this chapter in terms of managing operational pressures apply here too, but the political nature of interest groups also requires some unique approaches, having mainly to do with attitudes toward opposition and with creating structures and processes that provide ways of managing diverse concerns.

A first vital psychological disposition in the face of opposition is to avoid feeling personally aggrieved when things don't go as planned or when people do not get, or stay, onside. Reformers are often completely convinced by their own good intentions. When others fail to sign on, change leaders can easily get entirely frustrated. Yet that is just when it is most important to keep one's sense of proportion and direction, and to remain calm and focused. There will be opposition, thoughtful or not, so no point in being offended by it. There are many occasions when the first response to a problem should be something like counting slowly to ten before saying or doing anything else!

Keeping a positive orientation is important. It's helpful to assume that others are generally acting from some reasonable basis of understanding or from important pressures rather than just trying to be obstreperous or negative. As in any conflict, trying to understand another's thinking and see how to respond to their genuine issues is an important step in moving forward. Under pressure, the usual tendency is to jump to blaming the opposition; while satisfying psychologically, this is not a route to progress or a solution.

One way to stay positive is to keep talking about the big picture and how all the various pieces of change fit together. Reminding others of goals and purpose not only reinforces their work but also generates a greater sense of understanding and coherence as well as, often, more optimism.

Governments and districts could also do much to improve the political climate in schools and districts by helping school administrators at all levels learn more about effective community and labor relations—not just the legal elements, but even more how to build and maintain good working relationships with staff or parents in a school, since this has so much to do with the overall climate. These skills can be learned. Principals do not come into the job knowing them, but very few jurisdictions devote the effort to help them acquire what they need.

### Structures and places for debate and dialogue

The most important approach to managing political pressures is to create structures and processes for issues and concerns to be taken up in ways that are most likely to lead to constructive outcomes. Since political debate and disagreement are inevitable, it is important to have established mechanisms and places for these issues to be raised and discussed.

Inclusion and dialogue are good starting principles. Interest groups need to be given a seat at the policy table or a place in the dialogue. Efforts to marginalize others, tempting as they often are when things get difficult, will usually lead to more and bigger problems later. The goal must be to have all parties see themselves as part of the solution rather than as being primarily in opposition, since that is essential to real and sustainable improvement. Structured forums for debate also require organizations to put forward and defend their views to other partners, and to face and respond to the contrary ideas of others.

Just as improvement requires an infrastructure to support improved capacity on the part of schools and teachers, it requires an analogous infrastructure to manage political dialogue. However, very few reform programs give explicit attention to the political processes that will be required for success. Most settings do not have good formal structures that facilitate constructive dialogue, and in some places there are not even good informal connections among the parties.

In political dialogue, someone must always be looking for areas of common ground and mutual interest. Win-win is the fundamental premise for successful bargaining, and it seems to be possible more often than people think. For example, the interest of teacher organizations in more jobs and more members is quite complementary to some improvement strategies, such as efforts to reduce class size or to improve supports to high-need students. In Ontario one of the key elements in achieving four-year collective agreements from 2004 to 2008 was to create new teaching positions specially dedicated to the province's goals of higher high school graduation rates and improved literacy and numeracy.

Another example would be steps to improve professional learning opportunities for teachers, consistent with the ideas outlined in chapter 6. Essential to the goal of improved student outcomes, this is also a prime issue for teachers' professional organizations. The very large investment in Ontario in teacher learning, including developing an induction program for all new teachers, is an example of a change that is good for students and welcomed by teachers and their organizations. Districts, states, and countries with successful reform programs have made the same effort to support effective learning for teachers.

## Ontario's approach to managing political pressures

The Ontario education strategy did give specific attention to the need for such structures and processes. When Minister Gerard Kennedy began work on the Ontario education agenda in the fall of 2003, he knew the importance of building support and involvement from all parts of the education sector, especially after ten years of highly conflictual relationships. During the first year of the new government, in addition to managing the collective agreement process, Kennedy put in place a range of mechanisms to improve the overall policy climate. Some of the most important were:

* *Extensive informal discussions.* The minister, his political staff, and senior officials of the ministry all met frequently with various stakeholder groups. The minister spoke at many, many public events of all the key sector groups, both to state the government's views but also to hear feedback from the sector. The deputy minister and senior managers met regularly—usually quarterly—with the teacher organizations, the principal organizations, and the directors' (superintendents') association. All groups knew that if they had an issue or concern, they could get a hearing for it. This helped build trust, in contrast to the feeling among key groups, particularly teachers, that the previous government had no interest in their issues and opinions. However, to prevent the usual phenomenon in which political issues are primarily handled through such one-on-one discussions,

the minister also created a public forum for all groups to meet and work together.

- *The creation of the Ontario education Partnership Table.* The table was an open forum that brought together leaders from more than 20 key educational organizations. (Remember that Ontario has four publicly funded education systems—French Catholic, French public, English public, and English Catholic, hence the large number of stakeholder groups.) The table included the political leaders (such as presidents) and senior staff officers of Ontario's four associations of school boards, its five teacher organizations, the directors (superintendents), the three organizations of principals, the association of deans of faculties of education, the Ontario College of Teachers, three student organizations, and four parent organizations. Aboriginal organizations were added to the Table a little later. The Partnership Table met two to four times a year to provide a venue for all stakeholders to discuss the government's plans and policies. Partnership Table ground rules were established to promote open debate. The forum meant that all groups got the same information at the same time, and all groups had to hear and respond to other groups' issues and concerns. The minister attended and participated in all the meetings along with senior ministry staff.

- *Discussion papers.* As the basis for sector and Partnership Table discussions, the minister issued a series of discussion papers setting out the government's proposals in major policy areas. A half-dozen such papers were issued over the first two and a half years, dealing with such issues as teacher quality, the role of school boards, and student voice.

- *Providing more detailed input on key policy areas.* To this end, a series of Working Tables were created under the Partnership Table. Two of the four Working Tables initially created dealt with the government's main themes of literacy/numeracy and improving high school graduation rates. Another discussed issues of teacher development, including certification and professional development, which were the subject of a discussion paper in 2004, while the fourth focused on special education. Later, additional Working Tables were created on health in schools and on the role of support staff. The Working Tables were smaller in size because not all the organizations chose to participate in each one, could meet more frequently, and could give more intensive attention to key topics.

- *Involvement of the teacher unions.* A Student Success Commission was created to bring secondary teachers and district leaders (school boards and superintendents) together to discuss and resolve any conflicts over the initiatives to increase high school graduation rates. A Provincial Stability Commission was also set up with similar composition to resolve issues arising from the collective agreements in elementary schools, in particular concerning how to implement the reduction in assigned supervision time for teachers. In both cases these commissions have done important work to defuse conflict and find ways of resolving disputes. The ministry also provided a significant sum of money to the five teacher organizations to support their professional development work. A main intent of this funding was to support increased union involvement in professional development following ten years in which their entire emphasis had been on bargaining and working-condition issues.

None of these mechanisms has worked perfectly. Each has had its tribulations and disputes, sometimes heated. But the net effect of all of them has been to create a climate in which it is increasingly accepted that problems can be addressed and solved through collective action with a modicum of goodwill. Partners feel that they do have a way to be heard and that their concerns are taken seriously. The result has been a much more positive political atmosphere for education that has allowed schools to focus on the work of improving teaching/learning practices and student outcomes.

Analogous strategies can be used in a school or a district. In every organization, both formal and informal contacts between leaders and various stakeholders are vital to keeping people informed and feeling involved. Moreover, sharing as much information as possible tends to be associated with lower conflict. Smart principals make a point of checking out ideas and plans informally with some of the influential people in the school on an ongoing basis. They also try to tell the whole staff what is in the works and to share information and thinking on major decisions, in advance of a decision whenever possible. This happens above and beyond the kinds of input that may be solicited through staff working groups or committees or at staff meetings or parent meetings. Schools and districts can organize forums for staff, parents, and students to meet and discuss important issues and priorities, similar to the Ontario Partnership Table, but with whatever frequency and degree of formality seems suitable to a specific setting. It's particularly important in most settings, though it is also the kind of thing most of us would rather avoid, to reach out to people who may be opposed to an initiative. A few minutes in advance listening carefully to concerns can prevent many hours later spent trying to deal with more active grievances. People do not expect to get their own way all the time, but they are much more likely to be accepting of approaches that they do not endorse if they feel they have been given valid information, have had a real hearing, and that at least some of their concerns have been taken into account.

These principles of openness, shared ownership, and dialogue with external stakeholder groups are hard to put in place in most organizations, as they involve a fundamental reorientation of the typical tendency to see external relations primarily as a game in which the goal is to win. Most organizations, including schools and districts, are reluctant to share information externally (and often even internally). Consultation with "partners," if it happens at all, usually takes place after key decisions on direction have been made internally. Yet trust cannot be built in that way, and someone has to take the first step toward more open relationships.

This is why it is important to help the parties build capacity for constructive engagement. Especially in a setting with a history of conflict, people will not know how to work together. They have to be helped to learn this. School boards need to learn how to talk with teacher organizations, and vice versa. Principals may need help in building true learning communities in their schools. Groups representing marginalized communities may be so angry that they cannot easily take on a less combative stance. Sometimes external facilitators will be required to help people engage effectively. Building capacity for good dialogue is a key task in keeping focus and sustaining the momentum of school improvement.

One cannot be naïve in this process of dialogue and consultation. Extending a hand does not guarantee a good response. When it comes to conflict and competition, the habits learned over years, as well as genuine differences in views and interests, mean that trust-building is rarely easy or simple work. Some people and groups will be difficult, and not always for what seem to be good reasons. As mentioned earlier, people will not give up their ingrained habits nor what they take to be their real interests just because a new principal or superintendent or chief state school officer appears on the scene. Hard work must be done to understand, recognize, and adapt to diverse interests and points of view, and this work, just like the work of education reform in schools and classrooms, requires careful planning and ongoing attention.

### CONCLUSION

Keeping an effective focus on reform is challenging. There will always be multiple distracting elements in the form of other work, surprises, and competing agendas. These are facts of life that have to be accepted and accommodated in some way. This chapter has outlined some of the dispositions and techniques that can be used to minimize disruptions while building support for continued emphasis on the things that really matter. There is no more of a magic answer here than there is in any other area of school improvement. But there are steps that can be taken to lessen to some degree the mismatch that so many education leaders feel between what they believe to be important and what they actually seem to spend their time doing. Reducing this gap will improve both morale and productivity, which is a task worth our attention.

# 10

## What Can and Should Be Done?

This final chapter draws together the discussion in the rest of the book by reviewing some of the central messages and ideas, then by focusing on two equally important questions:

- What should school systems do to make the biggest positive differences for our students? *and*
- What can individuals at any level of the system do to make the biggest positive difference for students?

### CENTRAL MESSAGES

A first core idea in this book is that students have much more potential to do well than our schools and societies have so far tapped. The historic contribution of public schools to individual achievement and social mobility is one that deserves pride and recognition. At the same time, it is evident that much more should be possible. The stories and evidence from chapter 2 and elsewhere make it clear that many students who are now not doing well in our schools could do better, and that many people are able, given the right conditions and supports, to accomplish things far beyond what others thought possible. We may not know what the limits of human potential for accomplishment are, but we can be sure we have not reached them and probably have not even approached them. This appears to be true in every field of human activity, from language to science to human relationships to sports and the arts. Educators should approach their work, then, with a combination of pride in what has been achieved and humility in the face of how much more could be accomplished.

The current limits to student achievement arise primarily from conditions outside the school and largely beyond the power of schools to change. The most important of these is growing up in poverty. Schools did not create poverty, and schools alone, despite any rhetoric to the contrary, will not be able to eliminate or even substantially reduce poverty levels. That must be done primarily through other social and economic policies. But schools do have the opportunity, and the challenge, to help students do better than they otherwise might, to fulfill some of that untapped positive potential, no matter what the circumstances and limitations.

If school systems are to be able to bring more students than ever before to higher levels of accomplishment than ever before, they will need to do some different things and do them in different ways. Educators will need to dedicate themselves in a new way to the task and organize themselves so as to be able to accomplish it. The strategy that got us to our current level of achievement will have to be modified to get us to the next level. The central focus of this book is on how to do that.

I have defined the task as creating "lasting and sustainable improvement in student outcomes." Lasting and sustainable improvement means improving student outcomes across a broad range of important areas, not just reading and mathematics, and not just as measured by test scores. Lasting and real improvement also means greatly reducing the gaps in outcomes among different population groups, so that all elements of society benefit from public education.

These ends are important, but so are the means through which they are achieved. A main theme of this book is that real and lasting improvement cannot just be imposed from outside. Improvement has to take place in ways that support positive morale among educators, students, and parents, that do not demand impossible levels of energy on an ongoing basis, and that increase the capacity of the school or system to continue to be successful. It is only through this kind of strategy that public education can generate the level of public confidence and support that such a major social undertaking requires.

I have argued that we have learned quite a bit both about what needs to be done and about how to do it. Much of this learning has come from making mistakes, such as adopting the wrong reforms, failing to support them, or failing to implement them well. Trial-and-error remains a main form of human learning, and we are now in a position to benefit from earlier mistakes.

A strong program of improvement requires a focus on improving learning. To put it most simply, it is necessary both to build strong personal relationships with students, families, and communities and to improve core teaching and learning practices—not just in a few places, but broadly across entire systems. The necessary relationships and practices for this goal, however, can only be built and sustained in the right kind of organization. Changing organizational practices in schools and systems is not itself a goal, but it is an essential support for achieving any of our goals for students by making public school systems places where good people want to work and feel able to do good work in reasonable conditions.

Public schools depend on public confidence and support in the same way that each of us depends on the atmosphere to breathe; public understanding is "the environment" for public education. Taking this support and confidence for granted is as big a mistake as taking the quality of our air and water for granted. Building public support is challenging but both possible and necessary.

All of the above elements require effective leadership focused on school improvement, the ability to manage ongoing operations of the system, and the skill to negotiate the inevitable distractions and political challenges of managing a public enterprise such as schooling.

The overall message that I hope these chapters deliver is that we can do better, even much better. It will not be easy, but then no significant accomplishment is easy! There is no single thing that will create the improvement we want. We should disregard any effort to convince us that if we just did "x" all would be well, whether "x" is school choice or decentralization or professional learning communities or any of the myriad other recipes being sold to anxious educators or a gullible public. Schools are complex organizations, rooted in even more complex social settings. Education is not a mass production process but something that everyone—students and educators—does in his or her own way. Improvement requires sustained effort by many people over a considerable amount of time. It is about, as Slavin et al. (1992) put it, "the relentless pursuit of success" for all students. It is, and will continue to be, very hard and demanding work.

I believe educators are up to this work. So many have already been doing it for years or decades, often under difficult conditions. Most of all, educators are motivated by the opportunity to make a real, positive difference in the lives of students and the students' families. There are few things more worth our struggle, our time and energy and sweat and tears, than being able to see young people become something more than they, or we, thought possible. To see people take steps they thought they could not take and reach goals they thought they could not reach must surely be one of the greatest rewards life can offer. With a new sense of confidence in what is possible, and a more systematic approach, even more can be accomplished.

## WHAT SHOULD SYSTEMS DO TO SUPPORT IMPROVEMENT?

This book has focused on what needs to happen at the district and broader levels to support better outcomes for students. As some governments start to turn away from some of the mistakes and policy excesses of the past twenty years, what advice can we give both elected officials and senior system managers as to the actions they should take and the strategies they should embrace?

We have known for a long time, as Ronald Edmonds said thirty years ago, that we can improve student outcomes in schools, even under difficult circumstances. The challenge has been to do so across large numbers of schools, which has turned out to be much more difficult than anyone had thought. It's hard to improve one school, or a few schools, on a lasting basis, but it has been done many times. System change brings new and special challenges. Yet over time and with effort, we are learning more about what is required to create and sustain meaningful improvement across large numbers of schools. This is not, and never will be, an easy task, but it is possible. If we assume positive intentions and motivations on the part of most of the relevant actors—elected political leaders at the district, state, and national level as well as their senior officials—then it is now possible to provide some sound advice on what to do, and what not to do.

Let's start with the key portion of the Hippocratic Oath that doctors take—to do no harm. The history of education reform shows how often that injunction has been violated. Here are some things systems should *not* do:

- Assume that a single change can create improvement in a short time frame.
- Assume that a few strong leaders can force a school or system to improve all by themselves, simply through charisma or force of will. Lasting improvement requires ongoing effort from large numbers of people.
- Assume that the simplistic application of incentives, such as the idea of paying people more for higher achievement, or punishing schools that do not improve, will be a successful strategy.
- Start with changes in governance and policy. While such changes may be necessary at various points to support good teaching and learning practices (and only when they are supportive in that way), on their own, governance and policy changes will not produce improvement.
- Assume that new curriculum and standards can by themselves foster betterment. Good curricula, appropriate standards, and quality resources matter, but only when educators know how to use them and want to use them.
- Assume that an accountability system with data on relative school performance will create improvement. Unless people know what to do differently, and want to do those things, no amount of accountability will, on its own, lead to improvement.

If districts, states, and governments simply stopped acting on these assumptions, it would be a major improvement. However, real improvement has to be a matter not just of negatives but of positives. Four main steps are most important, whether in a school, a district, or an entire national school system. These are not choices; all of them require attention simultaneously.

1. *Focus on a few key student outcomes that matter most and are most understandable for the public and for educators.* A repeated theme in this book has been the importance of focusing on a small number of goals that are easy to understand, have broad acceptance, and can be used as the center of an improvement strategy. These goals should be important and ambitious. They should stretch people to do things they value—to have their reach exceed their grasp—because that is what produces top performance. At the same time, people must believe that the goals are meaningful and potentially achievable; setting impossible goals produces weaker, not stronger, performance.

   Focusing on a few goals does not, however, mean adopting a narrow view of schooling. For one thing, progress in literacy or numeracy can be aided and supported by a rich and varied curriculum, both because other subjects can reinforce key skills and because students are more motivated when their overall experience at schools is varied. Spending more and more hours on literacy at the expense of everything else is actually counterproductive to getting good outcomes in many ways. Having a few priorities can and should be balanced against the necessity of a broad approach to what schools do.

2. *Put effort into building capacity for improvement (skill).* Most of the time, where performance is weak, so is people's knowledge or skill as to how to do better. Improving system performance requires a large and sustained effort to improve skills. Teaching being a complex activity, improvement is also complex. Better teaching requires stronger content knowledge, stronger pedagogical knowledge, better ability to motivate and engage students, skills in working closely

with colleagues, capacity to work effectively with parents, and so on. Not every individual will need to develop all these, but all will need to be made stronger across the system. The center of any improvement undertaking should, then, be this sustained effort to strengthen skills.

Improving capacity requires sustained effort—not just professional development days but various forms of coaching and mentoring, effective use of staff meetings and other in-school time, and support through related practices such as supervision and evaluation. This means that there are policy, leadership, and system-procedure implications to capacity-building.

3. *Build motivation (will) by taking a positive approach.* One of the fundamental lessons of research on human motivation is that people will do more of what they think they are good at or can become good at. Improvement in education requires a strongly supportive message for students, parents, and educators. To repeat, you cannot threaten or shame or punish people into top performance.

Educators are largely motivated—as are most people—by accomplishment, and for most educators accomplishment means the success of learners. So systems need to talk often about how important student achievement is, how important educators are to that success, and about the steps being taken to support greater success.

Being positive does not mean approving everything the system currently does or avoiding any criticism. Educators can accept a position which says that current outcomes for students need to be improved, provided that the overall approach is not about blame and recognizes past efforts and successes.

4. *Work to increase public and political support for an effective, thoughtful, and sustained program of improvement.* Schools need support as well as pressure. Endless public criticism of schools is both unfair and counterproductive. It ignores the real limits on what schools can do; more importantly, it erodes public confidence and support, leading to a downward spiral of declining resources, effort, and results. Schools and school systems need the support of their public

as well as the expectation that more can and should be possible. System leaders need to combine these messages in their public communications, stressing both the many accomplishments and the need for continued improvement.

It's also important for school systems to speak up about the importance of the broader public policy environment. Without in any way reducing their own commitment to students, schools can also be advocates for decent jobs with decent wages, adequate social supports, reasonable housing, good child care, and appropriate recreation programs, all of which can help support student success.

This kind of program of communication requires deliberation and effort. System leaders, both elected and appointed, are critical to building this kind of public dialogue and understanding. It should be a fundamental part of the work of any person in a leadership role.

## WHAT CAN ONE PERSON DO?

The systems focus in this book and the earlier part of this chapter is important, because so much thinking in education does not take account of the dynamics of large systems. Change in a single classroom or school is important, but it cannot be sustained without system-level support. But systems are also made up of individuals, and no system can improve unless many, many people are prepared to act.

While it's always nice to tell other people what they should do to solve a problem, each of us also has an obligation to change what we ourselves do rather than wait for somebody else to solve our problems. So the last part of this chapter focuses on the actions that can be taken by anyone interested in public education, whether as an educator, a parent, a student, or a citizen (and some of us combine all those roles).

Individuals face many of the same constraints and pressures that systems do—too many things to do, not enough time, not enough support, and so on. The suggestions here will already be familiar to readers, as they mirror points made earlier—perhaps to a degree that some readers may find annoyingly repetitive!

- *Pick a few issues for focus—that give the most result for least effort.* It's not just a matter of dedicating one's efforts to a good cause, though that is certainly the right starting point. Given limitations of time and energy, it's also important to ask what efforts are likely to yield the greatest return. To be sure, our societies and organizations need people who are unwilling to accept that some things can't be done, because those people help us see new possibilities. Most of us, though, have to put our energy where it can make a real difference, which means picking things that are as hard as we can accomplish, but no harder. Inevitably, that's a fine judgment to make.

- *Build a team and allies; look after yourself and other people.* Our popular culture seems to value lone heroes, but in fact almost all significant human accomplishment is a result of the work of many people, not one. Even great individual artists have teachers and patrons. In schools, everything of value comes from teamwork and mutual support. So every person wanting to make a difference has to look for teammates, supporters, and allies. These are the people who help do the work, who keep everyone's morale up, who contribute the elements that were somehow missing. Not only are collective efforts more effective, they are more satisfying, too. Much has already been said in this book about teams; the most important thing to remember is to build relationships with others and then rely on them to do their part.

- *Think long- and short-term.* Improvement requires a long-term vision and strategy and the persistence to stay with it over years. Those who make a difference in any field are those with long-term commitment who make continual efforts. We admire, rightly, people who can see something great and set out to create it. At the same time, organizations work mostly in the here and now. As noted earlier, organizations are subject to big surprises and sudden shifts of climate, so that plans have to be changed or even totally revised. Even a long-term strategy usually gets implemented in short-term pieces and should be reviewed in light of changing circumstances. Sometimes an opportunity arises that begs to be taken advantage of, even if it was never part of the original plan. Effective promoters of improvement are able to stay true to their larger intentions but also take advantage of or react to the moment.

• *Pay attention to public confidence and the political environment.* Public education lives and breathes to the extent that the citizenry is willing to support the schools with their children and their taxes. Although educators want, with reason, to focus on the work they do every day with students, the stance in this book is clear. Education is part of the political world, so that anyone who cares about public education must be, at a minimum, alert to the foibles and vicissitudes of that world. The important work of improvement in classrooms and schools must be complemented by equally important engagement with citizens and taxpayers so they understand and support the purposes and approaches, not to mention the costs, of public education.

• *Stay positive and optimistic.* Creating meaningful improvement in a school or system is hard work. It won't always go right. Sometimes things will seem to get worse before they get better. A case in point: Steve Munby, now chief executive of England's National College for School Leadership, was previously head of education for the Knowsley Education Authority, near Liverpool in England. When he took over the authority's education system, it was ranked second to last in the country in achievement in secondary schools. Munby announced that he would change that within a year. And, he reports, he did. The next year Knowsley was dead last—before beginning an amazing improvement over the next few years under Munby's leadership.

One has to be persistent to improve large institutions, but one also has to be positive. The introduction to this book ended with a story about balancing realism and optimism. That balance remains important.

In fact, much of leading improvement is about balance. One has to be impatient for improvement, yet recognize that things do not change overnight. One must be deadly serious about how important education is, yet see how important good humor is also. School systems need pressure to improve and support for their efforts. Professionals need autonomy in their work but also a strong sense of standards and accountability. The balance between these various elements changes from place to place and time to time. Leaders always need to be alert to these balances.

## CONCLUSION

The time is right. There is a growing understanding that we can improve public education systems in ways that are positive and sustainable. We know more than ever before about how to improve student outcomes, increase student engagement, build educators' skills, create positive morale, and strengthen public confidence in public education all at the same time. We know that doing so requires a well-grounded education strategy, the right supporting conditions, and the appropriate political efforts and supports. When put together in this way, progress is clearly hard work, but it is not impossible. The combination of vision, optimism, and realism remains an essential grounding. I have tried to turn this combination into specific ideas and proposals that educators can use to advance the cause we all believe in. The stakes are considerable. To bring more students to higher levels of achievement than ever before, in ways that are positive and sustainable for education systems, is a worthwhile purpose for all the energy and skill we can summon.

# References

Anderson, L., and Pelliger, L. (1990). Synthesis of research on compensatory and remedial education. *Educational Leadership* 48(1), 10–16.

Argyris, C., and Schon, D. (1974). *Theory in practice: Increasing professional effectiveness.* San Francisco: Jossey-Bass.

Arkes, J. (2004). *Does schooling improve health?* Working Paper. Santa Monica, CA: RAND Corporation.

Arrow, K. (1951). *Social choice and individual values.* Monograph no. 12. Cowles Commission for Research in Economics. New York: John Wiley & Sons.

Aspen Institute. (2006). Strong foundation, evolving challenges. Washington: Aspen Institute. Retrieved August 19, 2008, from *www.aspeninstitute.org/site/c.huLWJeMRKpH/b.1737085/k.7592/Program_Publications.htm#urban.*

Audet, W., et al. (2007). The impact of the literacy and numeracy secretariat: Changes in Ontario's education system. Unpublished report, Canadian Language and Literacy Research Network.

Barber, M. (2007). *Instruction to deliver.* London: Methuen.

Bernhardt, V. (2003). *Data analysis for continuous school improvement.* Larchmont, NY: Eye of Education.

Berryman, S. (1992). Learning for the workplace. In L. Darling Hammond (ed.), *Review of Research in Education* 19. Washington: American Educational Research Association. 343–401.

Black, J.S., and Gregersen, H.B. (2002). *Leading strategic change.* New York: Prentice Hall.

Burbules, N. (1990). The tragic sense of education. *Teachers College Record* 91(4), 469–479.

Campbell, D. (1975). Assessing the impact of planned social change. In G. Lyons (ed.), *Social research and public policies: The Dartmouth / OECD conference.* Hanover, NH: Public Affairs Center, Dartmouth College.

Campbell, D. (2006). What is education's impact on civic and social engagement? In R. Desjardins and T. Schuller (eds.), *Measuring the effects of education on health and civic engagement.* Paris: OECD. 25–118.

Campbell, J. (1972). *Myths to live by.* New York: Penguin.

Christman, J.B., Corcoran, T., and Corcoran, T.B. (2002). *The limits and contradictions of systemic reform: The Philadelphia story.* Philadelphia: Consortium for Policy Research in Education.

Cohen, D.K., and Hill, H.C. (2001). *Learning policy: When state education reform works.* New Haven, CT: Yale University Press.

Corter, C., and Pelletier, J. (2005). Parent and community involvement in schools: Policy panacea or pandemic? In N. Bascia et al. (eds.), *International handbook of education policy.* Dordrecht, Netherlands: Springer. 295–327.

Cross-City Campaign for Urban School Reform. (2005). *A delicate balance: District policies and classroom practices.* Chicago: Cross-City Campaign. Retrieved August 19, 2008, from *www.urbanstrategies.org/programs/schools/urbanschool reform.html.*

Cuban, L., and Usdan, M. (eds.). (2003). *Powerful reforms with shallow roots: Improving America's urban schools.* New York: Teachers College Press.

Daggett, W. (2007). A comprehensive process for improving student performance. Conference proceedings. Rexford, NY: International Center for Leadership in Education. Retrieved June 10, 2008, from *www.icle.net/pdf/2007MSC%20 Bill's%20PaperFINAL.pdf.*

Danielson, M., and Hochschild, J. (1998). Changing urban education: Lessons, cautions, prospects. In C. Stone (ed.), *Changing urban education.* Lawrence: University Press of Kansas. 277–295.

Datnow, A., and Stringfield, S. (2000). Working together for reliable school reform. *Journal of Education for Students Placed at Risk* 5, 183–204.

David, J. (2008). What research says about small learning communities. *Educational Leadership* 65(8), 84–85.

DfES (Department for Education and Skills) (2004). Statistics of education: Schools in England. London: TSO. Retrieved June 10, 2008, from *www.dfes.gov.uk/ rsgateway/DB/VOL/v000495/schools_04_final.pdf.*

Dror, Y. (1986). *Policy-making under adversity.* New Brunswick, NJ: Transaction Press.

Drucker, P. (1986). *The frontiers of management: Where tomorrow's decisions are being shaped today.* New York: Harper & Row.

DuFour, R., Eaker, R., and DuFour, R. (eds.). (2005). *On common ground: The power of professional learning communities.* Bloomington, IN: National Educational Service.

Dye, R. (1980). Contributions to volunteer work: Some evidence on income tax effect. *National Tax Journal* 33, 89–93.

Earl, L. (2003). *Assessment for learning.* Thousand Oaks, CA: Corwin.

Earl, L., Levin, B., Leithwood, K., Fullan, M., and Watson, N. (2002). *Watching and learning 2: OISE / UT evaluation of the implementation of the national literacy and numeracy strategies.* Toronto: OISE/University of Toronto. Retrieved August 18, 2008, from *www.standards.dfes.gov.uk/primary/publications/literacy.*

Earl, L., Watson, N., Levin, B., Leithwood, K., Fullan, M., and Torrance, N. (2003). *Watching and learning 3: Final report of the OISE / UT evaluation of the implementation of the national literacy and numeracy strategies.* Toronto: OISE/University of Toronto. Retrieved July 25, 2008, from *www.standards.dfes.gov.uk/ literacy/publications.*

Edmonds, R. (1979). Some schools work and more can. *Social Policy* 9(5), 28–32.

Elmore, R. (2002). *Bridging the gap between standards and achievement: The imperative for professional development in education.* Washington, DC: Albert Shanker Institute.

———. (2004). *School reform from the inside out: Policy, practice, and performance.* Cambridge, MA: Harvard Education Press.

EQAO (2005). *Annual Report 2004–2005.* Retrieved June 10, 2008, from *www.eqao. com/pdf_e/06/06P013e.pdf*

Eulina, M., and de Carvalho, P. (2001). *Rethinking family-school relations: A critique of parental involvement in schooling.* Mahwah, NH: Laurence Erlbaum.

Evan, A., et al. (2006). *Evaluation of the Bill and Melinda Gates Foundation's high school grants initiative: 2001–2005 final report.* Washington, DC: American Institutes for Research and SRI International.

Feinstein, L., Duckworth, K., and Sabates, R. (2004). *A model of the inter-generational transmission of educational success.* Wider Benefits of Learning Research report 10, London: Centre for Research on the Wider Benefits of Learning, Institute of Education.

Feinstein, L., Sabates, R., Anderson, T., Sorhaindo, A., and Hammond, C. (2006). What are the effects of education on health? In R. Desjardins and T. Schuller (eds.), *Measuring the effects of education on health and civic engagement.* Paris: OECD. 171–354.

Field, S., Kuczera, M., and Pont, B. (2007). *No more failures: Ten steps to equity in education.* Paris: OECD.

Fullan, M. (2006). *Turnaround leadership.* San Francisco, CA: Jossey-Bass.

———. (2007). *The new meaning of educational change* (4th ed.). New York: Teachers College Press.

———. (2008). *The six secrets of change.* San Francisco, CA: Jossey-Bass.

Fullan, M., Hill, P., and Crévola, C. (2006). *Breakthrough.* Thousand Oaks, CA: Corwin.

Fuller, B., Elmore, R., and Orfield, G. (eds.). (1996). *Who chooses, who loses?* New York: Teachers College Press.

Garmston, R.J., and Wellman, B.M. (1999). *The adaptive school: A sourcebook for developing collaborative groups.* Norwood, MA: Christopher-Gordon Publishers.

Gawande, A. (2002). The learning curve: Analyst of medicine. *New Yorker* 52.

Giguere, S. (2008). *More than just jobs: Work-force development in a skills based economy.* Paris: OECD.

Gleason, P., and Dynarski, M. (2002). Do we know whom to serve? Issues in using risk factors to identify dropouts. *Journal of Education for Students Placed at Risk* 7(1), 25–41.

Groot, W., and Van den Brink, H.M. (2006). What does education do to our health? In *Measuring the effects of education on health and civic engagement*. Proceedings of the Copenhagen Symposium. Paris: OECD. 355–363. Retrieved August 19, 2008, from *www.oecd.org/dataoecd/15/17/37425763.pdf*.

Gross, N., Giacquinta, J., and Bernstein, M. (1971). *Implementing organizational innovations: A sociological analysis of planned educational change*. New York: Basic Books.

Hart, D., and Livingstone, D.W. (2007). *Public attitudes towards education*. Toronto: Ontario Institute of Studies in Education. Retrieved May 22, 2008, from *www.oise.utoronto.ca/OISE-Survey/2007/survey_final_final.pdf*.

Hargreaves, A., and Fink, D. (2000). The three dimensions of reform. *Educational Leadership* 57(7), 30–34.

Helliwell, J.F. (2002). How's life? Combining individual and national variables to explain subjective well-being. *NBER Working Papers 9065*. Cambridge, MA: National Bureau of Economic Research.

Hesketh, B. (1997). Dilemmas in training for transfer and retention. *Applied Psychology: An International Review* 46(4), 339–361.

Hong, G., and Yu, B. (2007). Early grade retention and children's reading and math learning in elementary years. *Educational Evaluation and Policy Analysis* 29(4), 239–261.

Hong, G., and Raudenbush, S. (2005). Effects of kindergarten retention policy on children's cognitive growth in reading and mathematics. *Educational Evaluation and Policy Analysis* 27(3), 205–224.

Hopkins, D. (2007). *Every school a great school*. Buckingham, UK: Open University Press.

Hubbard, L., Mehan, H., and Stein, M.K. (2006). *Reform as learning: School reform, organizational culture, and community politics in San Diego*. New York: Routledge.

Hunter, H. (2000). In the face of poverty: What a community school can do. In J. Silver (ed.), *Solutions that work: Fighting poverty in Winnipeg*. Winnipeg: Canadian Centre for Policy Alternatives. 111–125.

Jeynes, W. (2007). The relationship between parent involvement and urban secondary school achievement: A meta-analysis. *Urban Education* 42(1), 82–110.

Knapp, M.S., Shields, P.M., and Turnbull, B.J. (1995). Conclusion: Teaching for meaning in high-poverty classrooms. In M.S. Knapp (ed.), *Teaching for meaning in high-poverty classrooms*. New York: Teachers College Press.

Kohn, A. (1999). *The schools our children deserve*. Boston: Houghton Mifflin.

Kretzmann, J., and McKnight, J. (1999). *Leading by stepping back: A guide for city officials on building neighborhood capacity*. Chicago, IL: ACTA Publications.

Lapia, A., and McCubbins, M. (1998). *The democratic dilemma: Can citizens learn what they need to know?* New York: Cambridge University Press.

Lawton, D. (1994). *The Tory mind on education, 1979–1994*. London: Falmer Press.

Leithwood, K. (2006). *Teacher working conditions that matter: Evidence for change.* Toronto: Elementary Teachers' Federation of Ontario.

Leithwood, K., Day, C., Sammons, P., Harris, A., and Hopkins, D. (2006). *Seven strong claims about successful leadership.* London: DfES.

Leithwood, K., and Levin, B. (2005). Assessing leadership effects on student learning: Selected challenges for research and program evaluation. In C. Miskel and W. Hoy (eds.), *Educational leadership and reform.* Greenwich, CT: Information Age. 53–76.

Levin, B. (1975). A case study of a Canadian school board and disillusion revisited. *Interchange* 6(2), 23–31, 39–40.

———. (2001). *Reforming education: From origins to outcomes.* London: Routledge Falmer.

———. (2004). Helping research in education to matter more. *Education Policy Analysis Archives* 12(56). Retrieved August 19, 2008, from *http://epaa.asu.edu/epaa.*

———. (2005). *Governing education.* Toronto: University of Toronto Press.

Levin, B., and Alcorn, W. (2000). Post-secondary education for indigenous peoples. *Adult Learning* 11(1), 20–25.

Levin, B., and Naylor, N. (2007). Using resources effectively in education. In J. Burger, P. Klinck, and C. Webber (eds.), *Intelligent Leadership.* Dordrecht, NL: Springer.

Levin, B., and Wiens, J. (2003). There is another way. *Phi Delta Kappan* 84(9), 658–664.

Levin, H.M., Belfield, C., Muennig, G., and Rouse, C. (2007). The public returns to public educational investments in African-American males. *Economics of Education Review* 26(6), 700–709.

Lindblom, C. (1990). *Inquiry and change.* New Haven: Yale University Press.

Livingstone, D. (2004). *The education-jobs gap: Underemployment or economic democracy.* Toronto: Garamond Press.

Livingstone, D.W., Hart, D., and Davie, L.E. (1998). Public attitudes about education in Ontario. Toronto: OISE/University of Toronto.

Lleras-Muney, A. (2005). The relationship between education and adult mortality in the United States. *Review of Economic Studies* 72, 189–221.

Loveless, T. (1997). The structure of public confidence in education. *American Journal of Education* 105(2), 127–159.

March, J. (1984). How we talk and how we act: Administrative theory and administrative life. In T. Sergiovanni and J. Corbally (eds.), *Leadership and organizational culture.* Urbana: University of Illinois Press. 18–35.

Marzano, R. (2003). *What works in schools: Translating research into action.* Alexandria, VA: Association for Supervision and Curriculum Development.

Matthews, D. (2008). The public and the public schools: The coproduction of education. *Phi Delta Kappan* 89(8), 560–564.

McCombs, B., and Whistler, J. (1997). *The learner-centered classroom and school: Strategies for increasing student motivation and achievement.* San Francisco: Jossey-Bass.

McLaughlin, M.W. (1990). The Rand change agent study revisited: Macro perspectives, micro realities. *Educational Researcher* 19(9), 12.

Merttens, R., and Newland, A. (1996). Home-works: Shared maths and shared writings. In J. Bastiani and S. Wolfendale (eds.), *Home-school work in Britain: Review, reflection and development.* London: David Fulton.

Metz, M.H. (1991). Real school: A universal drama amid disparate experience. In D. Mitchell and M. Goetz (eds.), *Education politics for the new century.* New York: Falmer. 75–91.

Meunig, P. (2007). How education produces health: A hypothetical framework. *Teachers College Record Online.* Retrieved September 12, 2007, from *www.tcrecord.org/content.asp?contentid=14606.*

Meyer, M., and Zucker, L. (1989). *The permanently failing organization.* Newbury Park, CA: Sage.

Miles, K.H. (1995). Freeing resources for improving schools: A case study of teacher allocation in Boston public schools. *Educational Evaluation and Policy Analysis* 17(4), 476–493.

Munro, E. (2004). A simpler way to understand the results of risk assessment instruments. *Children and Youth Services Review* 26, 873–883.

Nettles, S., Caughey, M., and O'Campo, P. (2008). School adjustment in the early grades: Toward an integrated model of neighborhood, parental, and child processes. *Review of Educational Research* 78(1), 3–32.

Newton, K, and Norris, P. (2000). Confidence in public institutions: Faith, culture or performance? In S. Pharr and R. Putnam (eds.), *Disaffected democracies: What's troubling the trilateral countries?* Princeton, NJ: Princeton University Press. 52–73.

Odden, A., and Archibald, S. (2001). *Reallocating resources: How to boost student achievement without asking for more.* Thousand Oaks, CA: Corwin.

Odden, A., and Busch, C. (1998). *Financing schools for high performance: Strategies for improving the use of educational resources.* San Francisco: Jossey-Bass.

OECD. (2007). *Education at a glance.* Paris: OECD. Retrieved May 15, 2008, from *www.oecd.org/dataoecd/36/5/39290975.pdf.*

Oreopoulos, P. (2006). The compelling effects of compulsory schooling. *Canadian Journal of Economics* 39(1), 22–52.

Petrovich, J. (2008). *Strategies for improving public education.* New York: Ford Foundation.

Pfeffer, J., and Sutton, R. (2006). *Hard facts, dangerous half-truths, and total nonsense: Profiting from evidence-based management.* Boston: Harvard Business School Press.

Pirsig, R. (1974). *Zen and the art of motorcycle maintenance.* New York: Bantam.

Quint, J. (2006). *Meeting five critical challenges of high school reform: Lessons from three reform models.* New York: MDRC. Retrieved August 19, 2008, from *www.mdrc. org/subarea_index_29.html.*

Reeves, D. (2006). *The learning leader.* Alexandria, VA: Association for Supervision and Curriculum Development.

Robinson, V., Lloyd, C., and Rowe, K. (2008). The impact of leadership on student outcomes: An analysis of the differential effects of the leadership types. *Educational Administration Quarterly* 44(5).

Rothstein, R. (2004). *Class and schools: Using social, economic, and educational reform to close the black-white achievement gap.* New York: Teachers College Press.

Sarason, S. (1971). *The culture of the school and the problem of change.* Boston: Allyn & Bacon.

——— (1990). *The predictable failure of educational reform.* San Francisco: Jossey-Bass.

Sheldon, S., and Epstein, J. (2005). Involvement counts: Family and community partnership and mathematics achievement. *Journal of Educational Research* 98, 126–206.

Shirley, D. (1997). *Community organizing for urban school reform.* Austin: University of Texas Press.

Slavin, R., et al. (1992). *Success for all: A relentless approach to prevention and early intervention in elementary schools.* Arlington, VA: Educational Research Service.

Sloane-Seale, A., Wallace, L., and Levin, B. (2004). The post-secondary education of disadvantaged adults. In J. Gaskell and K. Rubenson (eds.), *Educational outcomes for the Canadian workplace: New frameworks for policy and research.* Toronto: University of Toronto Press. 118–137.

Spasojevic, J. (2003). Effects of education on adult health in Sweden: Results from a natural experiment. Ph.D. diss., Graduate Center of the City University of New York.

Stannard, J., and Huxford, L. (2006). *The literacy game: The story of the national literacy strategy.* London: Routledge.

Stoll, L., Bolam, R., McMahon, A., Wallace, M., and Thomas, S. (2006). Professional learning communities: A review of the literature. *Journal of Educational Change* 7, 221–258.

Stone, C. (ed.). (1998). *Changing urban education.* Lawrence: University Press of Kansas.

Stone, C., Henig, J., Jones, B., and Pierannunzi, C. (2001). *Building civic capacity: The politics of reforming urban schools.* Lawrence: University Press of Kansas.

Thrupp, M. (1999). *Schools making a difference: Let's be realistic.* Buckingham: Open University Press.

Ungar, M. (2004). *Nurturing hidden resilience in troubled youth.* Toronto: University of Toronto Press.

Ungerleider, C. (2007). Evaluation of the Ontario Ministry of Education's Student Success/Learning to 18 strategy, Stage 1 report. Ottawa: Canadian Council on Learning. Unpublished report.

UNICEF (2002). A league table of educational disadvantage in rich nations. *Innocenti report card* no. 4. Florence: Innocenti Research Centre. Retrieved May 13, 2008, from *www.unicef-irc.org/publications/pdf/repcard4e.pdf.*

Vila, L.E. (2005). The outcomes of investment in education and people's well-being. *European Journal of Education* 40(1), 3–11.

Wallace Foundation. (2008). *Becoming a leader: Preparing school principals for today's schools.* Retrieved July 23, 2008, from *www.wallacefoundation.org/NR/rdonlyres/ 4AFFEBC7-9912-4F23-9250-573F64D4B9D8/0/BecomingaLeader.pdf.*

Whitty, G., and Mortimore, P. (1997). *Can school improvement overcome the effects of social disadvantage?* London: Institute of Education.

Wilson, S.M., Darling-Hammond, L., and Berry, B. (2001). *Steady work: The story of Connecticut's school reform.* Retrieved August 19, 2008, from *www.aft.org/pubs-reports/american_educator/fall2001/work.html.*

Witte, A.D. (1997). Crime. In J.R. Behrman and N. Stacy (eds.), *The social benefits of education* (chapter 7). Ann Arbor: University of Michigan Press.

Wolfinger, R.E., and Rosenstone, S.J. (1980). *Who votes?* New Haven: Yale University Press.

Woods, P., Bagley, C., and Glatter, R. (1998). *School choice and competition: Markets in the public interest?* London: Routledge.

World Bank (2005). *Expanding opportunities and building competencies: A new agenda for secondary education.* Washington, DC: World Bank.

Young, S., Levin, B., and Wallin, D. (2007). *Understanding Canadian schools.* Toronto: Nelson-Thomson.

# About the Author

Ben Levin is Professor and Canada Research Chair in the Department of Theory and Policy Studies at the Ontario Institute of Studies in Education (OISE), University of Toronto.

Levin's career has been in academia and in government. His career in education extends over many years, starting with his efforts while in high school to organize a city-wide high school students' union and his election as a school trustee in Winnipeg at the age of 19. Since then he has worked with private research organizations, school divisions, provincial governments, and national and international agencies while also building an academic and research career in education.

Levin has held leadership positions in a wide variety of organizations in the public and nonprofit sectors. From late 2004 until early 2007 he was Deputy Minister of Education for the Province of Ontario. From 1999 through 2002 he was Deputy Minister of Advanced Education and Deputy Minister of Education, Training and Youth for Manitoba. He is widely known for his work in educational reform, educational change, and educational policy and politics. His work has been international in scope, including projects in a dozen countries and with several international agencies.

# Index